APR 2 9 1992

f the Art *by Robert G.*

D1708584

Armor, J. Michael Pol

(*continued on back*)

The Psychological Examination of the Child

THEODORE H. BLAU

A WILEY-INTERSCIENCE PUBLICATION

JOHN WILEY & SONS

New York • Chichester • Brisbane • Toronto • Singapore

Recognizing the importance of preserving what has been written, it is a policy of John Wiley & Sons, Inc., to have books of enduring value published in the United States printed on acid-free paper, and we exert our best efforts to that end.

This publication is designed to provide accurate and
authoritative information in regard to the subject
matter covered. It is sold with the understanding that
the publisher is not engaged in rendering legal, accounting,
or other professional service. If legal advice or other
expert assistance is required, the services of a competent
professional person should be sought. *From a Declaration
of Principles jointly adopted by a Committee of the
American Bar Association and a Committee of Publishers.*

Library of Congress Cataloging-in-Publication Data

Blau, Theodore H.
    The psychological examination of the child / Theodore H. Blau.
       p.   cm.—(Wiley series on personality processes)
    Includes bibliographical references.
    ISBN 0-471-63559-6
    1. Psychological tests for children. I. Title II. Series.
BF722.B52   1991
155.4′028′7—dc20   90-39091
                                              CIP

Printed in the United States of America

91 92 10 9 8 7 6 5 4 3 2 1

Series Preface

This series of books is addressed to behavioral scientists interested in the nature of human personality. Its scope should prove pertinent to personality theorists and researchers as well as to clinicians concerned with applying an understanding of personality processes to the amelioration of emotional difficulties in living. To this end, the series provides a scholarly integration of theoretical formulations, empirical data, and practical recommendations.

Six major aspects of studying and learning about human personality can be designated: personality theory, personality structure and dynamics, personality development, personality assessment, personality change, and personality adjustment. In exploring these aspects of personality, the books in the series discuss a number of distinct but related subject areas: the nature and implications of various theories of personality; personality characteristics that account for consistencies and variations in human behavior; the emergence of personality processes in children and adolescents; the use of interviewing and testing procedures to evaluate individual differences in personality; efforts to modify personality styles through psychotherapy, counseling, behavior therapy, and other methods of influence; and patterns of abnormal personality functioning that impair individual competence.

IRVING B. WEINER

University of South Florida
Tampa, Florida

iii

Contents

SECTION IV.   DEVELOPING AND PRESENTING
THE RESULTS AND RECOMMENDATIONS

Introduction

Much of the history and development of clinical psychology in general, and of clinical child psychology in particular, is tied to the development and refinement of psychometric methods (Blau, 1979). Based on the early psychophysical methods developed in the classic psychological laboratory, the pioneer work in testing forms the foundation for the instruments and methods of evaluation used by professional psychologists today. Clinical psychology's debt to these test developers is great. Psychological assessment today is, of course, more than testing. The psychologist is a collector and interpreter of data. The title of *psychometrist* is reserved for the psychologically trained individual who administers, scores, but rarely interprets psychological tests. In the assessment of human function and potential, most of the basic data collected comes from standardized tests.

The effectiveness of professional psychological service is determined by outcomes. In psychological assessment, the outcome is a report of findings, meanings, and recommendations. The giving and scoring of a test is an important but preliminary step in the entire process. Test results must be clarified and interpreted to consumers so that understanding, conflict, resolution, and maximization of potential can take place. Education and training in psychology, at both basic and advanced levels, often involves the learning of individual testing techniques and provides only limited opportunity to learn to interpret these data directly to the patient (or parent, in the case of a child). Although the doctorate in clinical psychology generally indicates that the individual is qualified to deal with the broader aspects of understanding and delineating human problems, psychologists frequently serve as high-level psychometrists with insufficient training opportunity to organize, direct, and facilitate their diagnostic findings. In most institutional and agency settings, the results of psychological assessments are given to other professionals rather than directly to the consumer.

The majority of trained and experienced clinical psychologists have spent the bulk of their working time with adults. This is a scientific/professional paradox. The training and theoretical background of the clinical psychologist systematically depend on various extensions of the concept that family, social, developmental, and educational circumstances, together with environmental influences in childhood, have significant effects on eventual adult adjustment and behavior. Paradoxically, little of the activity of clinical psychologists is directed toward work with children. The majority of diagnostic work with children is done by school psychologists. No derision by comparison is intended, but the bureaucratic restraints of the educational system restrict the range and opportunities of school psychologists to effectively apply their skills in understanding and helping children and parents with wide variations of psychological problems. Research concerning children and how they grow has been a major focus in psychology for almost a century. Clinical application of this research is more recent. Descriptions of how to conduct a general psychological examination of a child are rare in the professional literature.

Examination and assessment procedures utilized in psychological settings are in no way standardized. Opinions as to the "best tests" vary considerably. Diverse viewpoints are usual (and desirable) in any professional application of specific knowledge. Science can never be complete, and any procedure or method of application must be open to question and discussion. Because psychologists regularly deal in probability, this book is written with the point of view that it is *probable* that certain methods of observing the psychological traits of children are more reliable and valid than other methods. We can further state the probability that through the examination of any child with available psychometric instruments, the resultant information can be of use in helping the child and his or her family deal with environmental pressures. This is the essential premise here: Psychological tools and methods are in a sufficient state of development to be organized and applied in order to better understand the behavior of children. These techniques are applicable to children who seem to do well with their environment and to those who are in distress, or who are a source of distress to those near them. In this book, I present a method for examining children, and a rationale for this method. I attempt to demonstrate not only the method, but its direct application. This general psychological examination, which is hereafter referred to as the Basic Psychological Examination (BPE), is designed to bring together diverse but generally accepted psychological techniques and knowledge for the purpose of understanding an individual child. The examination explores the following areas:

1. The environmental press
2. Behavioral responses
3. Intellectual factors
4. Neuropsychological status and response capabilities

5. Academic achievement
6. Social–affective factors (personality)

I propose that investigation of these areas can result in an analysis of function and capability that will be helpful in understanding the child, and in meeting his or her needs and the expectancies of the environment.

Chapter 1 presents a brief history of clinical child psychology. Chapter 2 outlines the purposes and goals of the BPE. Chapter 3 explores the training and experience necessary to function as a fully qualified clinical child psychologist. Chapters 4 and 5 describe the kind of physical setting appropriate to conduct the BPE, and the equipment and material that should be available.

The second section of the book focuses on intake procedures. Chapter 6 addresses the issue of determining the environmental presses upon the child. Chapter 7 explores the selection of the assessment battery and the scheduling of the assessment. In Chapter 8 the intake procedure is demonstrated on a clinical case.

Section III is concerned with the examination process itself. Chapter 9 explores the initial contact with the child and the establishment of rapport. Chapter 10 addresses the evaluation of the child's intellect, and Chapter 11 presents procedures for conducting neuropsychological screening evaluation. Chapter 12 focuses on the child's primary environment, school, and explores achievement testing. In Chapter 13 the evaluation of personality is examined extensively.

Section IV presents the organization of the results and the making of recommendations. In Chapter 14 the methods by which materials are brought together to write a psychological report are explained in detail. Chapter 15 presents the way in which the results can be interpreted to parents, for maximum benefit. The text concludes with Chapter 16, a discussion of further applications.

A list of test publishers and equipment manufacturers is given in Appendix A. Appendix B contains a list of sources for parent training material.

All psychological efforts and research, theoretical or applied, are subject to author bias. Insofar as I recognize, the bias in this book, simply stated, is that psychological instruments and knowledge can be successfully applied to the evaluation of problems in childhood, and the results can be used to help children and their families move more successfully and comfortably through subsequent stages of growth and development.

SECTION I

Preliminaries

Development of Clinical Child Psychology

Understanding the child has been a matter of studied attention, clinically and theoretically, for almost two centuries. Tiedemann's biographical observations of a child's growth and development, published in 1787, can be viewed as a pioneering effort long antedating the longitudinal studies of the past 75 years.

EARLY SCIENTIFIC EFFORTS

The psychological study of child development began at the close of the 19th century. At that time the University of California was a growing center for the clinical study of the child. Millicent Skinn's (1893) carefully documented studies of the child's first year of life predated work on developmental rating scales. Moore, as early as 1896, studied patterns of early growth and development and attempted to scale and objectify clinical observation of the child. Binet's work from 1903 until the time of his death in 1911 brought the concept of measuring the development of the individual child in comparison with that of other children to the attention of psychologists and educators (Binet & Simon, 1909).

Early views held that the child was a *homunculus*, that is, a little man, a miniature. Both Locke and Hartley (1949), following their associationist concepts, held that the child was born without associations and had a simple capacity for sensory experience. Growth to adulthood was viewed as the establishment of associations and later complex objects of thought. Upon reaching full maturity, philosophical and religious conceptions would emerge, via the process of association. One might look upon Hartley's position as a kind of Victorian field theory.

PHILOSOPHICAL CONTRASTS

Hartley's position met with strong opposition from some of his contemporaries. Thomas Reid, a doubting and apparently vitriolic Scot, opposed the associationist viewpoint as rather weak tea. He proposed that children were born and endowed with an innate ability to identify "good" and "evil" and were thus free to choose right or wrong. Christian Wolf supported Reid by attaching the concept of *faculties* to the intellectualist view, indicating that the child had not only the awareness but the capacity for the soul to carry out activities.

Although these philosophical contrasts contributed to the eventual science of behavior, other events were occurring during the late 18th and the 19th centuries that led to the clinical study of the child. Humanitarianism, as characterized by Pinel's work at the Bicêtre, the French insane asylum, did much to repudiate the then current concept that a child "wills" the behavior that leads to disturbed adulthood. This essentially modern view of growth and development was vigorously seconded in the works of Beccaria, the pioneer criminologist who suggested that crimes were motivated by needs originally developed in childhood. He pleaded for a revision of the penal code so that punishment might be graded with recognition of childhood causes and rehabilitation potentials (Murphy, 1949). A hundred years later, the same view was expressed publicly by Karl Menninger (1959).

The attention of the world was focused on the growth process of the individual child through the reports of the Frenchman Itard on his work with "wild" or *feral* children. The concept of evaluating levels of mental efficiency in children began to emerge with Itard's view that some children are deficient in learning capacity. Sequin, following the associationist school with his concept of faculty psychology, began to evaluate and train children by the stimulation of sensory and motor functions.

Even the pioneer Wundt showed some interest in the evaluation of the child by applying his experimental methods to children's motor and learning behavior. One of his early students, G. Stanley Hull, brought these methods to the United States and became one of the founders of the field of child psychology. He established the *Journal of Genetic Psychology* in 1901. Most of his work with children was based on incomplete biographical data; however, interest was kindled and scientists began to study all aspects of child development (Watson, 1963).

EARLY CLINICAL CHILD PSYCHOLOGY

In 1896, Lightner Witmer established the first "psychological clinic" in the United States. He decided that his worker's task was to study individual children, using biographical techniques and limited "mental tests" (primarily form-boards). The intent or purpose in this clinic was to understand children and to help them overcome problems and frustrations, which in essence, is still the keynote in clinical child psychology practice today. The first concern at Witmer's clinic was the child's response to education; emotional factors were considered ancillary to a child's inability to learn. These American activities contributed to the budding study of the troubled child in the early part of the 20th century. One must return, however, to Binet to see this interest bloom (Murphy, 1949).

Trained in medicine, Binet showed a lifelong interest in psychological matters. His original training and research were influenced by the then predominant associationist school of Locke and Hartley, as well as by the teutonic precision of data collection established by Ebbinghaus and Wundt. Binet originated the first psychological laboratory at the Sorbonne. The scientist began to be the researcher–clinician as he became interested in hypnosis. Binet directed his interest and study to the individual, particularly to children. His reports of the psychological reactions of his daughters revealed not only the competent and diligent researcher, but the sensitive and empathetic clinical observer at work. These studies were significant in moving Binet to reject his early training in associationism, having observed too much evidence of unity, activity, and ego function in normal and abnormal children.

Binet's best known contribution to clinical child psychology began as a result of his broad interests as well as his scientific reputation. Appointed by France's minister of education to head a project to develop methods by which educationally inept children might be trained to become useful adults, Binet conceived that an instrument of measurement was needed to properly identify children unable to learn as well as most. After 2 years of intensive work with Theodore Simon, his associate, Binet reported in 1905 the development of a "test" to detect and measure mental defect. The test was based on a series of performances required of each child tested. The tasks were ordered for difficulty, and the child's successes indicated levels of performance ability.

In 1908, Binet announced the first revision of the Binet–Simon scale. Certain test items were omitted and new tasks were added. With this revision, Binet presented his concept of "age levels." The test items were arranged and graded to represent expected performance from age 3 through age 12. Each test item was placed according to the age at which most children were able to successfully perform it. In 1911, shortly after Binet's death, the final revision of "the Binet–Simon" was published. In this publication, Binet expressed his theoretical concept that intelligence was a combination of the capacity to understand or comprehend directions, the ability to maintain a mental set, and the ability to correct one's own errors. Binet considered this latter function to be the highest level of intellectual development, and he gave it the label *autocriticism.* In respect to current theory, Binet delineated what in current neuropsychological terms are called "functional systems of the brain" (Luria, 1973, 1980).

EXTENSION OF BINET'S WORK

Although Binet's work and certainly his theoretical position bear little resemblance to psychometric theory and practice today, the role of productive pioneer was surely his. The concept of the intelligence quotient (IQ) and the relative constancy of this ratio as devised by Stern (1912), the Americanization of the Binet–Simon by Goddard (1910), and the sudden flourish of interest in tests rapidly followed publication of Binet's work.

The years after 1915 were major growth years for applied psychology. Major advances in test construction influenced the growth of interest and activity in the clinical evaluation of the child (Terman, 1921). While test development became a prominent part of psychological affairs throughout the first half of the twentieth century, the question "why" began to accompany the sometimes feverish test-construction attitude of wanting to know "what" and "how much" (Doll, 1919). The search for theoretical constructs burgeoned among child psychologists.

The decade after 1915 produced great strides in understanding the nature of intelligence and learning. The most widely used American version of Binet's scale was the 1916 version by Terman. Age levels ranged from 3 to 18 years (the highest years on the scale were labeled *adult* and *superior adult*). Kuhlman published another revision of the Binet–Simon in 1922 which included tests below the 3-year-old level. This revision placed less emphasis on verbal factors and thus complemented rather than replaced the Terman scales. As a result of the extensive use of test instruments in educational practice during the 1920s, clinical child psychology had its greatest advance in study and practice since Witmer.

The use of psychologists to evaluate service personnel in World War I advanced the entire area of individual measurement. Major results of this applied phase were clearer understanding of the nature of intelligence, the value and need for refinement of test instruments, and considerable public awareness and acceptance of psychology as an emerging discipline (Brigham, 1921).

IMPACT OF THEORETICAL CONSTRUCTS

From this time on, separating the effects of test building from those of theory building on the development of clinical child psychology is difficult. Watson's behaviorism had significant impact in stimulating the growth of theories concerning normal and abnormal child development and behavior. Kurt Lewin's field theory also focused interest on the child as an individual and the need for methods to examine the process of development. Goodenough (1926), in developing her radically new approach to the examination of intelligence, the assessment of children's drawings, contributed a clinical technique that was to serve well as a measure of the child's emotional status, social perception, and intellectual development.

Beginning in 1923 and extending through the 1970s, Jean Piaget's work (1923, 1932) became a source of voluminous and productive research on the nature of the growing child. His early concepts of egocentrism, realism, and participation have strongly influenced child psychologists for over 50 years.

Anthropologists and sociologists also became important contributors to child psychology. Margaret Mead (1928, 1930), who described and evaluated child-rearing practices in widely divergent cultures, pointed out the significance of the family and the community in the formation of the child's values, concepts, and performance. Psychologists seeking to understand and assess childhood behavior problems owe much to the conceptualizations of environmental influence that emerged from the work of early social psychologists (Thurstone, 1931).

PSYCHOANALYTIC CONTRIBUTION

During the early 1930s, psychoanalysis, which had been developing in Europe and to a growing degree in the United States, began to have a forceful impact on clinical practice with children. Psychoanalytic theory emphasized the importance of childhood family experience on adult emotional adjustment and productivity (Freud, 1933/1966). Freud was disappointed in the results of his personal experience in attempting child analysis. To some extent this disappointment was based on his meeting of "Little Hans," his most famous child case, when the patient was a grown man. Hans had complete amnesia for the analytic experience that had occurred when he was 5 (Jones, 1953). Today, child clinicians know that this lack of memory is the rule rather than the exception and is not associated with success or failure of the therapeutic process.

The analytic view in the treatment of childhood behavior disorders was introduced in the United States in the clinic of Frederick Allen in Philadelphia. Melanie Klein's classic work on psychoanalytic treatment of disturbed children appeared in 1932. She described her method as play therapy: Sessions consisted of a series of activity techniques, at the child's perceptual level, designed to bring out underlying emotional structure for observation and amelioration. She proposed that play was sometimes the only communication possible with a disturbed child.

The contributions of psychoanalysis to child study were many. The concepts of sex role in personality development, identification as the modeling process for growth of character, and defense mechanisms, and the theory of ego development in the child were some of the constructs that helped psychologists to understand normal and abnormal child behavior.

Experimental studies of the influence of the family environment on the child's motives and behavior, such as those by Levy and, later, by Pauline Sears, did much to clarify the generalities of psychoanalytic theory (Stagner, 1936).

RECENT DEVELOPMENTS

The decade from 1935 to 1945 was characterized by the broadening of the concept of longitudinal research. Gesell's group at Yale (Gesell et al., 1943) and MacFarlane and her associates in California (MacFarlane, Allen, & Honzik, 1954) provided normative data on usual and unusual childhood behavior that have materially enriched the thinking and techniques of clinical child psychologists.

As more psychologists gained clinical experience working with children and their families, they began to expand their research interests from test construction to understanding and modification of affective behavioral responses. Interest began to grow in the detailed examination of the behavior of small groups of children using small-sample statistical techniques. A prime example was Sears's (1951) study of doll-play aggression in normal young children. The pioneering child research centers at Yale University, the University of California, the University of Iowa, and the University of Minnesota led in the production of significant research with children (Thompson, 1959).

Clinical child psychology as a training track and practice specialty emerged after 1955 (Ross, 1959). Psychologists in increasing numbers began to make available to the community at large, psychological skills aimed at understanding children, their growth, their problems, and their potentials. Child guidance centers were the main setting for such practice. Clinical psychological services for children rapidly became available in schools and in social agencies. Psychologists, and to a lesser extent psychiatrists, began to offer such services independently (Blau, 1959).

Research interest in specific clinical aspects of child development increased in the 1960s. Exploration of the sleep patterns of children, the relationship of sibling position to behavioral response, early learning facility, and the validity of psychological measuring instruments characterized some of the research efforts (Campbell & Thompson, 1968). Also, much activity was directed toward evaluating Piaget's conceptions of cognitive functions in children (Wright, 1966).

CURRENT DIRECTIONS

As the 100th anniversary of the founding of Witmer's child clinic in Philadelphia draws near, the study and practice of clinical child psychology remains a significant and growing area. Greater attention to the understanding and measurement of children's personality, social adaptation, and vulnerabilities characterized clinical child psychology of the 1970s and 1980s. The rapidly developing specialty of child neuropsychology has brought new understanding as well as new techniques for the assessment of children (Hartlage & Telzrow, 1986).

Because the purpose of this volume is to present a method for the psychological examination of the child, the historical development presented here is at best brief. The properly trained psychologist, in preparing to make a clinical examination of a child, is influenced by a historical imperative of almost a century. At this point in history, the public has a much more accepting image of psychology, and people are more aware of their need for information, understanding, and guidance in preparing their children to be comfortable and useful in a complex society. Since the world seems to become more complex with each passing year, parents' seeking guidance is likely to increase. The clinical child psychologist can help to meet these important community needs.

CHAPTER TWO

Purposes, Procedures, and Goals of Psychological Assessment of the Child

The ultimate goal and purpose of the psychological assessment of a child is to help promote the child's best interests. To accomplish this effectively, the psychologist must be capable of identifying and evaluating the significant forces, expectancies, and opportunities in the child's life, as well as the child's abilities and disabilities.

The complete psychological assessment of the child should proceed through five distinct phases. Phase 1 is a needs assessment (Kaufman & English, 1979), to determine the environmental presses that affect or are likely to influence the child. Phase 2, the examination of the child, is directed to the issues raised in Phase 1. It includes all of the tests, measurements, and other data collection that are used to clarify the status and potential of the child. In Phase 3 of the complete assessment of the child, the aggregation of information from the earlier phases is used to develop intervention strategies and recommendations to deal with the gaps in the child's development that were demonstrated in the first two phases. In Phase 4, the results of the psychological assessment are reported and interpreted to parents, guardians, and others who are significant participants in promoting the child's best interests. In Phase 5, an assessment of outcomes allows for revisions of intervention strategies and further recommendations in the child's best interests. An overview of these elements of the evaluation of the child is presented in this chapter, and the remainder of the book is devoted to the details of accomplishing these phases in practice.

NEEDS ASSESSMENT

During the needs assessment phase of the psychological assessment, the psychologist develops an array of questions about the child's development, psychological status, or potential from information provided by parents, guardians, teachers, and others in the child's environment. The older the child, the more likely it is that he or she will contribute questions or concerns to the needs assessment. In this phase, the psychologist schedules appointments to take formal and informal histories from significant parties in the child's life. The primary source of information is usually the parents or guardians with whom the child lives. Although a needs assessment may at times include extensive interviews, telephone calls, and examination of medical and other records, the needs assessment information in the majority of practical clinical situations will be provided by the child's parents during a structured interview.

EXAMINATION PHASE

To adequately address the issues involved in determining the best interests of the child, various psychological tests and inventories are administered. Some of these may be given to the parents or teachers in the form of behavioral rating scales or observational inventories. The older the child, the more the psychologist's examinations will include direct observation and measurement of performance and behavior. These procedures should be selected to produce a reliable picture of the child.

The domains to be explored should represent all important aspects of the child's inner and outer life. The coverage must be complete. No aspect of the child's psychological status should be left unexamined in the process of determining his or her best interests. The basic clinical examination of the child should include at least six elements: the clinical interview, direct observation, an intellectual evaluation, neuropsychological screening, evaluation of academic achievement, and a personality evaluation.

Clinical Interview

The initial contact between the examiner and the child allows for a mutual first observation. The clinician must create as safe and as comfortable a setting as possible for the child and give the child an opportunity to become acclimated to the setting and the examiners. At the same time, the initial interview with the child takes place. Inquiry into the child's views and opinions begins here.

Observation

During the entire examination phase, the psychologist has opportunities to observe and record the child's responses, noting confirmations as well as contradictions of parents' reports, teachers' observations, and test results. Additional questions for exploration often emerge.

Intellectual Evaluation

A complete and clear picture of the child's intellectual functioning and potential is likely to be of primary importance in understanding the child and making recommendations to the parents. Instruments selected to measure intellectual functions should provide information on as wide a range of the child's cognitive skills or deficiencies as possible.

Intelligence tests resulting in IQs or single indexes are of limited value as aids to the clinician seeking an in-depth understanding of the child. Some of the newer instruments classified as intelligence tests provide valuable information as to the child's individual learning style.

Neuropsychological Screening

Recent research in developmental brain–behavior relationships has provided test procedures that allow the psychologist to identify the presence of a variety of neuropsychological deficits. Where screening measures suggest such deficits, full neuropsychological assessment is indicated and should be included as part of the total psychological evaluation of the child.

Academic Achievement

Most children are tested for academic skills and/or achievement quite frequently in their schools. Such tests are ordinarily given to relatively large groups under conditions that may not result in a picture of the child's best performance. An accurate evaluation of the child's academic skills under carefully controlled conditions can provide valuable information about the child's maximum as well as functional performance capacities.

Personality

The personality structure of the child will help the psychologist understand sources of distress, explain unusual or unacceptable behavior, and clarify the child's developmental level. A thorough, properly conducted personality evaluation can indicate likely strategies for conflict resolution as well as age- and stage-appropriate learning experiences. The personality of the child may be both the most difficult technical challenge and the richest opportunity for the clinician during the psychological examination.

ANALYSIS PHASE

A standardized test should be scored and interpreted within limits and guidelines concordant with the instrument's standardization. The practical outcome should be information that provides relatively objective estimates of the child's psychological functioning. From this information, the clinician should be able to formulate conclusions to support a variety of interpretations and recommendations, which should usually include the following:

- A description of the child's current development stage
- Deficits and skills relative to developmental age and stage expectancies
- Special abilities and potentials
- Answers to questions posed by the needs assessment
- Recommendations for remedial procedures to deal with deficits or problems
- Recommendations for opportunities that might be provided to activate the child's potential
- Guidance for the parents and other involved parties to help create a support and enhancement network for the child

The recommendations must be developed as realistically as possible. The psychologist should always consider the resources of the family and the community and, as much as ethically possible, make recommendations that have a reasonable probability of being implemented.

INTERPRETATION OF RESULTS

The essential content of and the relationships among the first three phases of the psychological assessment should be presented in a written psychological report. This report should be of sufficient completeness, accuracy, and clarity that it can be used in any implementation of the findings that may be required.

For the psychological report to be communicated effectively, the psychologist should schedule an initial interpretation session with the child's parents or guardians. During this 2-hr session, the psychologist should review the needs assessment with the parents, describe the evaluation procedures, and report results clearly and concisely. Additionally, recommendations should be presented, the parents' questions answered, and concerns explored.

A full psychological evaluation usually results in a good deal of rich information about the child, some of which is complex and requires time and perhaps repetition and discussion before parents can fully comprehend the content. The psychologist can help by tape-recording the interpretation conference and suggesting that the parents take the tape and review the information one or more times before the next scheduled conference.

Hundreds of pamphlets and booklets are available that describe many common stages and problems of child development. At the time of the interpretation, the psychologist should provide materials specific to the child's problems, potentials, and developmental stage. Such materials should be chosen with appropriate regard for the parents' intellectual, cultural, and educational background and status.

During this first interpretation conference, the psychologist and parents should decide who will receive the child's psychological report: the school, agencies, and/or the child's physician. The school may or may not be an appropriate agency to receive (and file) a complete psychological report. The parents may prefer to have a letter sent to the school, and possibly to the doctor and agencies, summarizing the results of the psychological evaluation and recommendations.

This interpretation session is the first in a series of contacts between the psychologist and responsible adults in the child's world. Following this critical personal meeting, contacts between the psychologist and parents, teachers, guardians, and agencies may include telephone calls, conferences, correspondence, school visits, therapeutic ventures, or joint professional consultations.

OUTCOMES AND REVISION

The final, most variable phase of the child's psychological evaluation may include, in order of frequency, a second interpretation session, multiple sessions, or long-term tracking. This phase should be governed by whatever is necessary and feasible in the child's best interests.

In this phase of the evaluation, the psychologist determines how the results of the examination and recommendations have been received. The initial impact of the results can be evaluated and revisions made.

Second Interpretation Session

By the time the second conference takes place, the parents and other significant adults in the child's current environment should be aware of the results of the psychological assessment of the child and the recommendations based on those results. It is best if the parents, guardians, and teachers have discussed the results, and even better if the parents have tried some of the recommendations before the second session with the psychologist.

When the assessment and first interpretation have been done thoroughly and well, the parents are likely to report improvement in both the child's behavior and the parents' anxiety.

Questions concerning the evaluation results may suggest a need for clarification or even more extended consultations to help parents and teachers understand and implement the recommendations.

Additional Sessions

Additional meetings with parents, teachers, or others may be needed for further interpretation of results and clarification of recommendations. In some complex situations, additional sessions may evolve into parent counseling or school consultation. If original recommendations are ineffective or insufficient, additional sessions offer the opportunity to embellish or revise remedial steps originally recommended.

Tracking

A number of children who receive complete psychological evaluations at one stage of their lives will return later for reexamination. The psychologist may recommend reevaluations as part of the psychological assessment, to track progress and modify or adjust interventions. Parents sometimes bring children back to the psychologist for help in dealing with academic or developmental issues that arise as the child matures, frequently at key developmental milestones (preschool, postelementary, preadolescence, and high school).

The older the child, the more directly he or she should be involved in the planning and implementation of all phases of the psychological evaluation.

The psychological assessment of the child, as it has been generally described in this chapter and as it is presented in detail in the chapters that follow, is proposed as a Basic Psychological Examination. It is a framework within which the psychological status of almost all children at all developmental levels can be determined and the results used to support the best interests of the child. Specific instruments and procedures are bound to vary in respect to different problems, cultural status, and developmental levels. As new techniques and test instruments are developed, the details of the testing and data collection processes may change. The overarching structure and the goals of the Basic Psychological Examination are likely to remain.

CHAPTER THREE

Training and Experience Requirements

Chapter 1 describes some of the psychological interest in understanding children that has developed over the past 100 years. Perhaps a result of this development has been the emergence of the concept that psychiatrists work with adults, psychologists with children. The psychologist has been the primary professional to conduct psychological assessments of both children and adults. Psychological assistants are helpers who administer and score psychological tests, and are referred to as psychometrists. Although there is some crossing of the dividing lines, the fully trained psychologist has been considered the accountable member of the psychological assessment team. With the advent of licensing and certification of psychologists, this accountability has become a matter of law.

Qualifying for this clinical assessment role with children requires more than training and experience with test instruments. The fully trained clinical child psychologist must be capable of identifying and articulating the needs and best interests of the children, families, and community sources seeking help or guidance. A major element in this process should be the administration of a complete psychological examination. The selection of assessment procedures, the use of the resulting data, and the recommendations generated from this body of information are the major concerns of this volume.

To understand psychological tools and methods, the psychologist needs a broad educational background. Standards for education and training of clinical child psychologists are just beginning to evolve (Hoch, Ross, & Winder, 1966; Johnson & Tuma, 1983; Routh, 1985). Most of the psychological personnel who currently evaluate children complete their formal training at the subdoctoral level. Subdoctoral professionals who work in schools and community agencies are limited by a variety of traditions and bureaucratic constraints. A full range of assessment follow-up services can rarely be offered by these institutional clinical child psychologists.

BACKGROUND TRAINING

Psychological examination of the child consists of a series of behavioral observations which must be put into a framework that should eventually lead to understanding and prediction. For the person who is preparing to conduct psychological assessment of children, a basic foundation in psychology as a science is a necessary first step. Course work in general psychology and the experimental method are essential minimum requirements. Elementary courses in statistics would help the person to understand probability theory, which is necessary in deciding the usefulness and limitations of assessment instruments. Basic and intermediate courses in personality, the dynamics of human adjustment, and abnormal psychology should be taken. Ancillary courses in sociology, cultural anthropology, criminology, and marriage and the family would broaden the person's cultural awareness, which is vital for effective recommendations and interventions. Courses in child growth and development enable the examiner to have a series of developmental guideposts against which to view the performance of children. The broader the background training, the more effective the examiner.

Before the student clinician is exposed to practicum experience in the application and use of specific assessment instruments, the following formal course work in tests and measurements should be completed:

- The nature and history of psychological assessment
- Measuring and scaling
- Types of psychological tests
- Test construction, standardization, and development of normative data
- Reliability and validity
- Administration procedures
- Scoring procedures
- Reporting
- Ethical issues and legal constraints.

At the present stage in the development of education and training in psychology, the above training is likely to occur in graduate school. In practical terms, all of the above material can be adequately presented in courses that lead to the bachelor's degree in psychology.

The Basic Psychological Examination (BPE) proposed in Chapter 2 is intended to be a meaningful, composite, applied psychological procedure that the psychologist can use to understand the child, plan remedial work, and help the child and his parent figures reach their respective potentials. Current education and training systems, however, are not able to provide sufficient numbers of professional child psychologists to meet service needs as the general public becomes more aware of the value of such services.

A tendency, particularly among harried agency psychologists, is to decrease the use of psychological tests to save time or cost. Shortening the BPE, however, dilutes the potential value of the procedure. Another solution to the problems of cost efficiency and cost-effectiveness is the *assessment team.*

The psychological assessment team would probably function best in a psychological service center or a behavioral science center where it might serve in an autonomous manner, yet have opportunity for liaison with other professionals. A team might consist of one doctoral level psychologist as director, two psychological assistants working at a middle-management and clinician level, and four to eight psychological assistants doing the bulk of the face-to-face assessment work with parents and children. The training, role, and function of each specialist are described below.

Such an assessment team could offer thorough psychological evaluation services to a considerable number of parents and children. Such teams currently exist in school systems and in some agency settings. School psychologists are the largest and most active group of clinical child psychologists.

The Psychological Examiner

Training for the psychological examiner is complete at the bachelor's level or below. Given the fundamental background in psychology, the behavioral sciences, and testing theory and practice, the examiner's training is completed in a 6-month clerkship at a psychological assessment facility. Professional duties include the following:

- Managing the test room
- Administering, scoring, and profiling group and individual tests
- Preparing materials for interpretation
- Making clinical notes and observations concerning the child's behavior
- Maintaining stocks of test materials
- Filing clinical materials
- Learning interview skills.

The Psychological Assistant

Academic training for the psychological assistant is complete at the master's level. In addition to the formal course work taken by the psychological examiner, the psychological assistant has taken courses in interviewing, intermediate statistics, learning and personality theory, projective techniques, and individual psychological examination procedures, including neuropsychological assessment. Didactic training in child growth and development and research in developmental behavior patterns are important parts of the curriculum. Academic training should be followed by a year of clinical training and supervision in a psychological service center.

Professional responsibilities would include the following:

- Supervising the work of several psychological examiners
- Interviewing parents
- Collecting environmental information, which included making school visits
- Conducting individual examination procedures
- Writing final reports with recommendations
- Interpreting assessments to parents and others
- Consulting with other agencies and individuals to implement assessment results and recommendations
- Training and upgrading of psychological examiners
- Participating in assessment research
- Reviewing work of psychological examiners and serving as assessment consultant where difficulties arise.

The Clinical Child Psychologist

The doctoral level psychologist serves as the director of the assessment team. Formal academic training should be followed by a year or more of intensive postdoctoral training and supervision at a major clinical child assessment center. As director of the assessment team, the senior psychologist has the following duties:

- Supervising the entire assessment facility
- Training, supervising, and upgrading assistants and examiners
- Initiating assessment research
- Serving as a final review for unusual assessment problems
- Conducting special assessment procedures and demonstrating techniques with unusual assessment problems
- Establishing liaison with community agencies needing assessment services, and serving as consultant to these agencies
- Establishing channels for implementing recommendations resulting from assessment procedures
- Organizing workshops and advanced training seminars for the assessment team.

PERSONAL REQUIREMENTS

It is more difficult to specify the personal requirements for working with children than the necessary academic and practicum training. For the psychologist to function effectively in a diagnostic situation, he or she needs both the ability to elicit test behavior from the child and the sensitivity to create a flexible, open environment within which the child may demonstrate perceptions, capabilities, and potentials. To establish rapport with children, one must respect them as human beings. In the examination setting, the examiner must be aware that the child has certain rights and privileges despite being a visitor in the examiner's setting.

Although knowledge of developmental ages and stages is invaluable in helping the clinical child psychologist establish rapport and communicate with children in the examination setting, the examiner must be willing to try to understand and accept the child's level of function before introducing levels of function required by the assessment. Traits of warmth, acceptance, flexibility, authenticity, and transparency make for success in dealing with children. Honesty, some enthusiasm, and much patience can enhance the examiner's ability to create a setting and a relationship likely to encourage a child to respond and perform in such a way that the examiner can make valid observations of the child's psychological functioning. The effective child clinician must be able to create a structured setting that presents reasonable, clear limits, but that simultaneously allows and encourages the child to demonstrate the breadth and depth of his or her levels of development, problems, and potentials.

The effective clinical child psychologist must know his or her community as thoroughly as possible. The geography, history, cultural and economic diversity of a community govern the restrictions and opportunities to be considered when conducting and implementing a psychological evaluation of a child.

As discussed in some detail in a later chapter, an open mind and a willingness to modify responses will serve the new clinician well. Skill in dealing with children will develop as the clinician gains experience. Didactic preparation can help the psychologist understand the way in which children work. In the final analysis, it is the child who teaches the psychologist.

CHAPTER FOUR

Clinical Setting

The setting and surroundings in which the child is evaluated may enrich or detract from the examination. Tradition or availability of space usually dictates the physical setting. Experience suggests that examinations of children that take place under certain comfortable or comforting conditions are likely to be more productive and valid than those that occur under distracting or stressful conditions (Anastasi, 1982). Although ideal conditions are not always possible, this does not lessen the importance of the concept of ideal conditions.

INITIAL IMPRESSIONS—THE WAITING ROOM

Because a child is rarely seen immediately upon arrival at a psychologist's office, a waiting room is necessary. It is here that the clinical interaction begins. The child tends to "judge a book by its cover," and the waiting room and the receptionist constitute the psychologist's "dust jacket."

The waiting room should be light and airy. A small desk might be provided for the convenience of the adult who intends to wait for a child during an examination. In addition to adult seating, several pieces of children's furniture should be available. A child-sized table (16 in. high), several children's chairs (8-, 10-, or 12-in. seating height), and a drawing board make a comfortable play corner. The drawing board can be a blackboard with chalk or a marker board of white plastic on which the children can draw with crayons or felt-tipped marking pens. Children's books, puzzles, coloring books, and drawing implements can be arranged on shelves within the play area. Experience suggests that when the child participates in play activity in the waiting room, establishment of rapport between the child and the clinician has begun. Figure 4.1 presents a suggested waiting room arrangement.

Because the waiting room is part of the clinical setting, someone must be in charge. The receptionist is, to some extent, a clinician who directs and

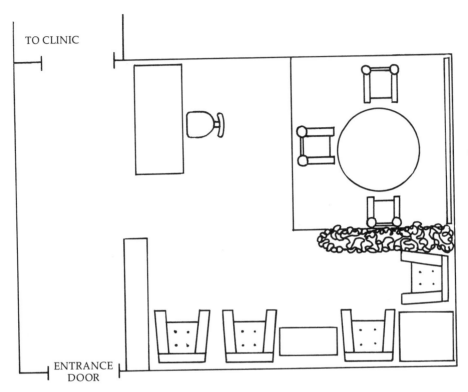

FIGURE 4.1   Waiting Room

controls the child's initial experience at the psychologist's office. The receptionist's ability to make the waiting room a comfortable experience for both parent and child can greatly aid the task at hand. By suggesting play activity, helping the child become acquainted with the play area, and in general welcoming the child—essentially by taking the child "off the parents' hands"—the receptionist tries to make the child aware that he or she is expected, accepted, and welcomed. The receptionist need not be in the waiting room at all times. He or she may greet the child and adults, help the family settle down, and leave. One clever receptionist has charmed frightened or withdrawn children with her electric eraser. Psychologists should help their secretaries and receptionists to become aware of the important role they play as the introduction to the clinical examination for the parents and the child. The receptionist should be trained to be a part of the family's total clinical experience.

THE PARENT CONFERENCE ROOM

The intake interview and history taking that precede the examination of the child ordinarily take place in the consultation office. Every effort should be made to make this a comfortable setting for the parents. Parents are often frightened and guilt ridden, and they may exhibit aggressive, punitive, and defensive attitudes that reflect their underlying sureness that the child's problem represents their own inadequacy. The first contact between the clinician and the parents usually takes place without the child present. When the appointment is first made, it should be made clear that the child is not to accompany the parents for this initial interview. In addition to obtaining information during this appointment, the psychologist can evaluate and encourage the parents as potential change agents. The psychological assessment expert is introduced as the professional who will hopefully provide the information necessary to guide the parents in creating meaningful changes for the child and the family. A successful intake interview is

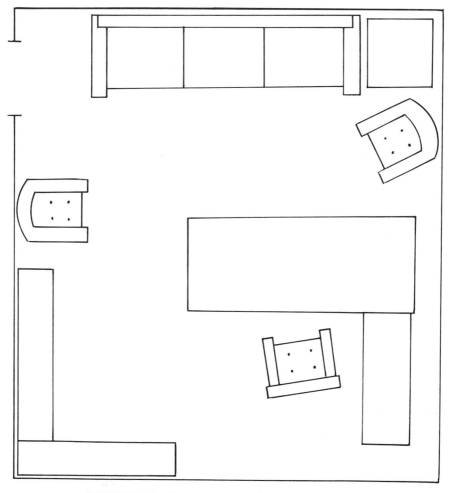

FIGURE 4.2   Traditional Consultation Office

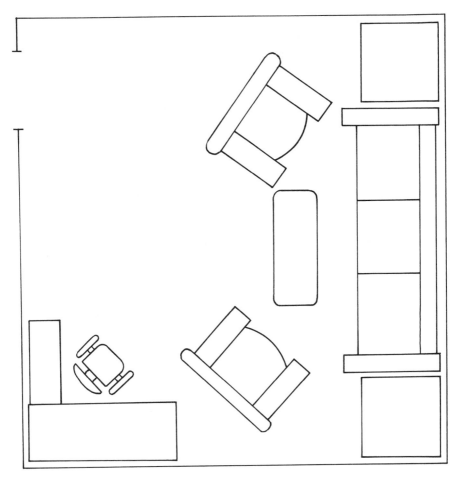

FIGURE 4.3   Informal Consultation Office

characterized by the psychologist's open communication and warmth, and by the parents' decrease in tension and agreement to become involved in a worthwhile joint venture.

The furnishings and decor of the consultation office should be attractive and restful. An office that displays clinical equipment, many diplomas and certificates, or an extensive library may stimulate parents to be defensive and uncomfortable. This office should be decorated in such a way as to encourage free expression of feelings and family attitudes. Richer and more complete information is likely to come from parents who feel secure during intake procedures. Although the clinician's attitude, skill, and experience are primary in motivating good response, the appropriate physical setting can enhance or detract from a clinician's talents. Some clinicians prefer a consultation office without a desk; in such an office the clinician faces the family in an informal manner, to encourage the family to be comfortable and forthcoming. Figure 4.2 illustrates a traditional consultation office, and Figure 4.3 shows a less formal arrangement.

EVALUATION FACILITIES AND PROCEDURES

The Test Room

Proper space is a critical requirement of a good test room. Lighting should be planned to create shadowless working spaces. The room should be sound conditioned. Soft colors and minimal decorative features will help the child to concentrate on the task at hand rather than on extraneous elements in the room.

A large table is the main working area. A height of 22 in., 5 in. shorter than ordinary desks, seems to be the best working height. A desk or table of standard height (27 in.) can be set at right angles to the testing table to serve as the clinician's work space as well as a testing table for adolescents and adults. Small children can stand to work at form-boards and other manipulative tasks, whereas older children can sit easily at a standard desk in a standard chair.

An additional table, approximately 16 in. high, should be available for children between 3 and 6 years of age. A sturdy chair for the child should have a seat height of approximately 10 in.

The various tables will prove useful, since the clinician may use one to lay out material while the child is using the other for testing. A 27-in. high cabinet or credenza with sliding doors can be used to store materials and for additional space for laying out tests. Figure 4.4 illustrates a suggested test room.

Furniture constructed of Formica or other durable veneer is preferable to natural wood surfaces since test room furnishings undergo considerable assault from feet, fingernails, pencil points, and stray equipment available to an active child.

The Playroom

Although considered the traditional sanctum of play therapy, a well-equipped playroom is also helpful in the psychological evaluation of children. Formal testing is impossible in some instances, and the playroom offers a semistructured setting in which the clinician can institute and observe children's behavior.

The ideal playroom should be designed to provide a maximum of facilities with a minimum of space restriction. Sufficient space should be available for jumping, stomping, throwing, and rolling. A climbing pole in the center of the room and a chinning bar in the doorway provide an opportunity to observe

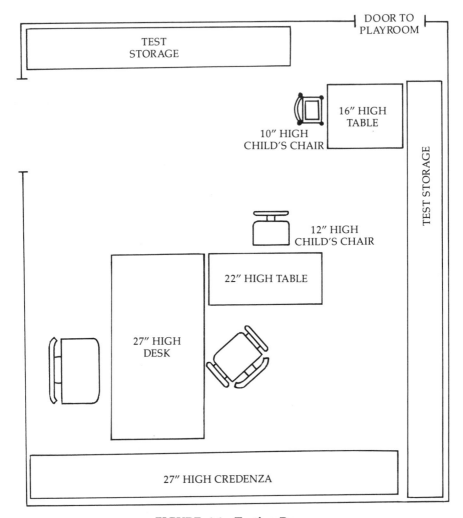

FIGURE 4.4   Testing Room

children's physical expressions and reactions even in moderately limited space. Materials not intended for the child's free choice should be stored in wall cabinets hung out of the children's reach.

Figure 4.5 shows a suggested playroom plan. The playroom allows the child a wide variety of activities, including jumping, climbing, finger painting, or building. Materials available for the child should include the following:

- Clay
- Finger paints

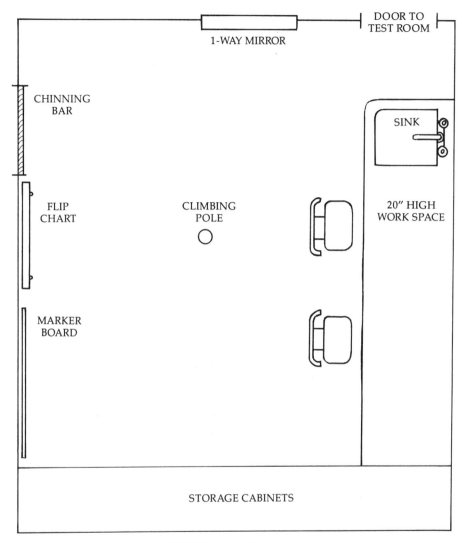

FIGURE 4.5 Playroom

- Water-soluble markers
- Colored chalk and crayons
- Large puzzles
- Balloons
- Suction darts (will stick on marker board)
- Simple construction kits (airplanes, boats, kites)
- Animal noses and masks for fantasy play.

To protect the child from paint smudges and ink, a supply of washable smocks should be available. (Large-sized men's shirts put on the child in a reversed manner and buttoned up the back serve well.)

Playrooms have been the traditional setting for play therapy. Experienced clinical child psychologists have found the playroom useful as a place to observe and sometimes test younger children. A one-way mirror is a traditional adjunct useful for training, instructing parents, videotaping test procedures, or monitoring test activities.

By providing specific places where child-oriented activity is expected and encouraged, disruption or destruction is less likely to occur in the remainder of the clinical setting. The test room, the playroom, and the play corner in the reception room should be constructed to encourage response without undue concern for neatness or defacement. These areas require sensible selection of sturdy furniture and synthetic wall coverings.

The child who shows interest in and positive response to the clinical setting is most likely to participate in the process. This kind of participation can determine the richness of information available for the final evaluation of the youngster's psychological potential. Test administration procedures are standardized and leave little room for individualizing the assessment situation. Certain techniques, however, can help to create a comfortable and inviting atmosphere for the child.

Fantasy Play. Except for the unusually disturbed or deficient child, almost all children are willing to enter into fantasy play. Through such play, the clinician can establish a strong and early rapport with the child. Some clinicians establish a "theme" or story line during the child's visit. The purposes of fantasy play are:

- To lessen or eliminate separation anxiety when the child leaves the parent in the reception room
- To help the child relax
- To encourage the child to develop an active, positive identification with the testing procedures
- To make the testing procedures move more rapidly and efficiently
- To ensure the child's willingness to return for subsequent test sessions.

Fantasy play as part of the testing sequence is discussed in greater detail in Chapter 7.

Treasure Chest. Filled with yo-yos, plastic bathtub boats, Chinese handcuffs, small kaleidoscopes, children's rings, balloons, puzzles, compasses, miniature cars and trucks, bracelets and necklaces, and other small toys of the dime store variety, the treasure chest is best used as the final stop in each session of the child's assessment. The container for these toys should be built and decorated as a pirate's treasure chest or other theme appealing to children.

At the end of each test session, the child can be brought to the playroom and allowed to select an arbitrary number of toys as a reward for working well. A large, old-fashioned lock on the treasure chest, with a key available on a nearby hook, increases the child's interest, glee, and participation.

Candy Store. Used also as a posttest reward, a cabinet with 15 or 20 glass or plastic apothecary jars filled with a variety of bubble gum and small colorful candies is a helpful adjunct to the assessment process. A supply of white candy bags completes the arrangement. At the end of each test session (with the parents' permission), the child is allowed to take any 10 pieces he or she wants. These candies and the old-fashioned candy bag provide positive reinforcement following the child's assessment experience.

Dart Board. The plastic marker board on the wall of the playroom can provide a rapport-building and tension-breaking device by serving as a dart board. Usually the child's first stop during the first assessment visit, the playroom is strange but exciting. Most children become comfortable and involved with the concept of participating and scoring by throwing or shooting suction darts. A sign above the marker board can read "If you score 40 points with 4 darts, you win a special prize." The child is asked to help draw a target with marker pens. Most children above 4 years of age can "win" in three or four tries. The special prize can consist of a kite and a ball of string, or a bollo paddle and ball. The child should be told that the special prize will be waiting in the reception room when he or she has finished for the day.

The anticipation of this "prize" seems to motivate children to participate in the long, sometimes uninteresting assessment process. Observation of the child's behavior during dart play provides material for the clinical observation of coordination, motor control, and laterality.

The use of these special facilities and procedures significantly reduces the number of "untestable" children. These settings and procedures are most useful for children between 3 and 12 years of age. Alternative approaches for younger and older children are presented in later chapters.

The main purpose behind careful preparation and a supportive, comforting examination setting is to allow the child to demonstrate his or her best performance. The child's poorest performance or behavior will be well documented in the descriptions of problems and concerns received from parents, teachers, and others. The psychologist's responsibility is to explore, document, and represent the child's latent skills and maximum potential.

CHAPTER FIVE

Equipment and Material

Although the assessment of adults can be conducted with a relatively limited number of tests and testing equipment, a thorough psychological assessment of a child requires access to a potentially large amount of equipment and materials. Because a wide range of results, answers, and recommendations are required and expected by parents, teachers, and others, the psychologist who conducts examinations of children should have the facilities and equipment to meet these expectancies.

With adults, rapport can be established in most instances during history taking at initial interviews. With children, trust, security, and cooperation must be established, reestablished, and embellished each time the child is seen during the assessment series. Very few children approach psychological assessment as willing participants. They are usually sent or brought by someone who is worried about them, displeased with their behavior, or angry at them. No matter what may be said to encourage the child to view the assessment in a positive way, wariness or fear can be expected as the child's initial response. Special materials and procedures can moderate or eliminate these negative affects.

Tests to measure various aspects of the child's life and nature are designed and standardized within relatively narrow age ranges. To be prepared to examine children from infancy through adolescence, the clinician must have available an appropriate range of test levels and forms. Some children must be retested to validate initial findings or for tracking purposes (discussed in later chapters). Alternate forms of intelligence, reading, and neuropsychological test instruments must be available to the clinician when necessary.

TEST MATERIALS

The range and quality of psychological tests available today enable the psychologist to choose batteries that focus on the specific requirements of the individual assessment. Because the quality of these instruments varies considerably, the psychologist must be willing to evaluate the reliability and validity of various instruments to ensure that the appropriate instruments are used. Clinical psychologists are trained to evaluate the adequacy of a test's standardization (Anastasi, 1982). Reviews are also helpful in deciding which tests are most useful for specific clinical purposes (Buros, 1960–1985, 1970–1975).

The reliability, validity, and appropriate utilization of any test or assessment technique are not static or fixed. The psychologist must weigh the needs and expectancies of the assessment against the "degree of fit" of the instrument; its standardization; its applicability to the child's age, ethnic background, and handicaps; and other factors.

The clinical child psychologist should decide on a basic stock of tests and equipment and be willing to add and discard assessment materials and techniques as dictated by research and experience, which the psychologist should constantly review.

The specific tests and equipment described in the following sections should be considered currently acceptable. Each clinical child psychologist may have individual preferences for tests to assess the various domains of child behavior and performance. This is understandable and desirable because instrumentation for the assessment of children continues to be developed and revised. Some general rules for the selection of assessment tests and instruments include the following:

1. *Applicability.* The clinical child psychologist should be reasonably sure that the instrument yields information that advances the goals of the evaluation. For example, a test of musical talent is unlikely to be helpful as part of the assessment of a 7-year-old who has regressed significantly after the divorce of his or her parents.

2. *Standardization.* Testing instruments should have a standardization history that suggests that the child is reasonably within the subject group upon which the test was standardized.

3. *Contemporaneity.* In most instances, tests contain language, cultural, and historical references that may be relatively unique to the era during which the test was developed and standardized. The clinical child psychologist should be sure that the test materials used to test a child are appropriate to the child's era of development.

In addition to the previous suggestions for selecting and using psychological and educational tests, clinicians should be relatively familiar with the standards for the development of educational and psychological tests (American Psychological Association, American Educational Research Association, and National Council in Measurement of Education, 1985).

TEST EQUIPMENT

Testing, in a sense, is psychology's birthright (Blau, 1979). Some child specialists may conduct an assessment without using formalized instruments, but rarely should psychologists take a nonpsychometric approach.

Thousands of test instruments and batteries have been developed for evaluating children's performance and behavior. Most have both advantages and disadvantages. The professional clinical child psychologist should be wary of becoming wedded to a particular test instrument or test battery. The purpose of each child's assessment should dictate the selection of test instruments. The value of any particular test must be gauged by the clinician in respect to the needs of the assessment goals and the quality of the instrument chosen. Judgment of quality requires that the clinical child psychologist have the skills and incentive to evaluate standardization data on tests used and current research relating to the base rates, reliability, validity, and applicability of all instruments used as part of the assessment process.

Excellent texts are available that describe and recommend a broad range of psychological test instruments and their proper utilization (Aiken, 1987; Sattler, 1982, 1988; Simeonsson, 1986). In a sense, such texts are outdated before they are published. Test development and utilization are two of the most dynamic areas of research and development in the fields of applied psychology. The changes and extensions of test standardization represent opportunities for more skillful practice.

Keeping current on the status of tests used with children requires the clinical child psychologist to read the appropriate clinical and research journals that publish reports and utilization information about test instruments and procedures. Also, brief reviews of major test instruments are available (Keyser & Sweetland, 1987). The professional and skillful clinical child psychologist should be familiar with these expert reviews for test instruments customarily used.

Although the various compendiums of test reviews and evaluations are continually revised, these revisions tend to reflect instruments that may have been available for some period of time or in some cases may be no longer published. To be able to order appropriate assessment material for children, the psychologist should create a test publisher and distributor catalog file. Once a test user is on the mailing list for a test publisher or distributor, new catalogs arrive on an annual or semiannual basis. Appendix A lists the major test publishers and distributors whose catalogs include clinical instruments and materials for the evaluation of children.

GAMES AND TOYS

The time allowed for the clinical child psychologist to communicate with the child is necessarily limited. Because only a certain number of hours can be spent in conducting the examination, initial impressions are extremely important and influential. The entire tone of the examination may be determined by the first contact between child and clinician. Except for the extremely young child, almost every child whom the clinician sees will have experience in games, toys, and fantasy. Appropriate use of this kind of material at the beginning of the session can set a positive tone for the examination. The use of toys and fantasy objects can also encourage maximum performance on the part of the child, which is one goal of the assessment. Adults in the child's environment will provide the clinician with many examples of the child's minimum performance; thus, in almost all cases, the clinician has to use the assessment to determine the child's potential.

The choice of games and toys that will be provided depends, to a large extent, on what the clinician finds comfortable. A traditional playroom may be the choice of some clinicians, although shelves and cabinets containing dolls, puppets, mustaches, wigs, and other fantasy materials may be sufficient. Other clinicians may want objects available in the consultation room, in the test room, on the walls, and in the hallways. The hallway may be a good place to set up a children's zoo approximately 48 in. off the floor. Photographs or lithographs of various animals attract the attention and positive responses of most children. The clinician may wish to have a drawer of hand puppets, balloons, and other toys with which to engage the child's attention and involvement while in the consultation office. The extent to which the clinician can utilize play materials to involve the child in the examination process depends on the clinician's experience, creativity, rapport-gaining skills, and, of course, personality. The use of these materials is addressed in some detail in Chapter 6.

FORMS

The recording of data and general information is an important part of any psychological assessment. The forms used in child evaluation vary considerably. Forms for recording the child's history, observations of the child's behavior, neuropsychological behavior observations, telephone contacts with teachers or playschool supervisors, and so forth, can be particularly useful for a variety of reasons: (a) A form is a convenient and time-saving device for recording important material that will be later used in formulating the assessment report; (b) by color coding forms, the clinician can easily retrieve data from a file full of materials collected during the assessment; and (c) by establishing a series of forms to be used in a child assessment, the clinician cycles his or her thinking into a pattern which, when repeated, allows the clinician to identify unique and essential elements of the child's behavior or performance for the purposes of the final assessment.

Throughout this book, examples of the uses of various forms are presented. The clinician may wish to develop forms similar to those presented or to create forms for specific purposes. In developing an assessment style, the clinician will find that forms represent the structure within which he or she can operate at the most efficient level.

THE ONE-WAY MIRROR

There is a long tradition of examining children in a room that contains a one-way mirror. On the examination side, the mirror indeed appears to be simply a mirror on the wall. Behind the mirror, however, is a room, usually slightly darkened, in which the testing process can be observed. Although the one-way mirror was originally developed as a teaching device, some clinicians have used it to allow parents to observe their children during assessments.

Most clinicians find that although the mirror is a traditional device, it falls into disuse very quickly. Having the parents observe the testing situation adds time and confusion to the assessment without accomplishing the goal of involvement or understanding. In addition, most children over the age of 5 ask, "What's behind the mirror?" It is probably unwise to incite feelings of suspicion and distrust in the child by having this kind of equipment.

MOTIVATIONAL EQUIPMENT

To help children produce maximum performance, the clinician should use a variety of motivational devices and situations. Some of the common devices that have been used successfully by clinicians who work with children include the following:

- *The Treasure Chest.* As discussed in the previous chapter, a large box, suitably decorated as a treasure chest, is filled with a wide variety of small, nondangerous toys that appeal to children ranging in age from 2 to 12. This chest may include whistles, compasses, stickers, a variety of rings, bracelets, necklaces, small games, balls, fans, kazoos, miniature figures of animals, dinosaurs, cars, trains, and other small objects of interest to children. These items can be obtained from a variety of sources. The way in which the treasure chest is used is presented in Chapter 9.
- *The Candy Store.* A special cabinet can be provided with a variety of glass jars to make an old-fashioned candy store. In these jars, the clinician can place bubble gum, candy corn, chocolate kisses, jelly beans, and so forth, that are generally not available to the child. Although this kind of reward should be used judiciously and with the parents' permission, it can be an effective motivational or reinforcement device.

• *Beards, Wigs, and Hats.* Dress-up materials in a chest or cabinet provide an opportunity to engage the child in fantasy play. This activity can be used for building rapport, breaking away from the rigors of testing, or observation of the child's capacity to participate in fantasy. Masks, hats with peculiar devices, and/or mechanical elements are interesting to children.

RECORDING DEVICES

The clinician who sees children regularly should have professional-quality tape-recording equipment. The clinician can tape-record the session during which he or she interprets the assessment results to the parents or other significant adults (see Chapter 15), and then give the tape recording to the adults. This tape serves as a therapeutic device and a continuation of the assessment interaction between the clinician and the parents. This procedure is addressed in some detail in a later portion of this volume.

Although much of the information presented in this book is suggestive, all of it has been tested and found to be effective. There are no absolute rules other than for the conduct of standardized tests.

SECTION II

Intake Procedures

CHAPTER SIX

The Environmental Press

The traditional team approach in child guidance clinics began with an intake worker or perhaps a secretary asking questions of the parents or other adults in the child's life. Next, an intake worker met with the adults to take the child's history. Following this, professional workers at a staff meeting might have decided to schedule an additional interview with the adults or to refer the child for psychological testing. Additional conferences with the parents or teachers might have taken place, often with another person conducting such interviews. At a staff meeting, all of the participants determined the conclusions and recommendations to be given to the parents at a subsequent meeting.

Many a client complained that, "Everybody listens to the story, but nobody tells me anything about what's going on." These reasonable complaints represent only one of the areas in which the clients spoke and we seldom listened.

To be of the greatest benefit to the child who needs help and to the parents and other community agents anxious to provide such help, a single clinician should be involved with the family from the beginning to the end. Effective use of clinical services and the quality of outcome are very much based on the inclusion of all significant family members and a single service provider throughout the process (Tolan, Ryan, & Jaffe, 1988).

To provide service with the greatest possible effect, the psychologist must provide an ambiance of security, professional skill, and support. Much of this is accomplished during the first contact. Because this first contact is usually with a secretary when a parent telephones for an appointment, it is important that the person receiving the telephone contact be warm, supportive, and encouraging, but not involved in the details of the problem. It is sufficient that the secretary take basic information, arrange an appointment, and ensure that case materials are ready for the clinician for the first meeting.

Figure 6.1 illustrates an intake form that can be used by secretaries or others to obtain basic information over the telephone, and to make the

___Card
___Letter
___Map   **INTAKE**

NAME_____ DATE_____ BY_____

ADDRESS_____ PHONE_____

BIRTHDATE_____ AGE_____ EDUC_____ SCHOOL_____

OCC_____ REL _____

REF_____ REP TO_____

REASON FOR REFERRAL:

QUESTIONS -- TERMINAL GOALS

HIST DATE: _____ _____ _____	_____EV.	_____TR.	DATE_____	HR_____
	_____EV.	_____TR.	DATE_____	HR_____
RESULTS: _____ _____ _____	_____EV.	_____TR.	DATE_____	HR_____
#2 _____ _____ _____	_____EV.	_____TR.	DATE_____	HR_____

FEES: DIAG: REC REQ:

                               THER:

                               RED. BASE

FIGURE 6.1   Intake Sheet

initial appointment. The intake sheet has blanks for the name of the young-ster, the family address, the date of intake, the birthdate of the child, the school grade, and the parents' name (with the high divorce rate, it is not unusual that the family name differs from the child's). The secretary should ask the parents the source of the referral. The secretary should be trained to ask what services are desired and why the contact is being made. In some instances, the parents or the referral agent cannot be very clear about why the consultation is sought. No effort should be made on the telephone to press the caller as to the exact nature of the difficulty. The purpose of the initial contact is to give the caller the feeling that he or she has come to the right place for consideration of the child's difficulties, that an appointment will be made, and that all things will be discussed during the first inter-view. Only the first history appointment should be made with the con-cerned adults. A 1-hr appointment is sufficient to begin the process.

Because it is from the child's environment that the request for an evalua-tion is generally made, the diagnostic process should proceed from the environment to the child. It is extremely rare for a child to ask for profes-sional help. Although important information may come from teachers, other professional people, a social agency, or other sources, the parents provide the broadest view of the child's environment. Even though some parents may be unable to present an entire picture of the child's life and times with accuracy and validity, they are important reporters and partici-pants.

The psychologist must have an opportunity to meet the parent or custo-dial figures with whom the child deals in his or her everyday life. The diagnostic process for the child may have therapeutic implications for the parents. Many parents are quite guilt ridden, and are entering into a proc-ess whereby the thought that "something is being done" can have helpful initial effects. Because the parents are so vital to the child, their involve-ment at the very beginning of the process prepares them to become part of the process. They thus become better able to participate in conflict resolu-tion, rehabilitation, or the pursuit of potential. Conversely, an intake proc-ess in which the parents feel threatened is likely to have negative effects on the child. Feelings of defensiveness that are stirred by the evaluation proc-ess may create hostilities that have a serious deterrent effect on implemen-tation of the recommendations that emerge from the evaluation process.

It should be standard procedure to call the responsible adults several days before the appointment to ensure that they remember the appoint-ment and that they plan to attend. If parents are coming from out of town and the psychologist's office may be difficult to locate, a map should be sent illustrating the easiest access routes to the office. Figure 6.2 illus-trates such a map. Everything should be done to make it easier for the parents to come to the appointment with a feeling that they will be met with consideration and professionalism. This graciousness will be helpful to the entire process.

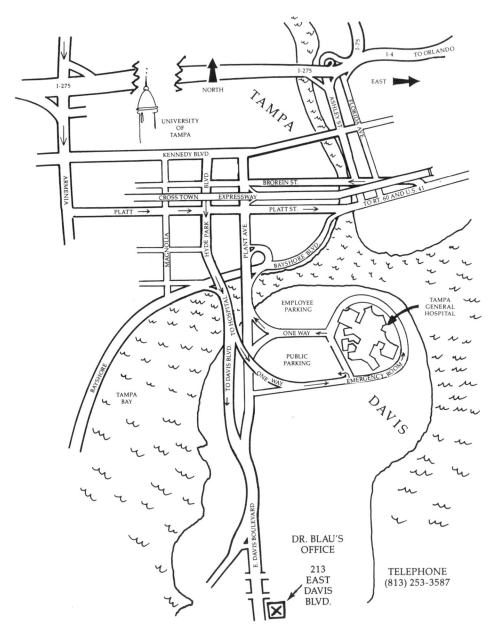

FIGURE 6.2 Map to Help Patients Find the Doctor's Office

THE INTAKE INTERVIEW

The initial appointment made with the parents should not include the child. The parents should be reassured that the child will be seen later. The secretary who makes the initial appointment should tell the parents in a supportive manner that the psychologist must spend some time with the people most important in the child's environment.

The psychologist should be prepared to provide a warm, supportive, yet structured setting for the first interview. The purpose of this interview is to involve the parents in the process, to obtain pertinent information, to provide a structure for understanding the child, and to inform the parents of the nature of the process and what may be expected. The first intake session is the time to make appointments for the examination and the results. Everything should be done in a manner so as to leave the parents with a positive feeling about the process.

The tasks of the psychologist during the intake interview include the following:

1. The collection of data to provide the psychologist with an understanding of the child's home and the child's parental figures
2. An opportunity to understand the child's manifest behavior or lack of performance as seen through the eyes of the closest adult figures in the child's life
3. The collection of data about the child's responses in the home, in the school, and in the community at large
4. An opportunity for the psychologist to set the stage for a comfortable process whereby the parental figures can be encouraged to participate in whatever remedial steps will be suggested
5. The collection of facts and figures about the child's progress through various ages and stages of development, to find anomalies that might explain or at least clarify some elements of the problems indicated by the parents.

Meeting the Parents

Most parents never consulted with a psychologist; they called for an appointment because, in most instances, they are concerned about a problem with their child. They often are tense, guilt ridden, perhaps even frightened. Starting off correctly is of great importance. The psychologist must do everything reasonable to involve the parents in a warm, supportive way. The psychologist can start by going to the waiting room to introduce himself or herself to the parents, offering to get them coffee or a cold drink, and ushering them into the consulting office. This simple gesture separates the psychologist in the mind of the parent from dentists, physicians, and other professionals who do not come out to greet the client, and sets a positive tone for the entire consultation.

After seating the parents comfortably, the psychologist should ask a very general question, such as "How may I be of service?" Most parents are somewhat puzzled by this question. They expect to be asked, "What's wrong?" They are surprised that a professional person is starting off with an offer of help. This can be advantageous and should be an important part of the introduction to the process. Many parents have difficulty deciding exactly what they are seeking. Others are very specific about why they have scheduled the appointment. In some cases, the parent may not be having any problem with the child, but may simply be seeking guidance in helping the youngster's development.

In any event, the psychologist's first order of business is to try to get an initial view of the parents' expectations. If the parents are unable to respond to the first question, the clinician might ask, "If I could answer any questions that you might have about your youngster, what might be important to you to know, or what might be important for you to see changed?"

The following is a verbatim excerpt from an intake session with the parents of a 5-year-old child. The father said:

> Our boy's birthday is in December. This means that we have to decide whether to enroll him in the first grade in September, probably in a private school, or wait a year. A lot of kids start the first grade when they're under 6. We hear that this might not be a good idea. We'd like to find out whether John has the intellectual capability and the emotional maturity to do okay in the first grade.

At this point, the mother interjected:

> He's been pretty happy in kindergarten, but the work has been pretty easy for him. We've heard a lot about reading readiness tests that might help us to decide whether John is ready for the first grade. Maybe you could give him some tests? His doctor says he's in good shape and may be a little large for his age.

In this initial statement, the parents have clarified their need quite well. They have anticipated a part of the basic test battery in asking about reading readiness. First statements by parents are not always so clear. The following is a portion of an intake interview with the mother of a $10\frac{1}{2}$-year-old boy. She was asked, "How may I be of service?" and she replied as follows:

> The pediatrician said that I should come to see you. I want you to do something for my boy. His teachers say he's lazy and always wants to be babied. I sent him 3 years ago to the chiropractor and after that to the neurologist, but I've had my problems, too, because I had my pituitary glands removed. I've

broken almost every bone in my body. I'm hurting constantly and my spine is out of place, too. He saw my first husband knock me down, and that's why I broke one of my bones and also punctured a lung.

I've had 12 operations and I think I'm going to need another one. Sometimes he's very brilliant, but he doesn't like being named after his father. He's angry at his father and has good reason, too, because his father was no good, so I told him to call his father "uncle." I married another man 2 1/2 years ago, but he is real nice. He's never home enough. After I had the tumor in my breast out and the bottom of my spine broke, I had so much surgery and the other baby has been so sick that I'm short with him.

We get along fine, of course, and we love each other and he's always slept with me and told me that I'm "his honey." The baby's been sick too. She's 2 1/2 years old and has been in the hospital three times. She's a very nervous child and this may be doing something to the boy. His grandmother always sat beside him during the time he did his homework. His grandmother died last year and now he wants me to sit with him. He looks at his grandmother's picture and says that she isn't smiling. He once told me he got so angry at her that he told her that he wished she was dead. I told him I didn't believe this, but he still keeps looking at the picture and asks the picture to smile at him. I think he wants some kind of forgiveness. The trouble might have started because my milk turned green at the end of 6 weeks after he was born. He was a very sickly child. He had convulsions when he was a baby and I think he had some 2 years ago, but it's hard to remember. He once had a brain wave test, but I never went back to find out what it meant. Last year, my husband gave him a doll because he was jealous of the baby when she got a doll. He loves the doll.

This initial interview demonstrates the difficulty a clinician might have during an intake interview in clarifying the needs of the child, let alone those of the parent.

Setting Goals

At any point during the intake interview, questions or goals may become apparent. These may be set down in the appropriate space on the intake sheet (Figure 6.1). This important step establishes the outcome structure and recommendations section of the final report, which is illustrated as the history-taking process presented in Chapter 8.

TAKING THE HISTORY

Once the parents are comfortable and the initial questions have been asked, the psychologist can take the detailed history. Although open-ended questions can be valuable, it is more efficient and effective to structure the history. This allows the psychologist to compare the child being evaluated with all the children whose histories the clinician has taken.

Figure 6.3 illustrates a coded form for taking the parent information portions of the family history. At the top of the form the clinician writes the date of the history taking, the names of the persons giving the history, and the clinician's initials. The coding for the MOTHER and FATHER information is as follows:

N—Name

A—Age

O—Occupation

E— Formal Education

H—Health (now and during the child's lifetime)

P— The parent's view of his or her own personality when interacting with the child. This can sometimes be best elicited by asking, "Tell me a little about your personality or your reactions when you spend time with your youngster."

The information provided by each parent or surrogate is noted on the form. The extra space between MOTHER and FATHER allows additional entries for stepparents.

SIBS is where information regarding name, age, and status of each sibling can be entered.

OTHERS is where the clinician can write information about any significant relatives or other adults or children who may have regular contact with the child.

SOC-EC is where the psychologist places the family's gross annual income and other information relative to socioeconomic status.

CLIMATE is where the clinician writes the parent's response to the question, "Tell me about the way you like things to go at home. Do you like things to be pretty much on schedule, or are you more easygoing?" Some parents seem to have difficulty with this question. They should be encouraged to express, in their own words, their preferred style of doing things at home.

CLIN is where the psychologist can write a brief description of his or her impression of the personality, style, or presentation of the parent figures.

F AND M INTERACTION is where the clinician writes each parent's response to the question, "Tell me about some of the things that you do together with your youngster." If the family is fractured by separation or divorce, the visitation schedule should be noted here, as well as any conflicts regarding the child's contact with each parent.

Examples of how this and other sheets in the history are filled out are provided in Chapter 8.

FAMILY HISTORY

DATE _____ INFORMANT _____ BY _____

MOTHER   FATHER

N

A

O

E

H

P

SIBS

OTHERS

SOC EC

CLIMATE   F   INTERACTION

CLIN:

M:

F:

M   INTERACTION

FIGURE 6.3   Family History Form

Figure 6.4 shows the second page of the history form. On this page, the clinician notes the details of the developmental history and related information obtained from the parents or surrogates.

PRE & POST NATAL is where the clinician writes the response to the question, "Was there any difficulty for mother or child at the time of birth?" Where problems are reported, the psychologist should attempt to get a brief but accurate description of the difficulties.

The clinician should write the responses to the following questions in the appropriate spaces.

BIR: "What did he weigh at birth?"

FEED: "Was she breast or bottle fed?" (Write the ages in months when shifts occurred from breast to bottle to cup.)

TT: "At what month was toilet training first started?"

1ST YR: "Were there any unusual events or problems during the first 12 months?"

2–5TH: "Were you satisfied with the youngster's development during the second, third, and fourth years?" (Bring up walking, talking, socialization, etc.)

MEDICAL is where the psychologist not only should write about any significant physical problems the child has or has had, but also should note whether the child has had a recent physical examination. If it has been a year or more since the child has been examined, the psychologist should insist that the child be seen by the pediatrician or family physician before the evaluation is completed. The parents should be asked at this point if they have any objections to the psychologist contacting the child's physician if it appears that this might be helpful during the evaluation. Specific questions under this section are:

PHYSICIAN: "Who is his doctor? When was his last physical?"

T&A: "Has she had her tonsils out? Any other surgery?" (Get details and ages where such occurred.)

OTHER: "Has he had any severe illness or injuries?" (Obtain details where such occurred.)

U.C.D.:   "Has she had the usual childhood diseases—mumps, measles, chicken pox? Any of them severe?" (Get details.)

IMMUNIZ: "Has he been immunized?" (Should the parents or surrogates say "no" or "don't know," referral to the family physician or pediatrician is indicated.)

REG. COMPL.: "Does she have any regular complaints, say, two or three times a week? Headaches, stomachaches, chest pains, leg aches, or anything?"

```
                                              HISTORY - 2

PRE & POST NATAL:                     GRANDPARENTS:
BIR:
FEED:
TT:

1ST YR:

2–5th:


MEDICAL:                              RELIGION:
PHYSICIAN:
T&A:
OTHER:
U.C.D.:
IMMUNIZ:
REG. COMPL:
PUB:
SEX ED:
ADD'L:


UNCONC:
FEVER:
SEIZURES:
DURING 1st 8 YRS:                     TRAUMA:
DIZZINESS:
HEADACHES:
POOR SLEEP:
SINISTRALITY IN FAMILY:
```

FIGURE 6.4   Developmental History Form

PUB: "Has she shown any signs of puberty? Breast development, broadening of hips, menstrual cycle?" (For boy—broadening of shoulders, pubic hair, cracking or lowering of voice.)

SEX ED: "Has he been given any sex education? By whom?"

ADD'L: "Have there been any unusual physical or social problems in her development that I haven't asked about?"

UNCONC: "Has he ever been unconscious?" (Get details.)

FEVER: "Has she ever had high fevers for more than a couple of hours?" (Get details.)

SEIZURES: "Has he ever had convulsions or seizures?" (Get details.)

DURING 1ST 8 YEARS is where the psychologist records symptoms which, when they occur frequently during the first 8 years of life, may indicate perinatal or postnatal brain disorder (Golden, 1987c; Satz, Taylor, Friel, & Fletcher, 1978)

DIZZINESS: "During the first 8 years of his life did he suffer dizziness frequently?"

HEADACHES: "During her first 8 years did she seem to have headaches regularly?"

POOR SLEEP: "During the first 8 years of life did he have a lot of trouble sleeping?"

SINISTRALITY IN FAMILY: "Is anyone in the family left-handed? On either side?" (Sinistrality and mixed cerebral dominance may have important implications for a child's personal, academic, and neuropsychological development. This is addressed in a later chapter.)

GRANDPARENTS: "Does she have living grandparents? Does she see them regularly? What kind of interaction is there?" (Children who have a positive experience with their grandparents tend to be better adjusted in a number of ways in later life; Blau, 1984.)

RELIGION: "What are the religious practices in the home, and to what extent does he participate in religious activities?"

TRAUMA: "Has she had any shocking or unfortunate experience in her life? Being lost? Almost drowning? Anything like that?"

Sufficient space is provided on the form to briefly record anything that the psychologist believes to be of value from the parents' statements. Such statements might include the following:

"She has lots of colds."

"He rocked his crib at night for 3 years."

"She would never let anyone hold her."

"We really didn't want a child at that time."

"He was hard to raise from the minute he was born."

"Because of her asthma, she couldn't do a lot of the things other kids could do."

At some time during the intake interview, the psychologist should ask the parents if the child has a nickname. This name can serve as a rapport device when the child is examined.

Figure 6.5 shows the third page of the history form. This section has to do with school activities and socialization.

SCHOOL is where the psychologist should write the brief details of school history. The initial question is "Did he attend preschool." This should be followed by the following questions:

1. "How did she do in the first grade?"
2. "Tell me how he did in each grade following."
3. "How is she doing now?"

To the right of the school grade information, the following items appear:

PERFORMANCE BELOW POTENTIAL: "Have you ever been told that she performs below her potential?" (Get details.)

SOCIALLY EMBARRASSING: "Has the school ever reported, or for that matter
have you ever observed, behavior on your child's part that is
socially embarrassing to him or those around him?" (The appropriate details to these questions should be put on the form.)

HOMEWORK: "Does she have a regular homework schedule?" (Get details.)

FRIENDS: "Does he have friends at school?" (Get details.) (This question
may be followed by further questions about whether the child
spends times at the friends' homes or whether the friends spend
time with him at his home. It is also appropriate to ask whether
the child tends to be a leader or a follower.)

HOME is where the psychologist records descriptions of the youngster's behavior in and around the home. The psychologist should ask, "Do you own your own home?" Questions about the size of the yard and play facilities are appropriate. Questions for the rest of the section are as follows:

ROOM: "Does she have her own room? Does she like her room and spend
time there?" (Get details.)

RECR: "What kind of things does he like to do for pleasure?" (Get details.)

SIBS: "Tell me a little bit about how she gets along with her brothers and
sisters."

MEALS: "Is he a good eater? Is he picky about anything?"

DISCIPL: "What kind of discipline have you found necessary? What has been
effective for you when discipline is necessary?"

CAMP: "Has she ever been to camp? How did she like it, and how did it
seem to affect her?"

SPORTS: "What kind of things does he like to engage in? Does he belong to
any teams?"

HISTORY - 3

SCHOOL: _____ Performance Below Potential

FRIENDS: _____ Socially Embarrassing

HOME: HOMEWORK:
  ROOM:

  RECR:

  SIBS:

  MEALS:

  DISCIPL:

  CAMP:

  SPORTS:

  HOBBIES:

  DATING:

  ALLOW:

  BEDT:

  CHORES:

FIGURE 6.5   School and Home Environment History Form

HOBBIES: "Does she have any hobbies or collections?"

DATING: "Does he show any interest in the opposite sex? Has he been spending a lot of time on the telephone talking with friends of the opposite sex?"

ALLOW: "Does she receive a regular allowance? Who gives her this allowance? Does she have an opportunity to earn extra money?"

BEDT: "What is his usual bedtime on school nights? Do you have any trouble getting him to bed at this time?"

CHORES: "Does she have any regular chores around the house? How effectively are these done?"

These questions will result in a brief but rather broad picture of the child's life and times at school and at home. Detailed questioning is always appropriate. Where copious notes are required, the reverse side of the form can be used.

Figure 6.6 is a history form that presents behavior problems that occur in normal children between the ages of 21 months and 14 years. MacFarlane et al. (1954) studied a large number of normal children during this 12-year developmental period and found that many so-called neuropathic traits or behavior problems appeared to be common in normal children during certain stages of development. These behaviors are often of great concern to parents. By recording the occurrence of these behaviors during the history taking, the psychologist has an opportunity to use these data for one or more of the following purposes:

- To summarize the behavior that distresses parents and/or teachers over the child's developmental years
- To record the occurrence of such behavior in respect to significant events in the family life cycle, such as births of other children, deaths, divorce, and remarriage
- To compare the occurrence of the child's behavior with the occurrence of such behavior at expected ages and stages.

The commonality of occurrence of these behaviors in children has been confirmed in Byar's (1983) cross-validation of the MacFarlane et al. studies using a more contemporary sample of children.

The personal adjustment page of the history shown in Figure 6.6 is completed in the following manner:

1. Whenever a significant event that might affect the child is mentioned during the history taking, the psychologist should draw a vertical line from top to bottom indicating the child's age at which this event occurred. Thus, if the parents divorced when the child was 7 1/2 years old, the psychologist draws a vertical line down the entire page between "7" and "8" on the "age" line.

HISTORY - 4

PERSONAL ADJUSTMENT

	AGE: 0	1	2	3	4	5	6	7	8	9	10	11	12	13	14
NAIL BITING	0	0	0	0	0	0	0	0	0	0	0	0	0	0	0
CRYING	0	0	0	0	0	0	0	0	0	0	0	0	0	0	0
THUMB SUCKING	0	0	0	0	0	0	0	0	0	0	0	0	0	0	0
ENURESIS	0	0	0	0	0	0	0	0	0	0	0	0	0	0	0
SOILING	0	0	0	0	0	0	0	0	0	0	0	0	0	0	0
SOMNABULISM	0	0	0	0	0	0	0	0	0	0	0	0	0	0	0
VOMITING	0	0	0	0	0	0	0	0	0	0	0	0	0	0	0
STUTTERING	0	0	0	0	0	0	0	0	0	0	0	0	0	0	0
MASTURBATION	0	0	0	0	0	0	0	0	0	0	0	0	0	0	0
NIGHTMARES	0	0	0	0	0	0	0	0	0	0	0	0	0	0	0
NIGHT TERRORS	0	0	0	0	0	0	0	0	0	0	0	0	0	0	0
FEARFUL	0	0	0	0	0	0	0	0	0	0	0	0	0	0	0
CRUELTY	0	0	0	0	0	0	0	0	0	0	0	0	0	0	0
TANTRUMS	0	0	0	0	0	0	0	0	0	0	0	0	0	0	0
DESTRUCTIVENESS	0	0	0	0	0	0	0	0	0	0	0	0	0	0	0
QUARRELSOME	0	0	0	0	0	0	0	0	0	0	0	0	0	0	0
JEALOUS	0	0	0	0	0	0	0	0	0	0	0	0	0	0	0
UNCOOPERATIVE	0	0	0	0	0	0	0	0	0	0	0	0	0	0	0
EXCESS ENERGY	0	0	0	0	0	0	0	0	0	0	0	0	0	0	0
LYING	0	0	0	0	0	0	0	0	0	0	0	0	0	0	0
STEALING	0	0	0	0	0	0	0	0	0	0	0	0	0	0	0
SHYNESS	0	0	0	0	0	0	0	0	0	0	0	0	0	0	0
DEPENDENCY	0	0	0	0	0	0	0	0	0	0	0	0	0	0	0
LACK SELF-CONF.	0	0	0	0	0	0	0	0	0	0	0	0	0	0	0
SENSITIVENESS	0	0	0	0	0	0	0	0	0	0	0	0	0	0	0
MOOD SWINGS	0	0	0	0	0	0	0	0	0	0	0	0	0	0	0

FIGURE 6.6   Behavior Problems of Normal Children Form

2. For details to be marked on the horizontal next to the key behavior items listed on the left, the parents are told the following:

> I'm going to ask you about some common behaviors that almost all children do at some time during their growth and development. I'd like you to tell me if your youngster presently does any of these or if the behaviors occurred in the past.

3. When the parents indicate that a behavior is currently happening, the clinician should mark an X on the line beside the behavior, under the numeral indicating the child's current age. The parent should then be asked, "When did she start doing this?" The psychologist can then mark another X under the age when the behavior began. The two Xs are then connected, indicating the period of the child's life during which the behavior occurred.

4. If the parent indicates that the behavior occurred intermittently, this can be indicated with a dashed line rather than a solid line connecting the Xs.

The exact manner in which this page is completed will be illustrated in the case presentation in Chapter 8, on page 85.

Questions to elicit information for each of the items listed under personal adjustment are as follows:

NAIL BITING: "Does he bite his nails regularly?" (If so, "At what age did he start to do this?")

CRYING: "Does she cry more frequently than a youngster her age should? (If so, "At what age did she begin to do this?")

THUMB SUCKING: "Does he suck his thumb or fingers regularly?" (If so, determine when this began.)

SOILING: "Does he mess his pants because he forgets or because he's too busy to go to the bathroom?" (If so, determine when this began.)

SOMNAMBULISM: "Does she walk or talk regularly in her sleep?" (If so, determine when this began.)

VOMITING: "Does he gag or vomit easily?" (If so, determine when this began.)

STUTTERING: "Does she stutter or block when she tries to tell you something?" (If so, determine when this began.)

MASTURBATION: "Does he show any unusual interest in his sexual organs or in those of others?" (If so, get details.)

NIGHTMARES: "Does she report bad dreams to you frequently?" (Get details.)

NIGHT TERRORS: "Does he wake up screaming or crying frequently?" (Get details.)

FEARFUL: "Is she afraid of anything regularly, such as the dark? Lightning? Riding in the car? Being alone? Anything?" (Get details.)

CRUELTY: "Is he cruel or hurtful to other children? To animals?" (Get details.)

TANTRUMS: "Does she throw tantrums or fits? Scream, yell, throw things when she doesn't get her way?" (Get details.)

DESTRUCTIVENESS: "Does he break up his possessions a lot? Other people's?" (Get details.)

QUARRELSOME: "Does she pick, pick, pick until someone will finally argue or fight with her?" (Get details.)

JEALOUS: "Is he jealous when you show affection to each other or to someone else?" (Get details.)

UNCOOPERATIVE: "Is she as cooperative as you would expect for a youngster her age?" (If not, get details.)

EXCESS ENERGY: "Does he usually show an average amount of energy? More than average? Less?" (Get details.)

LYING: "Has she been lying regularly?" (If "yes," get details.)

STEALING: "Has he been taking things that don't belong to him?" (If so, get details.)

SHYNESS: "Is she unusually shy around strangers or when she first meets people?" (If so, get details.)

DEPENDENCY: "Does he ask you to tell him what to do a lot? What to wear? What to pick out?" (If so, get details.)

LACK SELF-CONF.: "Does she seem to lack self-confidence?" (If so, get details.)

SENSITIVENESS: "Are his feelings easily hurt?" (Get details.)

MOOD SWINGS: "Do her moods change suddenly for no reason?" (If so, get details.)

A comparison of the child's behavior with base rates for each behavior can be made by consulting the tables beginning on page 156.

After the completion of the personal adjustment sheet, the history taking is essentially done. At this point the clinician should ask the history informants, "Are there any other things about your youngster that we haven't talked about that would be important for me to know?" Any details provided after this question can be noted in the margins of the appropriate history page.

While taking the history, the clinician must always be mindful that the diagnostic task should lead to the answering of questions and the making of recommendations that meet the child's best interests and the needs of the family and society. This may be an impossible task in some cases. The psychologist is duty bound, however, to use all reasonable methods and procedures to attempt to reach these goals.

The psychologist may find it helpful to conceptualize the diagnostic task in terms of fairly simplistic questions, hopes, or goals. Early in the intake interview, the psychologist asks the parents what questions they would like answered about their child. The responses are entered on the intake sheet (Figure 6.1). Throughout the history taking, however, the psychologist should be sensitive to other questions or goals that may become apparent as the parents answer questions and provide a broad picture of the child's life.

These questions and goals should be noted on the intake sheet. Some of the more common questions include the following:

"Why is he having trouble in school?"

"Is she learning disabled?"

"Why is he so hard to control?"

"Why doesn't she have friends?"

"Why does he always seem to be in trouble?"

"What can we do to stop her from fighting with her sister?"

"Is he depressed?"

"Is she dyslexic?"

"What is the best school setting for him?"

"Is she eligible for the gifted child program?"

"Is he retarded?"

"What would be the best custody and visitation arrangement for him?"

"What are we to do with her?"

"How can he improve at school?"

By no means is this list of common concerns complete. The results of a thorough psychological evaluation are likely to be helpful in answering many of the above and similar questions.

CHAPTER SEVEN

Selecting the Assessment Battery
and Scheduling the Assessment

After the history is taken, the child is scheduled for the examination. The parents should be present when the appointments are made, to further involve them in the process. At the same time the child is scheduled for examination, a time should be arranged for interpreting the results to the parents. Although psychologists traditionally conduct examinations of children and then send these reports to other professionals or to agencies, parents benefit a great deal more by understanding and participating in the process. Scheduling the parents to receive the results produces a sense of security in parents and creates a feeling of involvement that may be useful in ensuring that recommendations are carried out.

No single list of procedures can be scheduled for every thorough psychological examination, since much depends on each child's age, environment, education, and family structure. The psychologist needs to determine what is required so that every child is examined thoroughly. Brief examination and "screening" examinations may be useful, but they also may hide more than they reveal.

The psychologist should be thinking in terms of specific examination instruments from the time the initial appointment is made. The structure of the examination can be mentally formulated and reformulated throughout the data collection process with the parents and with other significant influences from the environment. By the time the history taking is completed, the psychologist should have a fairly clear idea as to the particular instruments that will be most useful.

As part of the trend of associating psychological services with medical treatment, a movement has emerged recently to link psychological assessment and intervention to medical cost containment (Cummings, 1988). The movement is to limit, restrict, or shorten psychological services and procedures. This trend is particularly unfortunate where children's services are concerned, because extensive diagnostic services for children have a very high probability of paying long-term benefits. The secondary prevention benefits that can occur from thorough psychological evaluation of children in terms of preventing future service utilization are extensive. Because many of the psychological conditions that can emerge or develop in adult years can be remediated or prevented by thorough and competent evaluation and intervention during childhood, being "penny-wise and pound foolish" through cutting costs and services with children should be opposed.

Clinically as well as logically, a thorough psychological assessment of the child has both preventive and remedial advantages. Whether a child has specific deficits or difficulties or is being evaluated simply to track development, the results of a complete psychological evaluation can serve as a navigational map for parents and teachers to better understand the child's development to date and to enhance future development. All of this is in the best interests of the child and, in turn, the family and society.

The specific procedures and tests that can be used to develop a meaningful description of the child in all significant domains vary according to many factors, including the following:

- The child's age
- The child's cultural background
- The quality and appropriateness of available tests and procedures
- The child's level of expressive and receptive language
- The child's capacity to participate in an examination
- The availability of the child, and the cooperativeness of the parental environment.

The test instruments are the products of psychological research during the past 100 years. The range of factors, age levels, and depth of coverage provided by standardized psychological and educational measurement devices is considerable (Buros, 1960–1985, 1970–1975; Keyser & Sweetland, 1987). Tests should never be viewed as absolute measurements or final definitions of any child's psychological nature; however, tests are invaluable in helping to provide a broad and deep picture of the psychological status of the child (American Psychological Association, 1985; Anastasi, 1982; Blau, 1979).

Choosing the appropriate tests to include in a complete psychological evaluation of a child requires a high level of professional skill. Although certain standardized tests are so useful that they may be given during almost every evaluation, the properly trained and experienced psychological clinician must always be prepared to vary the choice of tests for a child evaluation in response to the child's situational requirements. Thus, although the Stanford–Binet (Thorndike, Hagen, & Sattler, 1986) or the Wechsler Intelligence Scale for Children–Revised (Wechsler, 1974) may be almost universally chosen to evaluate an 8-year-old's intellectual function, should the child be a product of a bilingual environment, a test such as the Peabody Picture Vocabulary Test–Revised (Dunn & Dunn, 1981) or the Non-Verbal Test of Cognitive Skills (Johnson & Boyd, 1981) may be substituted or given in addition to the more frequently chosen instruments (Mitchell, 1985). The starting point in selecting specific tests for the evaluation battery should be the original needs assessment that was done with the parents.

In general, the complete psychological test battery should include instruments that cover the following areas:

- The child's intellectual capacities and learning styles
- The child's neuropsychological development and status
- The child's achievement levels in all significant areas of academic activity
- The child's personality and character.

SELECTING THE EXAMINATION COMPONENTS

Although the specific test instruments ordinarily are selected after all aspects of the environmental press are available, most experienced clinicians select elements of the test battery as the history is being taken from the parents or the parent surrogates. As the examination proceeds, test instruments may be added or deleted. Figure 7.1 presents a test room schedule form that may be used to select and schedule the child's examination. By no means does this form include all test instruments that might be used with children or their parents. The form should be modified according to the availability of instruments to the clinician, and to reflect new assessment procedures that replace outmoded tests.

Intellectual Assessment

The examination of every child should include a full assessment of intellectual capacity and/or potential. Levels of intelligence and variations in intellectual capacity can have great impact on both the understanding and resolution of conflicts that appear to be emotional, and that relate to family interaction, school activity, and social adaptation. Although the definitions of intellectual capacity may vary considerably, instruments for measuring those traits that are associated with the capacity to perceive material, incorporate it into the cortex, classify the material, organize it, store it, and retrieve it appropriately are of considerable importance in the general evaluation of the child.

The history of psychology parallels the development of intelligence tests. Rather elegant and well-formulated instruments are available to examine

TEST ROOM SCHEDULE

Birthdate _____

Age _____

Date Scheduled _____

NAME _____

	PSY	TR	DATE	DAY	HOURS	TOTALS	
SCHEDULE: History ___ ___ ___ ( )	___	___	___	___	___	___	PSY.
XIT ___ ___ ___ ( )	___	___	___	___	___	___	TR
XIT 2 ___ ___ ___ ( )	___	___	___	___	___	___	Workup
	___	___	___	___	___		
	___	___	___	___	___		

INTERVIEWS

___ History
___ Int
___ Int
___ Int
___ _____

INTELLIGENCE/DEVELOPMENT

___ AFRPV ___ QT
___ PPVT L/M
___ Binet L M
___ Bayley
___ Cattel
___ KABC
___ Chicago NV
___ Minn Develop
___ Vineland Adap ___ Soc
___ WPPSI-R   Mat
___ WISC-R
___ WAIS-R ___ WAIS
   ___ Inf ___ P Comp
   ___ Comp ___ P Arr
   ___ Arith ___ Bl Des
   ___ Sim ___ Cod
   ___ DigSp ___ Object
   ___ Voc   Assem

NEUROPSYCHOLOGY

___ Reitan Sens Def___A___C
___ Category (BK) Test
___ Wells & Reusch-A,A,A
___ MFD-Graham-Kendall
___ Indiana-Retain SF
___ Torque___ Rpt___ Parents
___ Hand Dynamometer
___ LNNB___I___II___Child
___ Neuropsych Sym/Sign

NEUROPSYCHOLOGY (Cont.)

___ Neurobehav Cog Status
___ Spiral AET
___ Fla Kind Screen (Satz)
___ Wisconsin Card Sort
___ ABC Vision

ACHIEVEMENT

___ Metro Achiev FM JS
   ___ Pre Primer
   ___ Primer
   ___ Primary 1
   ___ Primary 2
   ___ Elementary
   ___ Intermediate
   ___ Advanced 1
   ___ Advanced 2
___ Amer Schl Read/Arith
___ Gates MacG Rdg Readiness
___ Nelson-Denny___E___F
___ Gates MacGin Rdg___Prim
   ___ D FM 1 2 3
   ___ E FM 1 2 3
   ___ F Form 1
___ Stanford Task
___ WRAT
___ Metro Rdg___I___II

INTEREST +

___ Strong
___ Kuder
___ Wren S-H

MISCELLANEOUS

___ _____
___ _____
___ _____

PERSONALITY

___ TAT
  ___ 1 ___ 2 ___ 3BM ___ 4
  ___ 5 ___ 6BM ___ 6GF ___ 7BM
  ___ 7GF ___ 8BM ___ 8GF ___ 9BM
  ___ 9GF ___ 10 ___ 11 ___ 12BG
  ___ 12M ___ 12F ___ 13MF ___ 14
  ___ 15 ___ 16 ___ 17BM ___ 17GF
  ___ 18BM ___ 18GF ___ 19 ___ 20
  ___ Dictation ___ Write
___ Rorschach
___ H-T ___ DAP
___ Self Portrait
___ TASC ___ CSC
___ TA?
___ MMPI
___ MIllon
___ 16PF
___ CAQ
___ FIRO-B
___ Family Drawing
___ PIC
___ Haggarty - OW
___ Child Behavior Profile
___ Mother-Child Rel Eval
___ Parent Stress Index
___ Multidim Child Pers
___ Holmes Stress Scale (SRE)

MARITAL

___ Marital Audit ___ SRA
___ Marital Audit Inv
___ Marital Diag ___ Mar Roles
___ Mar Satisfction ___ MHP

FIGURE 7.1 Test Battery Checklist

children throughout their developmental years. Landmark work by Binet, Terman, and Merrill, as well as by Wechsler and his colleagues, resulted in instruments that help us understand how children think and respond through a wide range of capabilities (Sattler, 1982).

Although various instruments are available to measure the intellect of handicapped children, the focus of this chapter is on children who are able to operate within reasonable limits in all sensory modalities. Evaluating the intellect of children who are blind, deaf, speech impaired, and so forth, is a specialty in both clinical psychology and education, and is addressed in numerous texts (Anastasi, 1982; Goldman, Stein, & Guerry, 1983; Sattler, 1982).

The selection of the instrument for measuring a child's intelligence is frequently a matter of the individual clinician's background and personal experience. The child should always be given an individually administered intelligence test instead of a group-administered paper-and-pencil instrument. The individual psychological tests tend to be better standardized and have been more thoroughly researched than the narrower paper-and-pencil tests.

A number of major instruments can be used for testing children between birth and 18 years. The most frequently used instrument is the Wechsler Intelligence Scale for Children–Revised (WISC-R). WISC-R is the instrument of choice for the discussion in this chapter for children between 6 1/2 and 16 years of age.

For children younger than 6 1/2, the Wechsler Preschool and Primary Scale of Intelligence has long been available. The recent revised edition (Wechsler, 1989) appears to have addressed problems with the parent instrument, and may become the instrument of choice in the near future for children from age 3 to age 7. Other scales that might be utilized for evaluating the intellect of very young children include the Bayley Scales of Infant Development (Bayley, 1969) and the Stanford–Binet. Detailed review of these instruments is available elsewhere (Keyser & Sweetland, 1987).

It should be clearly understood that the purpose of intelligence testing is *not* to develop an intelligence quotient (IQ). Although the IQ has been a traditional way of describing children's intellect, this oversimplification of the cognitive responses of children has fallen into professional and scientific disrepute (American Psychological Association, 1985). Clinicians today are interested in a child's ranking in respect to cohorts. The percentile is clearly the preferred method of describing a youngster's level of intellectual functioning. In addition to this, summary scores are only partially useful. Most clinicians find that variations in subscale scores are helpful in understanding how the child thinks and behaves from an intellectual frame of reference. Again, weighted scores or percentiles are the most useful ways of aggregating the child's response. This scoring system is illustrated in the case material that follows the description of the basic test battery. It is sufficient for the moment to indicate that, except in most unusual cases, every youngster should have a complete, individually administered intelligence test as part of his or her basic psychological examination.

Neuropsychological Assessment

The basic aim of the neuropsychological assessment of children is to produce a reliable and valid demonstration of the relationship between the brain and behavior (Rourke, Bakker, Fisk, & Strang, 1983). Where there is reason to believe that the child has some disruption of the normal fluctuations of development in the functional systems of the brain, a full neuropsychological assessment is necessary. The purpose of such an assessment is to develop a treatment orientation to help the child develop in the most complete way possible (Rourke, Fisk, & Strang, 1986). Although the full neuropsychological evaluation of the child is considered in this volume, for purposes of describing the basic psychological examination of children, the neuropsychological assessment is essentially a screening evaluation. The purpose of the screening evaluation is to determine whether further assessment is necessary (Fletcher, Smidt, & Satz, 1979).

Because the period of cognitive development in children is lengthy and is not completed until sometime during adolescence, the issue is not whether neuropsychological deficit exists, but rather whether there is a reduced rate of cognitive development or a constant degree of deficit during the developmental period. Should the screening assessments indicate some deficit, which is later confirmed by the full neuropsychological battery, a series of neuropsychological assessments over a period of time, usually every 6 months, is necessary to determine whether such deficit is constant and whether intervening measures have been effective. Serial examinations are vital for tracking the nature of a deficit and its impact on the child.

When a history of brain trauma or severe disease is found, a full neuropsychological battery is necessary. Unfortunately, damage to the infant brain may be associated with a very complicated array of events including mild shaking, falls, and relatively moderate fevers (Kolb, 1989). Some believe that even such anomalies as mixed cerebral dominance may indicate some degree of neuropsychological deficit (Satz, 1973). In such cases, particularly where children are having difficulty in school, a complete neuropsychological battery may be helpful in identifying the source of the difficulty, as well as directions for remediation (Myers, Sweet, Deysach, & Myers, 1989).

The younger the child, the more difficult it is to evaluate the neuropsychological status, either through screening devices or full batteries. Most major neuropsychological test instruments develop stable, normative data beginning at approximately age 8. Screening before this age tends to be of questionable validity and reliability. Certainly gross neuropsychological deficits make themselves known through significant discrepancies in behavior on intelligence and achievement tests.

The first level of screening for neuropsychological deficits takes place during the history taking. Information from the parents, the school, or other sources that indicates that the child has problems in communication, motor behavior, cognition, memory, vision, or learning serves as clues that a neuropsychological deficit may exist. If such information has been revealed, the screening battery is the first step in determining whether neuropsychological deficit exists.

The actual screening tests for young children may consist of nothing more than the intelligence tests. Observation of the child's motility, language, and drawing behavior in addition to the clinical interview may be sufficient to determine whether full scale neuropsychological evaluation is necessary. For older children, such instruments as the Florida Kindergarten Screening Battery (Satz & Fletcher, 1980) or the children's screening tests for the Luria–Nebraska Neuropsychological Battery (Golden, 1987c) can be used.

At any time during the clinical interview with or the testing of the child, behavior or test responses may indicate the need for a more thorough neuropsychological assessment. Where this occurs, a full battery may be required. Many tests are available for neuropsychological evaluation of children (Rourke et al., 1986). Again, this issue is taken up in the chapters that illustrate clinical examples of the assessment process.

Achievement Factors

There is no question that the major task of the child, at least between the ages of 4 or 5 and 18, is education (Incagnoli, Goldstein, & Golden, 1986). Schooling continues beyond age 18 in 35–40 percent of children.

The task of education actually begins before the first grade for those children who enter kindergarten or prekindergarten. Children who are not keeping up academically are often referred for psychological evaluation. Assessment of both academic achievement and preparation for academic achievement are useful measurements in the complete psychological examination.

Except in the most unusual situations, every child who is examined, regardless of the reason for referral, should be evaluated as to preparation for academic work, levels of achievement in fundamentals, and, in particular, reading skills. Although many elements contribute to academic achievement, the mechanics of reading have to be considered the primary goal of the elementary years, as well as the primary academic tool for all the years that follow. The instruments available to assess children's academic preparation and/or achievement are among the richest reservoir of tests available to psychology. Academic attainment and achievement have been issues of concern for the past 100 years in the development of psychological testing. The question of children's academic achievement was the basis for the original development of individual intelligence as introduced by Binet (Binet & Simon, 1905).

The choice of academic achievement instrument depends on the child's age, grade placement, and history and the currency of the instruments available at the time the choice is made. Reference to evaluative authorities should guide the selection (Buros, 1960–1985; Keyser & Sweetland, 1987).

For children who are not in a school setting and who are too young for preschool reading and arithmetic readiness, instruments are available to evaluate developmental achievement. Such instruments include the Birth to Three Developmental Scale (Bangs & Dodson, 1979), the Kaufman Infant and Preschool Scale (Kaufman, 1979), the Minnesota Infant Development Inventory (Ireton & Thwing, 1980), and the classic and traditional Vineland Adaptive Behavior Scales (Sparrow, Balla, & Cicchetti, 1984). The more recently developed Child Behavior Checklist (Achenbach, 1985) provides rating scales for a full range of ages and normative data on children from infancy through adolescence and from normal development through serious pathology.

These instruments are extremely valuable, but must be applied with caution. In effect, they are structured interviews with parents, teachers, and/or other significant adults in the child's life. The responses of each person are subject to his or her own emotional, intellectual, and social status (Conrad & Hammen, 1989).

Personality Factors

Techniques for assessing and reporting the social–affective elements of a child's life are less well known and practiced than similar techniques used for assessing adult personality. As with adult personality tests, however, the bulk of personality tests and measurements available for use with children unfortunately are directed primarily toward the evaluation of pathological states.

Objective tests and projective techniques are available that can be helpful in demonstrating a wide range of the child's overt affective responses, social-interactional capabilities, and interpersonal and intrapersonal potentials. These measurements, of widely varying reliability and validity, can provide rich and helpful insight into the child.

Many well-developed "objective" instruments are available for assessing a variety of elements of children's personalities. A few of the more popular and well-received instruments are the Child and Adolescent Adjustment Profile Scale (Ellsworth, 1981), the Child Behavior Checklist (Achenbach & Edelbrock, 1983), the Children's Personality Questionnaire (Porter & Cattell, 1975), and the Personality Inventory of Children–Revised (Wirt, Lachar, Klinedienst, Seat, & Broen, 1984).

Projective techniques for children, especially figure-drawing methods, wax and wane in popularity. Use of these techniques requires a good bit of background and training, but they remain popular among psychologists who specialize in assessing children's personalities. Such projective techniques for children include the drawing of human figures (Koppitz, 1968; Meyers, 1989), the House–Tree–Person Technique (Buck, 1981; Hammer, 1978), the classic Thematic Apperception Test (Murray, 1943; Murstein, 1963; Rabin, 1981), and various sentence-completion tests and tasks.

The kinds of personality tests available for assessing children are numerous and continue to appear in different formats and for different populations. The selection of a battery of personality tests is based on the age of the child, any special conditions or handicaps suffered by the child, and questions that are raised in the needs assessment. Equally important are the skill, experience, and particular predilections or prejudices of the psychologist conducting the assessment. Methods of selecting personality tests are considered in later chapters.

Summary

The foregoing description of various tests does not constitute a total or a specific list of the measurements that can or should be used with children. The selection of specific tests should be based on the combination of factors noted previously, as well as the clinician's perception of the needs assessment and the questions that are to be answered. As the information is taken from the parents and combined with material obtained from other significant adults in the child's environment, the psychologist should be checking off possible examination procedures on the test battery checklist (Figure 7.1).

When the history taking is completed and the various test instruments have been checked on the test battery checklist, it is then time to schedule the assessment.

SCHEDULING THE ASSESSMENT

The clinician must estimate the amount of time necessary to complete the assessment by calculating how much time is necessary for each procedure checked on the test battery checklist. The total number of hours should be divided into components that are appropriate for the child's age. Children from 2 to 3 years should not be tested for more than an hour at a time. Children between ages 4 and 6 can tolerate about 2 hours in the test room. Children older than 6 seem to do well with a 3-hr test sequence, assuming that they have opportunities to move about and to break from the test situation. (Breaks are discussed in some detail in later chapters that focus on the test process itself.) This scheduling of time must be flexible. Some children who suffer attention deficit disorders may have to be tested in 30-min sequences. Again, this is a matter of individual judgment which must remain flexible throughout the assessment.

The psychologist at this point should structure the parents for the process to come and make an effort to involve them in that process. The psychologist should say something similar to the following:

> All of this information you've given me is important and interesting. It helps me to understand the kinds of problems you have and the kinds of things you're interested in knowing about your child. It is important for you to know that a number of the things that you have told me about your child and some of the things that you are concerned about are actually quite normal for the ages at which they have occurred. I will tell you more about that after we complete the examinations.
>
> I want to schedule some appointments to conduct various tests and examinations with your youngster. I am estimating that it will take X hours to complete the assessment. I would like to split this into three separate sessions of X hours each. During that time I will be talking to your youngster, having your youngster do a number of psychological tests, and observing those things that are important to understand about your child in order to help you and to help your youngster.
>
> I would also like to schedule an interpretation time. This is a 2-hr block of time in which I will tell you what we have done, what I believe it means, and what I recommend for you to do with your youngster. I will at that time explain all the tests that we have given, what they mean, and how they will help you and your youngster. I would also like to schedule an appointment time for you about 2 weeks after the first interpretation session. During the first interpretation session I will be giving you so much information that it will be difficult for you to absorb all of it and to ask questions. To help you with this, I'm going to make a cassette tape of all we talk about at that time. You can take this with you, play it as often as you like, develop questions that you might want to ask me, and identify things that are not totally clear to you. In the second interpretation session we can answer your questions and help you to implement those recommendations that you believe you can carry out.
>
> Between now and the time we give you the interpretation, you may have questions. Please feel free to contact me. I'm not sure what I will say, but I will do my best to answer whatever questions you may have.

The purpose of this structuring is to let the parents know what is about to take place and that it will come together in a meaningful interpretation at the end. Only rarely do parents ask questions about the examinations to come.

It is also important at this point to suggest ways in which the parents can structure the child for the evaluation. To some extent, this depends on the age of the child as well as the child's condition as estimated by the psychologist from the information already received. It is helpful to suggest to the parents that they encourage the child to look forward to the examination. For example, the psychologist might say the following:

> Jane will probably want to know why she is coming to see me. I suggest that you tell her that I am a person who helps people to find out what they can do best. Tell her that while she is here, she will play some games with me, and we will have a good time. Tell her that I am interested in her and that I am looking forward to meeting her.
>
> It's important that you don't share your worries or fears about the examination with the the child. This is new to you, and you have some natural concerns. Try to take the position that this is going to be very helpful to you and to your youngster. Try not to explain too much in detail what will happen here. Once you bring your youngster to our waiting room, it will·be my job to help her to be comfortable in going through the examinations and even to enjoy herself.

It should be clear that the intake procedure is the significant first step in the evaluation of the child. The purposes of this process include the collection of information about the child's immediate environment, the school situation, the child's behavior at home and at school, the parents' responses and their capacity to deal with the youngster, as well as other factors. During the intake interview, the psychologist is likely to become aware of the parents' needs as well as the needs of the child. It is an opportunity to lay the groundwork for the parents' acceptance of the assessment, the findings, and the recommendations. In agency practice, the intake process is often separated from the diagnostic examination by a significant time period; one person may actually do the examination whereas another gives the interpretation. This fragmenting is probably not in the best interests of the child or the parent. The procedures being recommended here involve a psychologist who sees the parents at the beginning, directs and conducts the examination of the child, and interprets the results. Others may assist in the interim, but it is clear to the parents that they are dealing with one professional person in seeking to resolve their concerns and to obtain help in working with their child.

Following this intake interview, the psychologist should take the parents to the staff member who schedules appointments. Every effort should be made to see the child early in the morning when he or she is quite fresh. It is also a good idea to schedule one test session in the afternoon, when the child is likely to be somewhat tired. This will give the psychologist a chance to observe the youngster under a variety of fatigue conditions, which will help round out the picture of the child. It is important to allow sufficient time between the last examination and the first interpretation to schedule additional testing should that prove necessary during the course of the assessment. It also should be kept in mind that interpreting the tests requires the psychologist's time and that this should not be rushed. Experience will dictate the amount of time necessary between the last examination and the first interpretation. Some clinicians find that a 1-week interim is quite sufficient, whereas others prefer to have 2 or 3 weeks.

Before the parents leave, it is important to have them sign any permission slips that are necessary to receive reports from the school, the child's physician, agencies, or other sources of information that would be helpful to the psychologist in understanding the youngster's past and present. It is wise *not* to ask permission to send the report at this time. The parents should be reassured that they will be the first to receive the report, and that the decision as to who will receive copies of the psychological report will be made after the interpretation.

CHAPTER EIGHT

An Intake Process:
The Case of Albert

The intake process described in previous chapters is illustrated in this chapter with an actual clinical case. Albert, a 7-year-old boy, is followed in this and subsequent chapters to illustrate the assessment process. All names have been changed, as well as other material that might identify any of the participants.

THE REFERRAL

First Contact

Jack Doe called to request a consultation concerning his natural son, Albert. He stated that Albert was in the second grade in a public school, and was not doing well. According to Jack, the school had evaluated Albert and found him to be a "learning disabled child." The father was very concerned, and wanted another opinion as well as some help in deciding what to do about the situation.

The father described a number of the child's symptoms, such as hyperactivity, difficulty in learning, and unresponsiveness in the classroom. Although the father was a high school graduate with little additional education, he seemed fairly well read, and had some questions about the specificity of a diagnosis of learning disability. In addition to having academic difficulties, Albert sometimes showed hyperactive behavior which got him into trouble with both his peers and his teachers.

The father, of course, had every right to be concerned about the labeling of his child. Labeling is not good for children, and there is a clear lack of specificity about the learning disabilities (Smith, 1978). The personality distress that Albert seemed to be suffering might not be associated with the learning difficulty at all, contrary to popular opinion. Many children with learning disabilities have few or no socioemotional disturbances (Rourke, 1988).

The issues brought up by Jack Doe in this telephone request are quite characteristic of the kinds of intake issues that initiate psychological assessment.

The Environmental Press

To complicate matters, Albert was the child of a fractured family. The biological mother and father divorced when Albert was 2 1/2. The mother remarried when Albert was 4 1/2. The father remarried when Albert was 6, entering the first grade. A new brother was born to Albert's stepfather and mother just before Albert turned 7.

Fortunately, both parents and both stepparents were on fairly equitable terms. They lived in communities 50 miles apart. All four agreed that a psychological assessment was warranted and were willing to participate.

Albert was additionally fortunate in that his second-grade teacher, Ms. Green at Willow Elementary School, was very interested in Albert, and encouraged the parents to have an additional evaluation. She forwarded a number of notes and observations about Albert during his first week of school, and retrieved tests of basic skills that had been given to Albert during the first grade as well as at the beginning of second grade.

Ms. Green wrote a very thoughtful and informative letter which, in part, stated:

> In the beginning of the school year, Albert often had problems staying in his seat. He talked out of turn and he had trouble staying on task. Albert continues these behaviors, and they seem to be happening more frequently. They seem to be worse than they were at the beginning. He falls out of his chair several times a day. He bothers other students by touching them. One student complained that Albert was constantly pulling her chair out. Albert's attention span is certainly short. He has trouble paying attention during instructional times.
>
> To give you some specific examples of Albert's "out of bounds" behavior— during a story time when the whole class is seated on the floor, Albert will get up and move from one side of the group to the other. Last week during one of these activities, Albert lay on the floor and rolled himself from the back to the front of the classroom several times. When Albert is out of the classroom, like before school, at lunch, or at recess, other students complain of Albert hitting or pushing them.
>
> There are times when I feel that Albert is not aware of these behaviors. I questioned him about his behavior and his reply shows that he's unaware of what he's doing. To give you an example, we were taking lunch count. The children stand to be counted. Albert was standing and when it came his turn to count, he replied, "I'm not standing."

Ms. Smith, Albert's first-grade teacher, provided a review of his activities during the first grade. Her letter included the following:

There are a number of areas in which Albert had some difficulty. One problem was with sitting. He couldn't stay in his seat. This was intermittent. On some days he seemed physically unable to remain seated for more than a few minutes at a time. Reminders would bring surprised looks from Albert, and he almost seemed unaware that he was standing up again.

Another thing that Albert tended to do was to hum and sing to himself. This again, brought to his attention, resulted in Albert's seeming to be surprised.

Albert sucked his thumb on occasion. He would thump pencils or fingers on his desk.

Certainly Albert had a short attention span, not too unusual for first graders. He was not able to stay "on task" for any sustained period of time. He had trouble understanding directions. He sometimes complained that he "can't think" because of background noises such as students in other classrooms, people walking the halls, and so forth. Headaches were another frequent complaint.

Albert ended the first grade functioning below his grade level in reading. He tended to read "word by word." His papers indicated a lack of comprehension.

Albert has had trouble relating to other children. While in line he would poke other children, grab other children, start "pencil fights" and grab items from another child's desk. His intent seemed to be "just playing" but it was quite disruptive.

I am pleased that you've decided to have a thorough evaluation. You are to be commended for the time, trouble, and money you are putting forth to help Albert. I am happy to be part of the team in working to help him achieve what I believe is his very good potential.

Albert's teachers provided the results of the Comprehensive Tests of Basic Skills given toward the end of the first grade. His results, in comparison with national norms, were as follows:

Test Area	Percentile (National Norms)
Word Attack	55th
Vocabulary	49th
Comprehension	51st
Total Reading	51st
Language Expression	70th
Math Computation	84th
Math Concepts and Application	82nd
Total Math	84th

There obviously are discrepancies between the observations of the teacher as to Albert's academic progress and his ability to compete at a national normative level. This finding is not infrequent and speaks for the importance of the use of psychological and educational tests in determining a youngster's status.

Albert was clearly an interesting youngster who was a source of concern to everybody significantly involved in his life and development. Many questions needed to be answered, but the opportunity to help this youngster, his parents, and his teachers seemed to be quite good.

THE INTAKE INTERVIEW

With over half of American families fractured through separation or divorce, psychologists frequently examine children who have two or more households and multiple parents and parent surrogates. In many cases a series of intake interviews must be scheduled for the psychologist to meet with all of the parent figures. In Albert's case, the families were willing to coordinate, and both parents and both stepparents met for the intake interview. The school material was not yet available, and this first appointment took place with a minimum of information available. Figure 8.1 illustrates the intake sheet that the psychologist had available when he first met Albert's family.

Albert did not attend this first meeting. Although adolescents of 15 years and older may be asked to attend a first evaluation session, having a younger child present when meeting the parents for the first time is often disruptive and usually not helpful.

At the first meeting, everyone was on time. Coffee and cold drinks were offered, and introductions were made. The stepparents knew each other slightly. Although the atmosphere was friendly, there was a moderate air of tension, as is generally the case when parent participants are unsure of the assessment process.

The psychologist began the session with cordialities. The parents were welcomed. They were praised for being concerned about their youngster at an early age, when remediation and problem solution tend to be easier than at a later age. They were told that the process would include the history taking, obtaining material from the school, examining the child, and then meeting to give results and recommendations. The parents were promised that before the end of the first session, the psychologist would tell them more about what would happen and what to expect. As soon as everyone seemed comfortable, the history taking began.

The mother, Jane, was a 32-year-old executive secretary with a high school education. She described herself as being in good health and never having had any significant health problems. When asked to describe her

X Card
X Letter
X Map

INTAKE

NAME __DOE, Albert_____ DATE __Sept. 15, 1988__ BY __S.C.__

ADDRESS __1651 Biltmore Road, Winston, FL. 33601 Ⓜ__ PHONE __(M) 661-3121.__ __Ⓔ(407) 219-3664__

BIRTHDATE __7/22/81__ AGE __7-2__ EDUC __2.2__ SCHOOL __Willow Elem.__

OCC __Ⓔ Police Officer Ⓜ Secretary__ REL __Ⓔ Jack Doe__ __Ⓜ Jane Smith__

REF __Ⓔ (A former patient recommends)__ REP TO __Parents__

REASON FOR REFERRAL: Teacher: Ellen Green

1. Ⓔ calls.

2. Albert not doing well at school:
   a. Behavior problems.
   b. Doesn't do work at school.
   c. May be a "hyperactive" or "Learning Disabled" child.

3. Parents are divorced but will come in together for history.

_____

QUESTIONS -- TERMINAL GOALS

1. Is Albert Hyperactive?
2. Is he "Abnormal"?
3. What can parents do to help him adjust?
4. How can Alberts attention span be improved?

_____

HIST DATE: __Tues 9/20 3:00pm__   ___| EV.   _3_ TR.   DATE __Oct. 17__ HR __10-12, 1-3__

RESULTS: __Tues 11/9 1-3pm__   ___| EV.   _3_ TR.   DATE __Oct. 18__ HR __10-12, 1-3__

#2   __Tues 11/23 3-4pm__   ___ EV.   _1_ TR.   DATE __Oct. 19__ HR __8-9am__

____ EV.   ___ TR.   DATE_____ HR_____

_____

FEES: __Ⓜ & Ⓔ will split the fee__   DIAG: __$1650.__   REC REQ:

THER: 1. School

RED. BASE   2. Pediatrician

_____

FIGURE 8.1   Albert Doe's Intake Sheet

personality when in contact with Albert, she said, "I like good behavior. I correct him when he doesn't behave well, but I try to do it constructively. I think I'm a fair person." The mother seemed straightforward, a bit stiff, but clearly anxious to help.

The natural father, Jack, was a 38-year-old police officer who had an associate's degree in criminal justice. He had been a police officer for 17 years. He described his health as "fine." He almost sheepishly said that when he is with Albert, he tends to be "a stern father." He laughed at his own statement, and said, "But we do have a good time, play a lot, and laugh a lot." The father appeared to be a traditional, fairly dominant, but flexible person.

The stepfather, Bill, was a 29-year-old insurance salesman who had completed 2 years of college. He described himself as being in good health. In dealing with Albert, he stated that he was "easygoing." The stepfather appeared to be a pleasant, somewhat passive person, not too revealing or forthcoming.

The stepmother, Mary, was a 31-year-old correctional officer who held a high school diploma plus a certificate of graduation from the Correctional Officer Academy. She described herself as "short tempered, but honest." She described her annoyance with Albert's misbehavior, but indicated that she loved him and enjoyed his visits. She appeared to be a somewhat easily threatened, defensive person.

The custody and visitation arrangements were quite flexible. The divorce had not been particularly grim. The mother was the primary caretaker, to which the father had agreed originally. Liberal visitation continued even after both parents remarried. Vacation times were negotiated, and Albert spent a good bit of time with both natural parents and both stepparents.

Albert's half brother, Bill, Jr., had been born approximately 10 months before the assessment began. The parents agreed that Albert was showing no particular difficulty in adapting to the half sibling.

Albert had some contact with his stepgrandparents, as well as with his paternal grandparents. Everyone agreed that these contacts were fairly positive. Albert had a fair amount of contact with the mother's aunt and the mother's cousins. No difficulty was noted among any of these interactions.

The annual income was $39,000 per year for the father's family and $55,000 per year for the mother and stepfather. The mother's household was located in a four-bedroom home, and the father's was in a three-bedroom apartment. Albert had his own room in each setting.

Figure 8.2 illustrates the notes taken during the family history described thus far. Various family members participated in answering the questions. No real difficulty occurred. Occasionally, one family member would answer, only to be corrected by another family member. It would appear that the history is fairly accurate.

Albert was the first child to his natural mother. He weighed 8 lbs 4 oz, and there was no difficulty before, during, or after birth for Albert or his

FAMILY HISTORY

DATE __9/20/88__   INFORMANT Ⓜ, Ⓕ, Step Ⓜ, Step Ⓕ   BY __THB__

	MOTHER	Step Ⓜ	Step Ⓕ	FATHER
N	Jane	Mary	Bill	Jack
A	32	31	29	38
O	Exec. Sect.	Correctional officer	Insurance	Detective - P.D.
E	H.S.	H.S. +	14	14 (A.A.)
H	Good	OK	Good	Fine
P	Likes good behavior Fair. corrects Constr.	short tempered, but honest	Easy-going	stern

SIBS
Bill Jr. 10 mo. loves him, no problems

Custody, shared
P. Caretaker Ⓜ
Visitation - Liberal
No conflicts
Negotiated holidays
& vacations

OTHERS
Step GP ⎫
P. GP ⎰ Good
Ⓜ Aunt & cousins - good

SOC EC
Ⓕ 3⁊ K 3 BR Apt.
Ⓜ 55 K 4 BR Home

CLIMATE
Ⓕ Pretty organized
Ⓜ Same

CLIN:
M: S.W. Stiff, wants to help.
F: Traditional, dominant, flexible
Step Ⓜ: Easily annoyed
Step Ⓕ: Pleasant, passive

F INTERACTION

We have a good time.
We play & laugh a lot.

Step F. Watch T.V.
help with homework

M INTERACTION

Firm but available.
Step M. Watchful & Critical

FIGURE 8.2   Albert Doe's Family History Form

mother. Albert was bottle fed and went to the cup without difficulty. No one could remember when this happened, but they agreed it was "normal." Toilet training began between 1 and 1 1/2 years, and Albert seemed to do quite well with this. When asked whether there were any difficulties during the first year of life, they said that there were none. They felt that his walking and talking, socializing, and development of skills between ages 2 and 5 developed within normal limits.

Albert's regular physician indicated that Albert was in good health. The parents reported that Albert broke his clavicle at age 2 but had recovered quite well. He had chicken pox quite badly and has quite a few residual marks on his face. He had had no surgery and had received all of his immunizations. Although Albert had no recent physical complaints, he regularly complained of headaches, leg aches, chest pains, and so forth until about a year previously. For a period of time, he had some sinus problems and nosebleeds. Albert showed no signs of early puberty. No adult in his family had given him any sex education.

All members of the family denied any episodes of unconsciousness, high fevers, or seizures during Albert's lifetime. They could recall no periods of dizziness or poor sleep. They all remembered that he suffered headaches regularly, but these had become less frequent. According to the natural parents, no left-handedness was on either side of the family. The father stated that redheadedness runs in his family, and the mother indicated that a number of twins have been born on her side of the family. Figure 8.3 shows the history form filled out from the material described above.

The parents sent Albert to prekindergarten, which they described as "play school." He seemed to have a good time and adjusted well. After he entered the first grade, he was described as hyperactive, although there were no academic complaints. His teacher remained concerned about his concentration difficulties and his lack of control in social interaction.

In the second grade, he remained hyperactive, and his academic work began to deteriorate. He showed a tendency to not complete assignments. His teachers in both grades indicated that his performance was below his potential. Both at school and at home, Albert tended to be socially embarrassing because of his touching and hyperactive behavior.

All of his parents agreed that Albert made friends easily but tended to be a follower. They indicated that he enjoyed his rooms at home. In both homes he had posters on the wall. Friends had slept over at both homes, but Albert had not slept over at the homes of his friends. His parents indicated that he enjoys movies and television. He was restricted to 1 hr of TV on school days and 2 hrs per day on weekends. They insisted that he got along well with his half brother and loved him. He was a picky eater, and the mother in particular had been concerned that he was not getting proper nutrition.

Both mother and the father disciplined Albert by depriving him of privileges. The mother occasionally spanked him when she felt frustrated. Neither the stepfather nor the stepmother participated in disciplinary action.

HISTORY - 2

PRE & POST NATAL:

BIR: 8'4" 1st No diff. -Ⓜor child

FEED: Bottle - cup? 9mo. No probs.

TT: 1-1½ yrs. OK

1ST YR: OK

2–5th: Normal

GRANDPARENTS:

Step Ⓖⓟ Local
            Good Rel.
P Ⓖⓟ Not as
            frequent but
            good

MEDICAL:

PHYSICIAN: Wm. Jason, M.D, Winston, FL

T&A: N

OTHER: Broken clavicle age 2. Did ok. Some sinus
       & nose bleeds.

U.C.D.: C.P. Bad. Facial scars

IMMUNIZ: Yes

REG. COMPL: Pain in legs, chest. Stopped a yr. ago.

PUB: No

SEX ED: No

ADD'L:

RELIGION:

Irregular attend
both families

UNCONC: N

FEVER: N

SEIZURES: N

DURING 1st 8 YRS:

DIZZINESS: N

HEADACHES: Until 1 yr. ago. Now infrequent

POOR SLEEP: N

SINISTRALITY IN FAMILY: Not known

TRAUMA:

None known

Ⓕ Family- red headedness
Ⓜ   "   " - twins

FIGURE 8.3   Albert Doe's Developmental History Form

Albert attended a day camp the previous summer and enjoyed it. He seemed particularly interested in active sports, especially soccer and skateboarding. He collected stickers. The mother had tried to give him an allowance, but this was stopped because he seemed irresponsible. Albert's bedtime was 8:30 P.M., and the parents had little difficulty getting him to bed. He awakened about 6:30 A.M. and seemed to have 10 hr of good sleep a night.

At the mother's home his chores were to keep his room clean, make his bed, dust his room, and sweep. At the father's home there were no regular chores, but the father indicated that Albert was a willing helper.

Various family members stated that Albert had wide-ranging emotional responses, was frequently irritable without apparent cause, and was impulsive. He did not seem to learn from experience, and made the same mistakes repeatedly. He was quite stubborn, was unable to follow directions, and had trouble completing projects. He created situations that resulted in conflict within the family. Often the parents felt impotent to help.

Albert seemed to be unusually kind to small animals, and all of the parents agreed that Albert seemed to have a "good heart." Figure 8.4 illustrates the notes in the history taking that describe the above information.

To record a visual picture of developmental anomalies and their time of occurrence, the psychologist asked the parents and stepparents about a variety of behaviors and when they occurred. The parents agreed that Albert had always sucked his thumb and fingers. He wet the bed regularly until about age 2 1/2 and continued to have sporadic "accidents." He occasionally walked in his sleep. He had had some mild temper tantrums all of his life. He had always been somewhat uncooperative and had exhibited excess energy. He was occasionally destructive, but not with any frequency, and quarrelsome, but not intensely so. All of the parents agreed that Albert had always lacked self-confidence and been quite emotionally sensitive; his feelings were easily hurt. Figure 8.5 illustrates these particular behaviors and their occurrence in relation to significant events. There are no indications that any of these behaviors were particularly associated with the major family changes that had occurred in Albert's life (his parents' divorce, the remarriage of each parent, and the birth of a half brother).

PLANNING THE ASSESSMENT

Choosing the Test Battery

Following the concept of the complete psychological evaluation, the psychologist decided that Albert would be evaluated with tests of intelligence, neuropsychological status, academic achievement, and personality. For the

HISTORY - 3

1st & 2nd

SCHOOL: Play school. Had good ___X___ Performance Below Potential
time & adjust. 1st Willow, "Hyperactive."
Poor concent. 2nd " " "remains" " "
D. not complete assign.

FRIENDS: ___X___ Socially Embarrassing
·Easily   Touching
·Follower   Hyperactivity
· Sleep over - both @ his homes. Not @ theirs.

HOME: HOMEWORK:

ROOM: Both homes - own room   None
       Enjoys posters
RECR: Movies, T.V. (1hr/day
       school, 2 hrs. weekends)
SIBS: OK

MEALS: Picky eater (M) concerned re: nutrition

DISCIPL: (F) - deprivation. (M) - also. Occasionally spanks
when frust. Step-parents d. discipline
CAMP: Day camp last summer-
       enjoyed   Wide range of emot.
SPORTS: Soccar. Skateboarding   response:
                                            ·Irritables cause
                                            ·Impulsive
HOBBIES: Stickers   ·D. learn from Exper-
                                               iences
DATING: N   · Stubborn
                                            · D. complete projects
ALLOW: Tried by (M) - irresponsible   · D. follow directions
stopped   · Creates conflict in
BEDT: 8:30 p.m. - 6:30 a.m.   family
                                            · Has good heart
                                            · Kind to small
CHORES: (M) Home - Keep room clean,   animals
make bed, dust & sweep room.
(F) Home - No regular chores. He helps out.

FIGURE 8.4   Albert Doe's School and Home Environment History Form

HISTORY - 4

PERSONAL ADJUSTMENT

Annotations (handwritten, top): Parents divorce · remarriage (N) · remarriage (E) · step-brother born · current age

PERSONAL ADJUSTMENT		0	1	2	3	4	5	6	7	8	9	10	11	12	13	14
NAIL BITING	N	0	0	0	0	0	0	0	0	0	0	0	0	0	0	0
CRYING	N	0	0	0	0	0	0	0	0	0	0	0	0	0	0	0
THUMB SUCKING	Y	X—0—0—0—0—0—0—0X								0	0	0	0	0	0	0
ENURESIS	Y	X—0—0—X0—0—0—0—0X								0	0	0	0	0	0	0
SOILING	N	0	0	0	0	0	0	0	0	0	0	0	0	0	0	0
SOMNABULISM	Y	0	0	0	X0—0—0—0—0X					0	0	0	0	0	0	0
VOMITING	N	0	0	0	0	0	0	0	0	0	0	0	0	0	0	0
STUTTERING	N	0	0	0	0	0	0	0	0	0	0	0	0	0	0	0
MASTURBATION	N	0	0	0	0	0	0	0	0	0	0	0	0	0	0	0
NIGHTMARES	N	0	0	0	0	0	0	0	0	0	0	0	0	0	0	0
NIGHT TERRORS	N	0	0	0	0	0	0	0	0	0	0	0	0	0	0	0
FEARFUL	N	0	0	0	0	0	0	0	0	0	0	0	0	0	0	0
CRUELTY	N	0	0	0	0	0	0	0	0	0	0	0	0	0	0	0
TANTRUMS	Y	X—0—0—0—0—0—0—0X								0	0	0	0	0	0	0
DESTRUCTIVENESS	Y	0	X—0—0—0—0—0—0X							0	0	0	0	0	0	0
QUARRELSOME	Y	0	0	0	X—0—0—0—0X					0	0	0	0	0	0	0
JEALOUS	N	0	0	0	0	0	0	0	0	0	0	0	0	0	0	0
UNCOOPERATIVE	Y	X—0—0—0—0—0—0—0X								0	0	0	0	0	0	0
EXCESS ENERGY	Y	X—0—0—0—0—0—0—0X								0	0	0	0	0	0	0
LYING	N	0	0	0	0	0	0	0	0	0	0	0	0	0	0	0
STEALING	N	0	0	0	0	0	0	0	0	0	0	0	0	0	0	0
SHYNESS	N	0	0	0	0	0	0	0	0	0	0	0	0	0	0	0
DEPENDENCY	N	0	0	0	0	0	0	0	0	0	0	0	0	0	0	0
LACK SELF-CONF.	Y	X—0—0—0—0—0—0—0X								0	0	0	0	0	0	0
SENSITIVENESS	Y	X—0—0—0—0—0—0—0X								0	0	0	0	0	0	0
MOOD SWINGS	N	0	0	0	0	0	0	0	0	0	0	0	0	0	0	0

FIGURE 8.5   Albert Doe's Behavior Problems of Normal Children Form

intellectual evaluation, the Wechsler Intelligence Scale for Children–Revised (WISC-R) was chosen. Although other instruments might have been used, research and clinical experience pointed to the value of the WISC-R.

To validate the level of intellectual function demonstrated by the WISC-R and also to determine whether Albert had any discrepancies in expressive speech, the Peabody Picture Vocabulary Test was selected as the second measure of intellectual capacity. A considerable discrepancy between Albert's responses to one test or the other could indicate sources of both academic and behavioral difficulty.

To evaluate cerebral dominance, the psychologist selected the Torque Test (Blau, 1977b). To measure the activity of the sensorimotor strip, the Hand Dynamometer (Reitan, 1981) was chosen. Graham and Kendall's (1960) Memory for Designs Test was selected to evaluate eye-hand coordination and visual memory. Rourke et al. (1986), in their review of neuropsychological assessments for children, described some techniques for selecting neuropsychological batteries. If neuropsychological deficits were indicated by screening tests, a full neuropsychological evaluation battery would have to be administered.

Although Albert had taken standardized school achievement tests, the Metropolitan Achievement Tests (Prescott, Balow, Hogan, & Farr, 1978) were selected to evaluate his academic capacity. Additional achievement testing is necessary for a number of reasons. School tests are given in group situations. There is no way of knowing how responsive the child may have been at the time the test was given. The child may not have understood the directions or may have been distracted or ill. The tests may not have been administered properly. To be able to advise the parents and the teachers as to the child's maximum academic achievement at the time of the assessment, the psychologist needs to administer a standardized examination in a face-to-face setting. The primer battery of the Metropolitan Achievement Tests was chosen for Albert. This battery covers achievement through the end of the first grade. Because Albert was just starting the second grade, the possibility that he would not perform well on a more demanding instrument was considered. Later it proved necessary to also administer the next level because Albert did very well on the primer version.

To evaluate Albert's personality, the psychologist decided to use selected cards of the Thematic Apperception Test, the House–Tree Test, the Draw-a-Person Test with inquiry, the Child Sentence Completion Test, and Family Drawing (Goldman et al., 1983). The parents might have been given various inventories to describe their youngster's behavior, but the specific history and the descriptive teachers' reports made additional inventories seem unnecessary.

During the course of an assessment, if the psychologist decides that the chosen test battery is insufficient, additional testing and information gathering can be added.

Time Sequence

Testing can be scheduled in many different ways. Albert's psychologist decided to schedule Albert on three separate occasions, spending 4 hr on each of the first two occasions and only 1 hr on the third occasion. It is important to observe the child under conditions that simulate the stresses of school. Because children spend more than 4 hr a day in school, a worthwhile element of the assessment process is to observe what happens when the child tires. This fact was discussed with the parents, and none of them felt that a 4-hr session would be too strenuous for Albert.

Figure 8.6 illustrates the test room schedule that was developed during the history taking session. This schedule is a map or guideline for conducting the testing. As each test is given, the marking is circled to indicate that the test was completed.

STRUCTURING THE FAMILY

At the conclusion of the history taking, and after the psychologist has determined what tests will be given and set the time schedule, it is important that the psychologist structure the family for a number of reasons.

Forming the Alliance

Involving the parents, as well as the teachers, in the assessment process is of considerable importance. The end result of the process is a series of recommendations, almost all of which can be carried out only by significant adult figures in the child's life. The more involved the parents and teachers are in the process, the more likely they are to participate in various efforts at resolution and remediation. The essence of forming the alliance is communication: The adult figures in the child's life should have the opportunity to express their ideas about the child, and they must receive communication from the psychologist as to what is being done and the outcomes of the process. At the end of the history taking, a number of elements that are important to the alliance bonding should take place.

Cautious Reassurance.   At the end of the history taking, the psychologist needs to reassure the parents that the information given is helpful. Parents also should be reassured that nothing is terribly odd or peculiar about their child and that many of the things they are doing with the child are correct and helpful.

A Picture of What Will Be Done.   The psychologist should tell the parents what will be done with the child during the course of the assessment and should ask their permission to use the candy store and the

TEST ROOM SHEDULE

Birthdate 7/22/81
Age 7-3
Date Scheduled 9/15 & 9/20

NAME DOE, Albert

SCHEDULE: History Tues 9/20 3pm (1)
XIT Tues 11/9 1pm (2)
XIT 2 Tues 11/23 3pm (1)

PSY	TR	DATE	DAY	HOURS	TOTALS	
1	3	10/17	Mon	10-12 & 1-3	2	PSY.
1	3	10/18	Tues	" "	7	TR
	1	10/19	Wed	8-9 am	3	Workup

INTERVIEWS

X History
X Int
X Int
X Int
___ _____
___ _____

INTELLIGENCE/DEVELOPMENT

___ AFRPV   ___ QT
X PPVT(L)M
___ Binet L M
___ Bayley
___ Cattel
___ KABC
___ Chicago NV
___ Minn Develop
___ Vineland Adap ___ Soc
___ WPPSI-R   Mat
X WISC-R
___ WAIS-R   ___ WAIS
  X Inf   X P Comp
  X Comp   X P Arr
  X Arith   X Bl Des
  X Sim   X Cod
  X DigSp X Object
  X Voc   Assem

NEUROPSYCHOLOGY

___ Reitan Sens Def___A___C
___ Category (BK) Test
___ Wells & Reusch-A,A,A
X MFD-Graham-Kendall
___ Indiana-Retain SF
X Torque X Rpt___ Parents
X Hand Dynamometer
___ LNNB___I___II___Child
___ Neuropsych Sym/Sign

NEUROPSYCHOLOGY (Cont.)

___ Neurobehav Cog Status
___ Spiral AET
___ Fla Kind Screen (Satz)
___ Wisconsin Card Sort
___ ABC Vision

ACHIEVEMENT

X Metro Achiev FM JS
  ___ Pre Primer
  X Primer
  X Primary 1
  ___ Primary 2
  ___ Elementary
  ___ Intermediate
  ___ Advanced 1
  ___ Advanced 2
___ Amer Schl Read/Arith
___ Gates MacG Rdg Readiness
___ Nelson-Denny___E___F
___ Gates MacGin Rdg___Prim
  ___ D FM 1 2 3
  ___ E FM 1 2 3
  ___ F Form 1
___ Stanford Task
___ WRAT
___ Metro Rdg___I___II

INTEREST +

___ Strong
___ Kuder
___ Wren S-H

MISCELLANEOUS

X Drawing of choice
___ _____

PERSONALITY

X TAT

X 1	___ 2	X 3BM	X 4
___ 5	X 6BM	___ 6GF	___ 7BM
___ 7GF	X 8BM	___ 8GF	___ 9BM
___ 9GF	___ 10	___ 11	___ 12BG
___ 12M	___ 12F	X 13MF	___ 14
___ 15	___ 16	X 17BM	___ 17GF
___ 18BM	___ 18GF	___ 19	___ 20

X Dictation   ___ Write
___ Rorschach
X H-T   X DAP
___ Self Portrait
___ TASC   X CSC
___ TA?
___ MMPI
___ MIllon
___ 16PF
___ CAQ
___ FIRO-B
X Family Drawing
___ PIC
___ Haggarty - OW
___ Child Behavior Profile
___ Mother-Child Rel Eval
___ Parent Stress Index
___ Multidim Child Pers
___ Holmes Stress Scale (SRE)

MARITAL

___ Marital Audit   ___ SRA
___ Marital Audit Inv
___ Marital Diag   ___ Mar Roles
___ Mar Satisfction   ___ MHP

FIGURE 8.6 Albert Doe's Test Battery Checklist

THEODORE H. BLAU, PH. D.
213 East Davis Boulevard
Davis Islands, Tampa, Florida

CLINICAL PSYCHOLOGY
CHILD PSYCHOLOGY

The following appointments have been made for

ALBERT DOE

Day _MONDAY_ Date _Oct. 17_ Time _10−12 + 1−3_
TUESDAY   _Oct. 18_   _10−12 + 1−3_
WEDNESDAY   _Oct. 19_   _8−9 am_

If for any reason the above appointments cannot be kept, please call
253-3587 at least 24 hours before the scheduled appointment.

RESULTS + INTERPRETATION

FIRST : Tuesday, Nov. 9, 1−3 pm

SECOND : Tuesday, Nov. 23, 3−4 pm

FIGURE 8.7 Albert Doe's Appointment Card

treasure chest as motivational devices. Any restrictions on candy, soft drinks, or certain kinds of toys should be elicited at this point.

The psychologist should give the parents an idea of what will happen without exposing them to actual test items. No matter what their good intentions, parents may "coach" a child before the examination. The parents should be told what kind of time schedule is required, and the appointments should be set. When everyone agrees on the appointment times, the parents should be given an appointment card. A copy should be kept in the child's file in the event that misunderstandings occur as to the agreed-upon times. Figure 8.7 illustrates Albert's appointment card.

Helping the Parents Structure the Child

A matter of some conflict for most parents is how they will tell the child about the examination. The psychologist should help in this respect by making a number of suggestions about what the child should be told and how the examination should be approached.

Availability of the Psychologist. Before ending the interview, the psychologist should tell the parents that if they have any questions before the assessment is completed, the psychologist is available to take telephone calls to discuss these concerns. Although this should not be encouraged, the door should certainly be left open for any additional comments the parents (or the teachers) may have. This availability also helps to cement the alliance that is so necessary for the successful application of the results of a psychological evaluation.

The Structuring of Albert's Family

After scheduling Albert's psychological assessment, the psychologist did the following structuring with the family:

> You've given me a very good picture of your son. While we were talking and you were giving me this information, you noticed that I was making some little marks on this sheet. This is the test room schedule. I have put together a custom-made psychological evaluation for Albert. The examinations will include tests of his intellectual capacity and function, observations of his behavior, opportunities for him to demonstrate his skills and abilities, measurements of his brain–behavior interactions so that we can compare him with others his age, and a very careful assessment of what he has absorbed from his school experience to date. I know that he has had school tests, but we would like to give him a test face-to-face and be able to tell you Albert's maximum ability to reproduce fundamental material necessary in school work.
>
> We will spend a lot of time examining Albert's personality—his reactions to different people, the things that stimulate him, the things he might be fearful of, and the sources of much of his behavior. As you recall, at the beginning of this session, I asked you what questions you might want answered. As I see it, from your comments, these are some of the questions whose answers we'll seek:
>
> 1. Is Albert hyperactive?
> 2. Is Albert abnormal?
> 3. How can his attention span be increased?
> 4. What can you as his parents do to help him in his adjustment?
>
> We are going to find out a lot about Albert as a growing person. I think you should know that what you have told me about Albert is most interesting, but not particularly unusual. I've seen many children who have similar behaviors. I should like to tell you that many of the things that you have been doing with Albert are, in my opinion, exactly right. The results of this evaluation are going to show you that you do a lot of things correctly.
>
> We're going to examine Albert according to the schedule I've given you on that appointment card. Then, after a week or so for me to work up the results, I'd like to sit down with all of you for a 2-hr session and tell you what we've done, what we've found, what it means, and what we recommend. During this session I will provide you with a lot of data on what we did with Albert, what the tests showed, and what it all means. There is so much information during these sessions that we like to put the session on a cassette tape and give it to you at the end of the session. We then want you to play that tape,

consider what we've done and what we've found, talk about the recommendations, decide what things might not be clear, and prepare for a second interpretation session where we will clarify any issues, and help you to implement the recommendations.

There will be a written report. We recommend that this report not be sent directly to the school until we have our interpretation and decide what information would be useful in helping the school to help Albert. As you probably know, any report sent to the school becomes part of the school record. We want to be sure that anything we tell the school will work in Albert's best interests and not in any way against those interests.

In your telling Albert about these examinations, I think a couple of things would be helpful. First of all, I think it would be most helpful for both mother and father to tell him about the forthcoming evaluation. I would suggest that your approach be very positive. I would tell Albert that he's growing up, and that there are doctors who can find a person's abilities and talents. I would suggest that you tell Albert that he will have a lot of fun while he's here. Our experience is that children do enjoy the clinic and we have a number of things that are very interesting and stimulating. I would suggest that you tell Albert that while he's here, he's going to have a good time, and he's essentially going to do a lot of playing. I would be careful not to overstructure Albert, but certainly to present a very positive attitude about coming here. Once you get him to the waiting room, it will be my responsibility to take over and make it a very positive experience for Albert. Do you have any questions so far about what we're doing and what we're going to try to do?

Between now and the time I see Albert and between then and the time I give you the interpretation of the results, you may have some questions. Please feel free to call me. The earlier during the evaluation that you ask questions, the less I'll know about Albert. The further we go, the more I will know. It's not necessary for you to wait for the interpretation if some issue arises that gives you concern. Also, if there are additional questions that arise as you think about it, please call me and tell me what these are and we will try to fit them into the assessment.

I want to tell you that it's gratifying to work with parents who, although split and in different family settings now, still are able to focus their concern on Albert and his growth needs. You must realize that I see many parents who are bitterly opposed to each other, and of course the child suffers from this. Your spirit of cooperation and interest I think is the most valuable thing that Albert has at the moment. I commend you on this and I have found that this suggests that we will all work well together in Albert's best interests.

The parents seemed quite positive about what had occurred. They agreed to share the task of bringing Albert to the clinic, and they agreed that they could all be present for at least the first interpretation and possibly the second. Arrangements were made so that each family could have a copy of the tape. It was decided that the mother would call Albert's teacher, since she had a very good relationship with her. The mother would tell the teacher about the process, and inform her that the psychologist would be getting in touch with her. This family intake session ended on a positive note.

The Examination Process

CHAPTER NINE

First Contact with the Child

THE CHILD IN THE WAITING ROOM

The psychologist, having spoken to the parents during the intake interview concerning the importance of the first visit, can expect that the child will be moderately well prepared for the first session. However, some parents, because of their own misunderstandings or anxieties, bring the child to the first session without any structuring or supportive encouragement. The psychologist should always be prepared for a child who does not know what is going to happen and fears the worst. Very few children come for their first psychological examination with a clear idea of what will happen. Psychologists should understand that the unknown is a source of great anxiety to children or to adults. Almost without fail, one can expect that children will feel some trepidation at the time of their first visit.

In Chapter 4, the physical structure of the waiting room was illustrated. Hopefully, the parents will be a few minutes early, and the child will use the play facilities to become somewhat acclimated and comfortable. Frequently, however, the psychologist finds the child sitting on the parent's lap or standing beside the parent's chair clinging to the mother's or father's hand, clearly very tense.

Initial impressions set the tone for future contacts. The psychologist can do several things to ease the tension of the child's first contact. First and foremost, the psychologist should be on time. The longer the child must wait in the waiting room, the less comfortable the child will be leaving the parents and entering the new setting. One way in which the psychologist can initiate a positive first contact is to disrupt any prejudgments the child may have about the examination. Most children associate the concept of "doctor" or "examination" with negative experiences. To disrupt any prejudgment about the atmosphere, the psychologist can introduce himself or herself in a playful, unserious manner. One way to begin an alliance with the child is to play "peek," a somewhat more complex form of "peek-a-boo" which every child knows and understands. To do this, the psychologist can "edge" his or her head around the door frame leading to the waiting room. As soon as the child sees the psychologist's head, a quick withdrawal behind the door frame usually attracts the child's attention and amuses him or her. Waiting 4 or 5 sec, the psychologist can then repeat putting the head around the door frame a foot or so lower so that the head appears unexpectedly in the child's line of vision. Children find this very amusing, and apparently relaxing. They inevitably laugh and point this out to the parent. After two or three repetitions, the psychologist steps into the room, points the finger at the child, and says, "You peeked!" Most children respond with, "No, I didn't!" The psychologist can then appear to be flustered and say, "Oh, yes. *I* peeked!" and follow this with a giggle. Very few children can resist this harmless interaction.

The psychologist should follow this by saying, "I am Dr. Jones," and offer to shake hands with the child. The first observation of the child's lateral dominance is made at this point. A certain number of children will stick out their left hand rather than their right hand, often checking themselves, correcting the motion, and then presenting their right hand. While shaking the child's hand, the clinician may feign excruciating pain and groan and say, "Oh, my goodness, you're so strong. Please don't hurt my hand." Most children respond to this kind of nonsense in a positive manner.

It is unwise to engage in conversation with the parent during this introduction. Focusing on the child in the pleasant and silly manner noted above is something to which most children relate. These procedures are inappropriate with youngsters older than 10 or 11, but extremely effective with younger children.

At this point the clinician may say, "We're going to have a good time today. Is that the truth or a lie?" This sort of approach continues the psychologist's effort to disrupt prejudgments that may be worrying the child. The child will usually shrug or say, "I don't know." The psychologist should say, "Well, that's the truth. Sometimes I tell the truth and sometimes I tell a lie. I'll let you guess which it is, and maybe you'll get a nice reward if you guess right."

Very few children can resist some form of the introduction noted above.

ESTABLISHING AND STRENGTHENING RAPPORT

Encouraging the child to leave the waiting room and accompany the psychologist to proceed with the first interview is a major step. In most cases, once this task is accomplished, the remainder of the consultation is relatively easy.

There are philosophical differences regarding the style in which examinations are conducted. Some psychologists prefer to conduct the examination in a very objective, straightforward manner, emulating in every respect the standardization procedures used in the various test instruments that form the test battery. The examination style proposed here is for the purposes of identifying the child's maximum functional ability, potential, and resources for both conflict resolution and enhanced developmental experience. To achieve this goal, the psychologist should make sure that the structure and the ambiance of the examination setting encourage the child to produce at his or her highest level of function. Thus, it is helpful to create a *token economy* system as part of the examination. One way to do this is to set up a theme around which the entire clinical experience revolves. Perhaps the clinic can become zoolike, or situationally like a playschool.

One psychologist, for example, focuses on the bear, a symbol that seems to engender feelings of warmth and security in children. (The popularity of bears as favorite toy animals for children has existed continually for over 100 years in the United States.) A large number of small bears are unobtrusively attached to curtains, window frames, bookcases, and other parts of the various rooms in the clinic. Most adults do not even notice these small bears, but children always seem to see them quite quickly. The theme of the bears is repeated in pictures or photographs of bears located in various rooms of the clinic.

The token economy can be associated with the selected theme. For instance, in a clinic with a bear theme, each child, once he or she leaves the waiting room, can be provided with a "bear ticket." Perhaps the psychologist can have the child put his or her hand on the copy machine; the resultant copy is a palm print that the child identifies as his or her own. This sheet can then be labeled "Bear Ticket." The child is then told that a treasure chest and a candy store are in the clinic and that, during the time that he or she is there, there will be opportunities to earn Xs on the bear ticket. The clinician can add two columns to the bear ticket labeled "treasure" and "candy." This ticket is then carried by the child throughout the testing experience. Figure 9.1 illustrates a bear ticket for Albert.

As described in Chapter 4, the treasure chest can be a box that is painted to resemble a pirate's treasure chest. The box contains small toys that are of interest to children between the ages of 3 and 11. After making the bear ticket, the psychologist may want to let the child glimpse the treasure chest and its contents. The psychologist may say, "When you're finished today, you can exchange your bear ticket for as many things in this chest as you have Xs under "treasure."

The candy store can be extremely effective if it is set up in a closet. As discussed in Chapter 4, the candy is placed in glass jars as were characteristic of candy stores in the era of the child's grandparents. It is best to provide candies that the child generally does not see in his or her everyday environment: Old-fashioned "chicken feed," licorice, and fruit-filled hard candies, as well as a wide variety of bubble gums, can be very attractive to children. The candy store should be equipped with white sacks or a carton of plastic zip-lock bags.

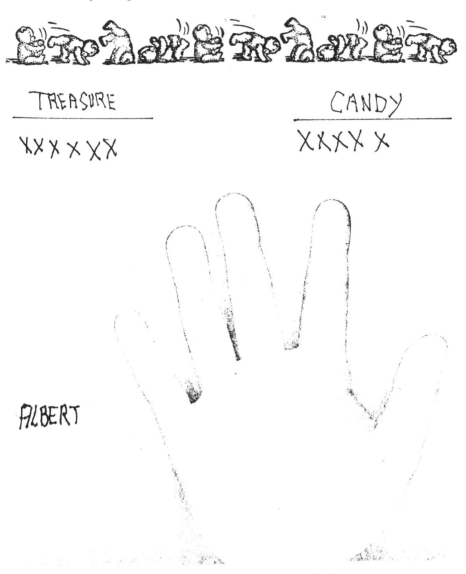

FIGURE 9.1   Albert Doe's Bear Ticket

As the psychologist shows the child these reward options, he or she should introduce the child to the entire staff of the clinic. Anyone whom the child is likely to see during the course of the assessment should be identified by the psychologist as someone who is there to work with the psychologist and to be helpful, friendly, and available. During this introductory time, the child and the psychologist will be walking through the clinic hallways and visiting the various rooms. This togetherness will help develop the bond with the child and will give the child the security of familiarity with the physical surroundings.

At this time, the child should be offered a cold drink from a refrigerator that has a wide variety of drinks that children enjoy: sodas (including diet sodas), juices, and milk. This offer helps meet the child's dependency needs and creates a more comfortable setting. Children often refuse the first time they are offered refreshments.

It is important that the psychologist receives the parents' permission before offering the child candy, toys, and drinks. Because some parents prefer that their children be given only natural fluids and sugarless gums, these should be available. After this familiarization with the surroundings, the child can be brought to the psychologist's office for the initial interview. The psychologist seats the child comfortably in the office and begins the initial portion of the assessment. This consists of talking and getting acquainted. The psychologist can ask the child a number of simple questions that are not particularly intrusive, such as the following:

- Do you know your birthdate?
- Do you have a favorite toy?
- Who is your best friend?
- What do you like to do most when you're in school?
- What is your favorite television show?

The psychologist can ask the child about hobbies, pets, sports, or particular interests that have already been described by the parents during the intake interview.

In keeping with the bear theme, the psychologist might carry a large stuffed bear into the interview room, have the child sit next to the bear, and take a Polaroid picture of the two to help bond the child to the testing experience in a positive way. (Figure 9.2 shows a picture of Albert with Harry the Bear.) Two pictures should be taken, one for the file and one for the child to take home. If the child is the product of a fractured family, an extra picture can be taken so that the child may have one in each family setting. Children often cherish these pictures and ask that they be put up on a bulletin board at home. The picture in the folder enables the psychologist to make physiognomic comparisons in the event that further evaluations take place in the future. Physiological growth occurs with psychological development, and where a sequential series of tracking assessments are made, the pictures in the folder can illustrate the child's physiological development.

The child can then be taken back to the refrigerator and again asked to choose something to drink. At this time it is wise to make sure the child

FIGURE 9.2   Albert with Harry the Bear (Albert is not the "real" Albert in the story, but gives you an idea of the age of the boy. The bear is the "real" bear.)

knows where the bathroom is in case he or she may wish to use these facilities.

By this time the child should feel fairly comfortable in the setting, and the psychologist can then introduce the child to the assessment process.

BEGINNING THE ASSESSMENT PROCESS

The child must be comfortable before beginning any formal assessment process. After the initial introduction to the clinical setting, as described above, the child should be seated comfortably in an office or in the test room. The psychologist begins to make the first observations and to ask the child some initial questions.

Albert showed a great deal of motor behavior, and seemed to enjoy walking around and touching things. For this reason, the beginning of the assessment took place in the consultation office, rather than in the test room, because there were more chairs, walking space, and objects that could be examined.

Albert adapted to the setting fairly quickly, and sat in the chair assigned to him. He readily responded to questions. He indicated that he lived with his mother and stepfather and that this was all right. He expressed fairly immediate and consistent negative attitudes toward his half brother. He said that he enjoyed visiting with his father and stepmother.

CLINICAL OBSERVATIONS

Patient's Name ___Albert Doe___   Date $\frac{10/17}{10/18}$ $\frac{10/19}{1988}$ By $\frac{THB}{AX}$

Initial Observ. & Test Behavior   Time $\frac{1:00}{7:15}$

- Blond hair
- Blue eyes
- Tall for age

SPEECH:
- High
- Crackley

- Sucks thumb on & off
- Drinks a lot of fluids
- Became irritable and resistant when tired

- Belches often
- Answers impulsively

☐ Glasses

☒ Other
Two front teeth missing

HEARING:
- OK

FAMILY:
- Lives with Ⓜ & step Ⓕ. OK.
- D. like ½ brother
- Likes to visit Ⓕ

MOTOR:
- Jumpy
- Explores & touches
- At times "hyper"
- Right-handed

SOCIALIZATION:
- Friendly
- Seems immature for age
- Very responsive to Bear Ticket and Rewards

SCHOOL:
- OK
- Hard to "stay still"
- Teacher likes me

COOPERATION:
- Answers very quickly
- Varies
- Pouts when limits are set
- Uses fake crying to get his way
- Did very well when given a lot of attention
- Often refuses at first, then cooperates.

Bobby & Carl are best friends

CONFIDENCE:
- Not good
- Doesn't want to risk "guessing." Later on achievement tests, does guess difficult items.
- Gets upset with himself.

OTHER:
Likes:
- Playing & friends
- Making paper airplanes
- "Who's Boss" favorite T.V.

FIGURE 9.3   Albert Doe's Clinical Observations Sheet

He felt that school was all right, but that it was hard to "sit still." He spontaneously remarked that his teacher liked him. He was able to indicate to the examiner that he had two best friends at school, and he named them.

Figure 9.3 shows a clinical observation form on which some of the above comments and other observations were written. The same form is used throughout the testing, and is marked by every examiner who participates in the assessment process. As noted on Figure 9.3, observations were made on three different testing dates.

When it became apparent that Albert was comfortable, he was provided with a blank sheet of paper, presented in the horizontal axis, and two lead pencils with erasers. He was given the following directions:

> Albert, I would like you to draw something for me. I would like you to draw a house and a tree. Any kind of a house and any kind of a tree will do. Just do the best you can.

Albert looked at the examiner, took the pencil, and drew a relatively small, primitive house structure. He immediately erased this (the residuals can be seen on the drawing) and drew a larger house. He then proceeded to draw the tree. Figure 9.4 shows Albert's House–Tree Test.

Following the successful completion of the House–Tree Test, the examiner gave Albert the bear ticket and inscribed an X for both candy and treasure. Albert was delighted, and immediately asked how he could earn more. Taking this as a cue, the examiner took Albert to the test room, and began the formal testing with the Information subtest of the Wechsler

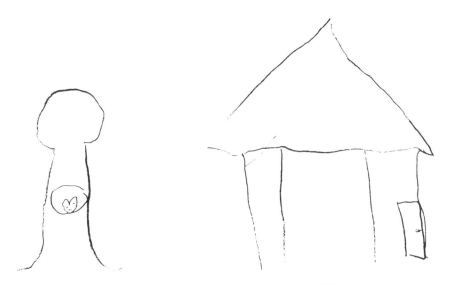

FIGURE 9.4   Albert Doe's House-Tree Test

Intelligence Scale for Children–Revised. Albert entered into this with energy and interest. As the items became difficult, he tried to avoid guessing, even though guessing was encouraged. When he did not know an answer, he was upset with himself. He did a certain amount of whining and pouting as the items became difficult. With support and encouragement, he continued to work in a fairly effective manner. Compared with other children his age, he seemed younger, more impulsive, and more reactive emotionally.

At this point, Albert was introduced to the psychological assistant and told that she would play some more games with him, and that he should not forget his bear ticket. He seemed cooperative and was able to proceed with several hours of testing. His responses to the situation can be noted in Figure 9.3 on the clinical observations form.

CONCLUDING THE FIRST SESSION

When Albert finished the allotted time in the test room, the psychological assistant escorted him back to the consultation room. Albert very happily showed the psychologist his bear ticket. He also produced a drawing that he asked to be allowed to make in crayon as a gift to the psychologist. Figure 9.5 shows the gift drawing that Albert made for the psychologist. Albert explained the drawing: The car represented his being driven to the office for the examination, and the flower was something that Albert had been praised for drawing well in school. The various lines throughout the drawing, in green crayon, represented grass.

The psychologist thanked Albert for his gift and then took him to the candy store and the treasure chest to select the number of items indicated by the bear ticket. Albert talked happily about the experience and asked whether he could return for more. The psychologist reassured him that he could return and that the staff would look forward to seeing him. He asked whether he would get another chance to win treasures and candy on a bear ticket, and the psychologist reassured him that the token economy would continue to apply.

After Albert retrieved his various rewards, he was taken to the waiting room where his mother awaited him. He dashed out and showed her his accomplishments and rewards, and seemed very positive about his experience. The mother seemed a little surprised about this, and made some comment about how nice it was to see Albert enthusiastic and pleased.

The psychologist confirmed with the mother the time and date of the next appointment. It is always wise to seek confirmation, even though an appointment card has been given, to ensure that no misunderstandings occur. Albert insisted on giving the psychologist a farewell hug, and the first session ended in a positive way.

FIGURE 9.5   A Gift Drawing Given to Examiner by Albert

Not all first sessions go as smoothly, although it is more the rule than the exception. If a child is excessively frightened, unsure, or in other ways uncomfortable, the first session may be spent mostly in free play, balloon breaking, discussions, and creating a comfortable alliance between the child and the psychologist. This is always a matter of clinical judgment, and the introduction to the test situation should not be rushed.

CHAPTER TEN

Evaluation of the Child's Intellect

No assessment area has received greater attention in the psychological literature than intelligence. The concept of intelligence is described and defined in many ways, from many different points of view, and hundreds of instruments have been developed and standardized to measure this trait, state, condition, or behavior. Terman (1921) pointed out that we must guard against defining intelligence solely in terms of a particular test or the ability to pass the tests of a given intelligence scale. Binet and Simon (1905), the originators of the first individually administered intelligence scale, regarded intelligence as a collection of faculties such as judgment, initiative, practical sense, and the ability to adapt oneself to circumstances. On this basis, the age scales were first developed.

Great thinkers in psychology have come to no absolute agreement regarding the definition of intelligence. Different tests emphasize different theoretical positions and focus on a variety of descriptive outcomes. Today, it is generally agreed that intelligence is a series of genetically determined response capabilities that are significantly modified by experience. In no other area is the concept of individual differences more clearly demonstrated (Sattler, 1974).

For the purposes of this book, the definition of intelligence achieves a form in terms of the end result that it serves. The only reason for any of the tests that are given to children is to answer questions associated with understanding the child, the child's best interests, and the sources of difficulty that the child may have. Thus, the definition of intellect relates to the end products that can serve the purpose of the evaluation of the child.

In no way do the procedures recommended in this book attempt to delineate the total parameters of the application of intelligence to human behavior. Rather, the purpose of measuring children's intelligence, insofar as the comprehensive examination of the child is concerned, is to apply findings and explanations to counseling and predictive situations that continually face clinicians to whom children are brought for help. Extensive clinical experience suggests that there are many ways in which the results of intelligence tests can be extremely useful during the comprehensive psychological examination as outlined in this volume. The more frequently useful applications of intelligence test data are considered in detail below.

USING INTELLIGENCE TEST DATA

A Measure of What Can Be Expected of the Child

Regardless of the reason for the initial consultation, parents have overt as well as covert expectancies for their children. Many of these expectations revolve around the child's capacity to cope or the child's capacity to perform. Almost universally, parents who bring children to psychologists are interested in some measure of brightness, coping capacity, or ability to compete in the world—essentially what is measured in intelligence tests.

Although the results of the intelligence tests do not always meet the parents' hopes and expectations, a meaningful measure of the child's potential is extremely important in helping the parents to work effectively in the child's best interests.

Sensible Guidance for the School

Most of a child's focused time and activities between the ages of 3 or 4 and 18 or older are spent in an academic setting. School is the child's and adolescent's job. Although school systems have a great deal of testing activity, it is generally on a group basis, and sometimes yields a less than accurate picture of what may be expected of a child. The school's job is not to provide individual comprehensive psychological evaluation of the children in the system, although this might be an altruistic goal. With the millions of children in American schools, a comprehensive psychological evaluation for each would be logistically impractical. Such a comprehensive evaluation should be the choice of parents, either when they perceive problems or when they choose to increase their knowledge of the child in order to avoid difficulties and to enhance opportunities.

The school may be very interested in a child's intellectual capacities, often as a way of relieving the school of responsibilities for difficulties faced by the child. On the other hand, individual teachers are frequently pleased to have external recommendations that will help them to help the child. Each part of the comprehensive psychological examination of the child can result in some useful information for the school and teachers. The results of a carefully administered individual intelligence test are ordinarily welcomed by teachers and guidance counselors. The interpretation of the individual test of intelligence, identifying areas in which the child is likely to perform easily, as well as areas where difficulty may occur and performance may be limited or scattered, is useful information for any teacher.

Explanation of Previously Noted Difficulties

Many difficulties exhibited by children are either caused by or significantly affect intellectual performance. These difficulties include brain disorders, severe emotional problems, developmental anomalies, endocrine disorders, and hereditary dysfunction (Rourke et al., 1983; Rourke et al., 1986; Sattler, 1982). Some children's difficulties both at home and at school may reflect extraordinary intelligence (Horowitz & O'Brian, 1985). Children of extraordinarily high intellectual capacity frequently have problems in communication, learning style, and value systems in relation to their peers. They may pose a threat to their teachers. These differences can lead to extremely unfortunate reactions for these children. Knowledge of a child's intellectual capacity is sometimes the first step to resolving such difficulties.

Opportunities to Resolve Problems

Because the most significant part of the comprehensive psychological examination of children is the outcome, or recommendations, the clinician must depend on the child's capacity to carry out or implement recommendations in order that these suggestions have some utilization. For instance, the child must have sufficient comprehensive capacity and attention span to tolerate a specified homework schedule. Knowledge of the comparative aspects of various intellectual capabilities allows the clinician to build a set of recommendations that have the highest probability of leading to a successful resolution of problems.

A Key to Reward and Esteem Building

Again, the clinician should always be thinking about the recommendations that he or she can present to the parents and to the school, to help avoid further difficulties and create a more enhancing reward system for the child. These recommendations are frequently based on a knowledge of what the child is able to do well and what the child approaches with difficulty and likely failure. Although every child is faced with learning certain academic and social fundamentals, these fundamentals may be learned in many different ways. The nature of the child's intelligence is often the most important information that a clinician can use to prepare recommendations that have the highest probability of achieving performance outcomes and of creating a sense of worth and fulfillment in the child. It is not enough to simply ensure that the child is adequately able to accomplish what the school expects, to acquire fundamental academic skills, and to function adequately, or reasonably adequately, within the expectations of society. The psychologist is also responsible for providing the significant adults in the child's life with the opportunity to create those circumstances in which the child can go beyond fundamentals and develop a sense of self-worth that can be useful not only to the child throughout his or her life, but in terms of meeting society's needs and even contributing to a more humanistic and fulfilling social milieu.

These are not all of the reasons for giving an intelligence test to the child. The clinical observations made during the presentation of stimuli during an individual intelligence test are extremely useful to the seasoned clinician in beginning to develop a concept of the functionality of the child. Although the measures of performance and personality are important, clinical observation is also an important part of the examination. The intelligence test is an excellent opportunity to observe how the child performs under mild, moderate, and intense stimulation.

CHOOSING THE TESTS

A comprehensive assessment of the child requires a measure of intelligence that goes beyond a single number or a percentile. Because the psychologist must interpret to the parents and to the teachers what a child can and cannot do, the fewer generalities, the better. To meet this need, individually administered tests of intelligence are the instruments of choice.

Many individual tests of intellectual functioning have been developed (Anastasi, 1982; Keyser & Sweetland, 1987; Sattler, 1982). In the case illustrated in this volume, testing was with the Wechsler Intelligence Scale for Children–Revised (WISC-R; Wechsler, 1974). The Wechsler scales— including the adult version, the Wechsler Adult Intelligence Scale–Revised (Wechsler, 1981)—are considered standards in the field of testing. Reliability is excellent, and the validity is acceptable for clinical utilization. The standardization procedures include excellent geographic sampling, as well as adequate sampling for sex, race, community size, and socioeconomic class. The administration procedures for the various Wechsler scales allow the examiner to evaluate a wide range of a child's knowledge and are organized in such a way that the examiner can readily determine whether the child really understands what is being asked. Scoring criteria are both well standardized and realistic.

The WISC-R is usable for youngsters from $6^{1}/_{2}$ to about 16 years of age. Younger children should be tested with another instrument, for example, the Wechsler Preschool and Primary Scale of Intelligence-Revised (WPPSI-R; Wechsler, 1989). The WISC-R is not particularly useful, however, for children who are severely or profoundly retarded.

Other individually administered tests of intelligence that can be used with children include the Columbia Mental Maturity Scale, the Culture Fair Intelligence Test, the Leiter International Performance Scales, the Slosson

Intelligence Test, and the Stanford–Binet Intelligence Scales (Keyser & Sweetland, 1987). Because the Wechsler scales are universally known and used, they are particularly useful in communicating results to school systems and other professional organizations where other psychologists may be called upon to apply findings of the comprehensive examination.

The 11 subtests of the WISC-R offer an opportunity for the psychologist to understand any fluctuations that may exist in the way the child views and meets the world. Such fluctuations can be extremely useful in understanding performance or behavior that is the source of distress in the environment.

Additional Intelligence Testing

Even though the Wechsler scales offer 11 different subtests of the child's intellectual performance, it is wise to add an additional intelligence test to the battery, preferably one that approaches the child's intellectual functions in a totally different way from that of the Wechsler scales. For people in the age range of 3 to adulthood, the Peabody Picture Vocabulary Test–Revised, Form L or Form M, is frequently the instrument of choice (Dunn & Dunn, 1981). This test does not require the child to use expressive speech; the answers are simply indicated by pointing the finger. It is also an excellent instrument to determine the intellectual potential of children who are frightened of responding or of trusting their own judgment. The use of an alternate instrument also allows the examiner to determine whether significant fluctuations occur in the child's intellectual responsiveness, at different times of the day or under different conditions. A number of these tests are reviewed thoroughly by Sattler (1982).

Conditions of Administration

One of the more significant characteristics of a good test is the availability of very careful and very specific directions for administration and scoring. Tests should always be administered under optimal conditions using standardized procedures. The test room should be well lighted, and the working space should be large and uncluttered. There should be no distractions of any significance in the room. The examiner's attitude is also important, and the child must be encouraged without coaching.

Of particular importance is the examiner's awareness that children are different. It is unacceptable to give a test in a standardized manner to a child who is the product of an ethnic minority and compare the results with those of children who had greater advantages in education or modeling. This comment also applies for testing handicapped children, emotionally disturbed children, brain damaged children, retarded children, physically handicapped children, and delinquent children. Children with hearing defects or visual problems may be tested, but their tests must be interpreted in light of these special conditions.

The examiner is responsible for carefully noting all of the child's behavior that may have some effect on the quality of the performance (Sattler, 1982).

The Examiner's Attitude and Presentation of Self

It is commonly understood by psychologists that the examiner may create a "halo effect." The children who are pleasing and attractive to the examiner are likely to have better scores than children who are angry, unresponsive to the examiner's expectations, difficult, or unattractive. Extreme care must be taken to avoid such effects or, if they exist, to make careful note of them in the clinical observation of the testing. The examiner must create an attitude of safety and an aura of encouragement. While being responsive to the child, the examiner must not create an aura of expectancy that is so strong that the child feels "pushed."

Optimizing Performance

During the history taking and examination of school records, the psychologist is likely to get a good picture of the child's intellectual response under difficult circumstances. One responsibility the psychologist has during the comprehensive psychological examination is to determine the maximum performance that the child can produce under the best circumstances. The tests allow an opportunity to find out why a child is not regularly performing at a maximum level. A significant difference between the child's intellectual performance during the examination and the reports of parents and teachers is an excellent starting place for clues to the sources of the child's difficulty.

In support of this responsibility, after a test has been administered according to standardized procedures, the psychologist may choose to "test the limits" and give the child an opportunity to perform beyond the time limits, at levels higher than standardized cutoff. Testing the limits may also be done during subsequent appointments when the child may be rested. The test must always be scored according to the customary standardization procedures, but discrepancies based on additional opportunities for the child to perform are noteworthy, and this manner of testing should be followed in all examinations.

Reporting the Results of Intelligence Tests

Psychologists have been more or less "stuck" with the concept of the intelligence quotient (IQ). Developed by Stern early in the century, this concept was popularized by Terman when he published his 1916 revision of the Binet test (Murphy, 1949). The concept of IQ is so widely accepted that we almost dare not omit it when writing to schools. Parents are frequently tenacious in seeking their child's IQ. If asked what it means to them, the parents are often puzzled but give a response indicating that they are worried that the IQ is not high enough, or, if it is high, that some special activity should be made available to the child. There may be some substance to these concerns, but focusing the concerns on a single number is rarely in the child's best interest.

It is the psychologist's job to reeducate the parents. No single number can accurately represent the intellectual abilities of the child. When interpreting the child's examination to the parents, the psychologist has an opportunity to clearly specify what the test results mean and to what degree they can be deemed reliable and valid. Very specific standards have been developed for the reporting of test results (American Psychological Association, 1985).

The concept of mental age can be a useful means of reporting intellectual results, but this concept is also easily subject to misinterpretation. The best descriptor is percentile. The parents can be guided by the psychologist in understanding that this statistic is a fairly exact comparison of their child's performance with the performance of other children of similar age. Examples of how these numbers should be interpreted to the parents follow. It is always important for the psychologist to clearly indicate that test results are estimates of factors that are measured, and are never to be considered absolute designations of the child's total abilities.

ALBERT'S WISC-R

The WISC-R was an ideal choice of instrument for Albert. He was in the second grade and was having difficulties at school. Neither the parents nor the teachers seemed to be sure of his basic intellectual ability. All parties were anxious for guidance in understanding how to deal with Albert. A full measure of intellect certainly seemed warranted.

Figure 10.1 shows the WISC-R summary sheet for the intellectual evaluation of Albert. Even at first glance, a number of interesting things may be seen on Albert's WISC-R results. Albert has what might be called "good" intellectual capacity. The sum of his Verbal tests places him in the Bright range of intellectual capacity; he exceeds 84 of 100 youngsters of his own age who take these tests. In the Performance tests, he is Very Superior, exceeding 96 of 100 youngsters of his own age in these tests. One could end this discussion by saying that Albert's Full Scale score places him in the Superior range of intellectual capacity. He is able to equal or exceed 94 of 100 youngsters of his age who have taken the same tests. This statement would not be inaccurate, but it would certainly be incomplete and perhaps misleading.

It is important to note that Albert has a range of performances. In Vocabulary he falls at the 50th percentile, as he does in Digit Span, which is not included in the scoring of the total Verbal score. Why is there such a

	Year	Month	Day
Date Tested	88	~~10~~ 9	~~19~~ 49
Date of Birth	81	7	22
Age	7	2	27

	Raw Score	Scaled Score	Percentile
VERBAL TESTS			
Information	8	11	(63)
Similarities	11	13	(84)
Arithmetic	11	17	(99)
Vocabulary	18	10	(50)
Comprehension	12	12	(75)
(Digit Span)	(8)	(10)	(50)
Verbal Score		63	
PERFORMANCE TESTS			
Picture Completion	17	14	(91)
Picture Arrangement	21	12	(75)
Block Design	18	12	(75)
Object Assembly	22	14	(91)
Coding	48	16	(98)
(Mazes)	(—)	(—)	
Performance Score		68	

	Scaled Score	IQ	Percentile Rank	Classification
Verbal Score	63	115	84th	BRIGHT
Performance Score	68	126	96th	VERY SUPERIOR
Full Scale Score	131	123	94th	SUPERIOR

FIGURE 10.1   Case A—Albert's WISC-R Scores

discrepancy between these subtests, which place him in the average range, and subtests such as Arithmetic, which put him at the 99th percentile, and Picture Completion and Object Assembly, which place him at the 91st percentile? Albert's Coding subtest scores place him at the 98th percentile. These differences, which are between 1 and 2 standard deviations apart, may also be significant in terms of Albert's intellectual responses to a variety of situations. A variable profile may be found in youngsters who are suffering a developmental lag, who have some kind of neuropsychological dysfunction, or who suffer a variety of conditions based on endocrinological or physiological deficiencies. Variations may reflect attention deficit disorders or ethnic disadvantage. Personality anomalies can be associated with scale score variability.

The responses in Figures 10.2 through 10.6 can be compared against a standard WISC-R record form.

Although Verbal–Performance differences may be significant, they also occur with some frequency, particularly at the lower end of the age norms, which is where Albert falls. Higher Performance subtest scores than Verbal subtest scores may simply represent that performance skills are better developed than verbal skills at an early age. There may be developmental lag, some auditory conceptual deficiency, or some mild language deficit. Since Albert is 7 years of age, one would be concerned about his reading performance in school. He also may have a visual, nonverbal response that is better developed than his auditory processing. To better understand Albert's intellectual response, the separate subscales should be examined.

Information

Albert was examined on 18 of the 30 Information subtest questions, in accordance with the standardization procedures. This subtest samples a broad range of general knowledge. Albert's responses provide clues about his general range of information, his alertness to the environment, and possibly his social or cultural background. Although individuals may acquire isolated facts without being able to use them effectively, intellectual capacity may account for high scores.

Research shows that the Information subtest is strongly weighted in the g factor of intelligence. It also contributes substantially to a verbal comprehension factor.

Albert had no trouble with the first 6 items, but missed Items 7 and 8. He believed that there are 5 days in the week (in point of fact, there are 5 days in his school week, but he received no credit for this possibility). The month following March, according to Albert, is June. He answered Items 9 and 13 correctly, but he missed the remainder of the items. He did not answer or stated "I don't know" to a number of items. He indicated no particular pattern of subscale variability (i.e., missing very easy items and getting very difficult ones).

1. INFORMATION		**2.** PICTURE COMPLETION		**3.** SIMILARITIES	
Item	Score	Item	Score	Item	Score
1.	(	1.	l	1.	l
2.	l	2.	l	2.	l
3.	l	3.	l	3.	(
4.	(	4.	l	4.	\
5.	l	5.	O	5.	l
6.	l	6.	l	6.	2
7.	O	7.	(	7.	l
8.	O	8.	l	8.	O
9.	l	9.	l	9.	l
10.	O	10.	l	10.	O
11.	O	11.	l	11.	2
12.	O	12.	(	12.	O
13.	l	13.	l	13.	O
14.	O	14.	O	14.	O
15.	O	15.	l	15.	
16.	O	16.	l	16.	
17.	O	17.	l	17.	
18.	O	18.	l	TOTAL SCORE: 11	
19.		19.	\		
20.		20.	O		
21.		21.	O		
22.		22.	O		
23.		23.	O		
24.		24.			
25.		25.			
26.		26.			
27.		TOTAL SCORE: 17			
28.					
29.					
30.					
TOTAL SCORE: 8					

FIGURE 10.2   Albert's WISC-R Subtest Responses

4. PICTURE ARRANGEMENT		5. ARITHMETIC		6. BLOCK DESIGN	
Item	Score	Item	Score	Item	Score
1.	2	1.	1	1.	2
2.	2	2.	1	2.	2
3.	2	3.	1	3.	2
4.	1	4.	1	4.	4
5.	5	5.	1	5.	4
6.	0	6.	1	6.	4
7.	0	7.	1	7.	0
8.	3	8.	1	8.	0
9.	3	9.	1	9.	
10.	3	10.	0	10.	
11.	0	11.	1	11.	
12.	0	12.	1	TOTAL SCORE: 18	
TOTAL SCORE: 21		13.	0		
		14.	0		
		15.	0		
		16.			
		17.			
		18.			
		TOTAL SCORE: 11			

FIGURE 10.3   Albert's WISC-R Subtest Responses

Albert performed at the 63rd percentile on this test, which placed him in the high Average range in comparison with his age cohorts.

Picture Completion

The Picture Completion subtest consists of 26 drawings of objects from everyday life. The child's task is to discover and to point out or name an essential missing portion. The child must understand the incompleteness of

7.

VOCABULARY

Item	Score	Item	Score
1.	2	17.	0
2.	2	18.	0
3.	2	19.	0
4.	1	20.	0
5.	1	21.	
6.	1	22.	
7.	0	23.	
8.	2	24.	
9.	2	25.	
10.	1	26.	
11.	2	27.	
12.	1	28.	
13.	0	29.	
14.	1	30.	
15.	0	31.	
16.	0	32.	

TOTAL
SCORE: 18

FIGURE 10.4   Albert's WISC-R Subtest Responses

the picture and acquire the concept that an *essential* portion is missing. It tests the child's ability to differentiate essential from nonessential detail. It requires concentration, visual alertness, and visual memory. This subtest is a fair measure of the *g* factor and contributes substantially to the perceptual organization factor.

As can be seen in Figure 10.2, Albert responded correctly to the first few items, missed Item 5, and then gave correct responses through Item 13. He missed 14, responded correctly through 19, and then missed 4 consecutive items. Albert's resultant raw score of 17 and weighted score of 14 placed him at the 91st percentile for this particular subtest, and indicates that Albert is in the Superior range in perceptual organization.

8. OBJECT ASSEMBLY		9. COMPREHENSION		10. CODING	
Item	Score	Item	Score	Item	Score
1.	6	1.	2	A.	48
2.	5	2.	2		
3.	5	3.	2		
4.	6	4.	2		
TOTAL SCORE: 22		5.	1		
		6.	2		
		7.	0		
		8.	0		
		9.	1		
		10.	0		
		11.	0		
		12.	0		
		13.	0		
		14.	0		
		15.			
		16.			
		17.			
		TOTAL SCORE: 12			

FIGURE 10.5   Albert's WISC-R Subtest Responses

Similarities

The Similarities subtest contains 17 pairs of words, and the child must explain how they are similar or alike. The subtest is heavily loaded in the g factor and also contributes significantly to the verbal comprehension factor. Verbal concept formation is measured and, probably, abstract thinking ability. Cultural opportunities are said to influence the capacity to perform on this subtest.

Albert's responses to the Similarities subtest indicated a bit of subscale variability. He finished Items 1–4, and then scored 1 point for Item 5, a full score for Item 6, and 1 point for Item 7. He missed Item 8, received partial

11. DIGIT SPAN		12. MAZES		DIGITS BACKWARD	
Item	Score	Item	Score	Item	Score
1.	2	1.		1.	2
2.	2	2.		2.	1
3.	0	3.		3.	1
4.		4.		4.	0
5.		5.		5.	
6.		6.		6.	
7.		7.		7.	
8.		8.		TOTAL SCORE: 4	
9.		9.			
10.		TOTAL SCORE:			
11.					
12.				FORWARD SCORE: 4	
TOTAL SCORE: 4				+ BACKWARD SCORE: 4	
				TOTAL: 8	

FIGURE 10.6   Albert's WISC-R Subtest Responses

credit on Item 9, missed Item 10, and received full credit on Item 11. He then missed 3 consecutive items, completing his work on this subtest. The poor responses to Item 5 and 7 in comparison with the excellent responses to Items 6 and 11 suggested that sometimes Albert may act impulsively and thus present a less than superior response. His score placed him at the 84th percentile in this particular measure.

Picture Arrangement

The Picture Arrangement subtest requires children to place a series of pictures in a logical sequence. The 12 sequences of items look like comic strips. This subtest measures the ability to comprehend and evaluate a total situation. This subtest requires nonverbal reasoning and some planning ability. A subtle element of social intelligence is also involved, since rearranging the cards involves some anticipation of consequences of initial acts.

Albert was asked to arrange the pictures in the correct order to tell a story that makes sense. His responses can be seen in Figure 10.3. Albert's performance placed him at the 75th percentile in this factor.

Arithmetic

There are 18 word problems presented in the Arithmetic subtest. The examiner reads the child the problem, and the child answers without using a pencil or paper. The subtest requires direct counting of concrete quantities, simple addition and subtraction, simple division, multiplication, and subtle operations in the later items.

This subtest is heavily weighted in numerical reasoning ability and moderately weighted in the g factor, with a high loading of the factor freedom from distractibility. It is thus one of the measures of concentration and attention span on the WISC-R.

To do well on the subtest, Albert was required to follow verbal directions, to concentrate on certain parts of the questions, and to have a knowledge of basic arithmetic operations. His responses are shown in Figure 10.3. Albert missed no items through 9. He missed Item 10 (he missed the same item on the Information subtest), gave correct responses on Items 11 and 12, and then missed 3 in a row to end the test. Albert's weighted score of 17 placed him at the 99th percentile, indicating unusual arithmetic reasoning ability for his age.

Block Design

In the Block Design subtest, a child is given a specific number of blocks, each side of which is totally white, totally red, or half red and half white. The child is shown designs ranging from simple to complex and asked to copy each with the blocks that are given. There are 11 items on this subtest. For the first 2 items, the examiner creates actual block models for the child to imitate. The remainder of the designs are constructed from pictures on cards. This is a timed test, and credit is received for accuracy and time.

Block Design tests the child's ability to perceive and analyze forms by mentally breaking down the design into its parts and then building equivalent parts into an identical design. Visual organization and visual–motor coordination are involved. Logic and reasoning, as applied to spatial relationships, are also required. In essence, the Block Design test is a nonverbal concept-formation test. A child who has slow motor activity or visual problems is likely to do poorly on this test.

The Block Design subtest is heavily weighted in the g factor and contributes a great deal to the perceptual organization factor.

Albert passed the first 3 items easily, and then passed Items 4, 5, and 6, but received little time credit. His work was relatively slow. He achieved a scaled score of 12, which placed him at the 75th percentile in comparison with his age group.

Vocabulary

The Vocabulary subtest contains 33 words. The child is asked to define each word orally. The child's responses are scored on a range of 0 to 2 for the quality of the response, according to specific criteria.

The Vocabulary subtest essentially tests word knowledge, but it also requires learning ability, fund of information, richness of ideas, memory, language development, and probably other factors. Of the WISC-R subtests, Vocabulary is the highest weighted on the g factor. Of course, the subtest contributes to the verbal comprehension factor.

Albert showed more variable response on this test than on any other test. He scored 2 points each on the first 3 items, scored 1 point on the next 3 items, missed an item, received several 2-point scores and a 1-point score, and then received another 2-point score. He answered Items 12 and 14 with 1-point scores and missed 6 consecutive items to end the test.

Albert's responses placed him at the 50th percentile. This score is one of his poorest, even though it puts him in the Average range. An examination of his responses indicates that he gave simplistic impulsive responses, and did not respond very well to the questioning intended to elicit a higher level of response. Thus, once he gave an answer, he stuck with it almost stubbornly, as can be seen from his tendency to repeat his answer when questioned.

Albert's responses had a concrete quality, which suggested that he may not have the language skills concomitant with a superior level of intelligence. The cause of this can be cultural, educational, neuropsychological, emotional, or even hereditary.

Object Assembly

In Object Assembly, each of four jigsaw puzzles forms a familiar object: girl, horse, car, and face. As with the other subtests, the complexity of the items increases. This subtest requires the youngster to operate within certain time limits, and extra points are given for more rapid completion of a correct figure.

The subtest requires visual–motor coordination, sensory–motor feedback, visual perception, perceptual skill, and construction skills. Object Assembly is essentially a test of perceptual organization ability, and youngsters who have neuropsychological deficits may do relatively poorly.

As with other subscales, Object Assembly is fairly loaded with the g factor of intelligence. It also has a high factor loading on perceptual organization. Some children approach this subtest in a trial-and-error manner, whereas others seem to grasp the total picture of what is required at the beginning of the test.

Albert achieved a total score of 22. He was able to put together all four of the puzzles perfectly, although he achieved no time credits for rapid construction. In spite of this, he scored 22 points, which translates to the 91st percentile in comparison with those his age.

Digit Span

Digit Span, a supplementary subtest, is not ordinarily used in total scoring unless interpolation is done. The child is asked to listen to a series of numbers and then repeat them in the exact order given. On a second portion of the test, numbers are given and the child is asked to repeat the numbers backward from the way they were presented by the examiner.

Digit Span is a classic test of short-term memory and attention. It is used in most neuropsychological batteries in one form or another. Rote memory is the primary requirement for this test, but receptive and expressive speech are also involved. The digits backward task involves complex cognitive processing at a higher level than the digits forward task.

Digit Span is relatively low in the g factor, but it is a strong measure of freedom from distractibility.

Albert was able to repeat four digits forward (twice) and to repeat three digits backward (once) and four digits backward (once). His results placed him at the 50th percentile in comparison with those of his age group. This subtest is one of the two in which Albert fell far below his performance on the other subtests. The reasons for this will be explored in further testing.

Thus, the WISC-R revealed that Albert is a bright youngster who should be skillful in arithmetic and in social and playground activity. The results also led to some interesting questions: Why was Albert's performance low in Vocabulary and Digit Span and moderately low in Information?

The percentile is the statistic to be used in presenting the data in the report and to the parents. It is important that subscales be converted to percentiles using Wechsler's tables (1974).

In addition to providing conversions to percentiles, Wechsler's (1974, p. 189) provided conversions from raw score equivalents to test ages. For some parents or teachers, the reporting of a mean test age can be meaningful. In actuality, it is equivalent to a mental age. To find the mean test age, the subtest ages are summed for all 10 subtests and divided by 10. In Albert's case, his two lowest scores (Vocabulary and Digit Span) yielded equivalent test ages of 7 years, 2 months, and 6 years, 10 months, respectively, His highest score (Arithmetic) resulted in a calculated mental age equivalent of 9 years, 6 months.

All in all, Albert appears to be a pretty bright youngster.

Ancillary Intellectual Evaluation

As discussed previously, it is always wise to administer more than one intelligence test. The Peabody Picture Vocabulary Test–Revised (PPVT-R) was chosen to give to Albert. It is an individually administered, norm-referenced, wide-range power test of hearing and vocabulary. The child is given five training items in which he or she is shown a card on which there are four pictures. The examiner says a word, and the child is asked to choose the picture that best represents that word. The range covered by this test in the normative group is from $2\frac{1}{2}$ to 40 years of age.

On the PPVT-R Albert received a raw score of 82, which converted to a standard score of 100. This score places Albert at the 50th percentile in comparison with children of his age. This level of response is exactly that achieved on Albert's Vocabulary subtest on the WISC-R. Clearly, vocabulary skills are the lowest of Alberts' current intellectual responses, which could certainly lead to all kinds of difficulties in school and at home. This issue will be explored in great detail as further testing takes place. At the present time, the intellectual evaluation provides some important information:

1. Albert generally falls in the Superior range of intellectual capacity.
2. A moderate amount of subscale variability is apparent in his results.
3. Albert's poorest intellectual responses include immediate memory, vocabulary skills, and acquisition of general information.
4. When given a nonverbal test that requires that he respond to vocabulary that he hears, Albert falls at an average level, which, based on his own potential, is relatively low.

Although some speculation can be made as to why these factors exist, it will prove helpful to await the full battery in order to put all elements together into a cohesive and most meaningful interpretation.

CHAPTER ELEVEN

Neuropsychological Evaluation

Neuropsychological evaluation of children is one of the newest assessment ventures of clinical psychology. Prior to the past decade, very little neuropsychological testing of children took place, and when it did, generally some form of adult test procedure, such as the Bender Visual–Motor Gestalt, was used. With the rapid growth in the clinical application of neuropsychological research and test instruments that began in the early 1970s, interest in evaluating children who might have neuropsychological deficits also grew. Although this development lagged somewhat behind the development of neuropsychological assessment of adults (Lezak, 1983), the past 10 years have seen significant developments in neuropsychological testing approaches and instruments used with children (Rourke et al., 1986).

The purpose of neuropsychological assessment of children is to produce a reliable and valid description of the relationships between the child's brain and the child's behavior. Complete neuropsychological evaluation of the child begins with the description of the child's neuropsychological status in respect to the functional integrity of the youngster's brain. The goal is to use a series of examinations and interviews to be able to understand and describe the pattern of abilities and deficits exhibited by the child, and to identify those that are due to compromised cerebral functioning. The full neuropsychological evaluation may include a diagnostic formulation, a description of the youngster's deficits and residual abilities, prognosis in some cases, and recommendations for rehabilitation.

The full neuropsychological assessment of the child yields information on sensory–perceptual responses (tactile, auditory and visual–sensory–perceptual processing); motor and psychomotor skills (grip strength, motor speed, psychomotor skills with upper and, in some cases, lower extremities); psycholinguistic abilities (receptive speech, expressive speech, associative language skills); and, depending on the age of the child, concept formation and problem solving abilities. Many of these abilities may be evaluated through elements of the intellectual tests. The Wechsler scales have been the primary instruments of neuropsychological assessment that rely on intellectual evaluation.

Screening Evaluations

The most popular development in the past decade has been so-called "screening" evaluations to be used with children during a general assessment. The primary purpose of screening is to determine whether children are "positive" in respect to some neuropsychological factor, thus leading to a recommendation for more complete neuropsychological assessment. Using a relatively small number of tests and procedures that can be applied cheaply and routinely, the screening process should yield low frequencies of false negatives for children who might be at risk, and a relatively low frequency of false positives. Screening techniques are likely to be used more and more as part of psychological batteries in the future (Satz et. al., 1978; Satz & Fletcher, 1979, 1982; Silver, 1978).

The assessment procedures recommended in the BPE are essentially screening tests.

Difficulties in the Neuropsychological Evaluation of the Child

Neuropsychological evaluation makes fairly careful measurements of various performance capabilities of the individual. One difficulty with using neuropsychological tests on a child is that they measure the performance response of the child at the time the child is tested. During the growing years, the brain is characterized by plasticity, which enables the child to tolerate a larger number of blows to the head, shakings, and high fevers than can the average adult. This plasticity is also associated, however, with developmental changes that occur during the years of growth. Since development does not occur in a smooth, predictable curve, but rather in spurts, the job of assessment is much more difficult. Thus, a 7-year-old may show a number of significant deficits in neuropsychological development at the time of testing, and several weeks later show none of these. Apparently development has occurred, and the testing simply took place at a stage when the youngster was unable to perform at the expected developmental age level.

Despite these difficulties, base rates are beginning to be available for young children. The younger the child, the greater the difficulty in establishing a stable mean performance score by age. Not all tests suffer from this particular difficulty. Certain developmental skills seem to follow a fairly linear increase with age. Table 11.1 shows a linear increase in the means for the Hand Dynamometer task in children aged 6 through 12 (after Spreen & Gaddes, 1969).

TABLE 11.1   Means and Standard Deviations for the Hand Dynamometer Task

Male				Female		
Age	N	Mean	SD	N	Mean	SD
		Right-hand grip strength (in kg)				
6	8	9.0	1.9	8	8.6	1.2
7	36	10.4	2.2	24	10.1	2.3
8	12	13.6	3.0	19	11.2	1.8
9	13	16.4	1.0	14	13.2	2.8
10	8	18.1	1.6	15	17.3	3.3
11	12	21.3	3.1	21	18.4	3.6
12	18	21.9	2.2	15	22.3	4.2
		Left-hand grip strength (in kg)				
6	8	8.9	1.8	8	7.0	1.2
7	36	9.6	2.1	24	9.0	1.7
8	12	13.0	3.0	19	10.2	1.5
9	13	16.3	3.1	14	12.1	3.2
10	8	17.0	1.4	15	15.6	2.8
11	12	20.7	2.5	21	17.8	3.7
12	18	22.6	2.8	15	20.6	4.3

Usefulness of Neuropsychological Assessment

As part of the BPE, neuropsychological assessment has a number of potential uses, including the following:

1. *The Screening Role.* The neuropsychological assessment should help the clinician decide whether a full neuropsychological assessment, or possibly referral to a neurologist, is indicated. If the signs are only vague, referral back to the pediatrician to evaluate the physical situation before making a neurological referral may be indicated. This referral is usually done when subsequent full neuropsychological assessment confirms deficits suggested by the screening tests.

2. *Relating Neuropsychological Status to Performance or Behavior Deficits.* Deficiencies in neuropsychological behavior or comparisons of various neuropsychological performances can help the clinician to understand difficulties the youngster is reportedly experiencing in school or at home. In some cases, anomalies in the intellectual evaluation confirm and/or support deficiency patterns.

3. *Relating Neuropsychological Status to Instructional Style.* In all instructional areas, particularly in the acquisition of verbal skills (vocabulary, comprehension, and speech), deficits in neuropsychological status can be a significant factor in choosing methods of instruction

that differ from the usual and customary method in which children are taught. Deficiencies in left temporal lobe function are sometimes associated, in growing children, with difficulties in reading, writing, and speaking. When the child has unusual patterns of neuropsychological function involving expressive speech, receptive speech, vision, tactile functions, body-in-space, planning and organization, and other areas, the psychologist may make recommendations to the teachers and guidance counselors as to how the school may maximize instructional opportunities for the youngster.

4. *Developmental Lag.* In a fair number of cases, the BPE reveals that the child suffers some form of developmental lag. Sometimes the school sees this as a "specific learning disability" or sometimes views it as a "dyslexia" in the case of reading problems. The neuropsychological examination may indicate that the child is merely behind the norm in certain neuropsychological development. The clinician may advise the school as to how it can enhance the youngster's opportunities, create rehabilitation situations, and in most cases tolerate some delay in expectation until growth and development resolve the difficulty. Understanding this lag is also helpful to parents.

SOME CURRENTLY UTILIZED SCREENING INSTRUMENTS

As stated previously, the primary purpose of a neuropsychological screening instrument is to determine whether further evaluation is necessary. Short screening instruments tap only a limited number of neuropsychological functions or systems. The more systems that are involved, the more complex the instrument. Some screening instruments may focus more on anterior cortical functions, whereas others, particularly those that involve visual activity, may emphasize the posterior cortical functional systems. Thus, false negatives on some screening tests may occur because the neuropsychological deficit is not "tapped" by the particular instrument. Any screening instrument used to identify neuropsychological deficit must be viewed within the limitations of what that screening instrument requires the child to do.

The Wechsler Intelligence Scale for Children–Revised (WISC-R)

The subscales of the WISC-R, particularly in comparison with each other, may serve as a neuropsychological screening instrument. WISC-R subscales that fall below the child's chronological age, and more particularly those that fall below the mean of the child's own performance, may represent specific neuropsychological deficits. The following sections describe some of the more common interpretations of "lowered" WISC-R scores insofar as neuropsychological deficit is concerned.

Information.   On the Information subtest, it is important to differentiate between failure due to ignorance and failure due to the loss of once-stored information. This rule applies more to adults than to children, but should be considered when testing a youngster who may have acquired language and then lost it due to some cerebral damage or disease. Although Information tends to be the least affected of the WISC-R subtests when a youngster suffers some brain deficit, any kind of brain damage tends to depress all of the subscales to some extent.

Information performance is heavily loaded in the kinds of skills that are developed and manifested by integrated activity in the left temporal lobe in most youngsters. Deficits in Information performance may suggest lesions or dysfunctions in the left hemisphere. The clinician's task is to separate significantly lowered Information responses based on cultural or educational deficiencies from those due to neuropsychological deficit.

Comprehension.   The Comprehension subtest measures the youngster's ability to reason in a practical way. Neuropsychological deficits are identified by responses that suggest that the youngster has not been able to learn to reason beyond a concrete level in accordance with what would be expected at his or her age. The subtest provides a chance for the clinician to observe how the youngster deals with common problem solving situations within his or her age expectancy. The clinician must be alert to deficiencies that represent cultural or educational problems rather than neuropsychological deficits.

Arithmetic.   Deficits on the Arithmetic subtest represent problems with immediate memory, concentration, or conceptual manipulation. Poor performance on this subtest can also represent concentration difficulties. If this is the cause of the poor performance, one can also look for poor performance on the Digit Span subtest. Deficits in auditory–verbal input also tend to result in poor performance on the Arithmetic subtest. Again, the clinician must determine whether the child has ever learned the fundamentals of arithmetic and forgotten them because of neuropsychological deficit, or has been unable to record the fundamentals in the first place. Both conditions may be the result of neuropsychological deficit, but the etiology may be unclear. Such deficit may be innate, developmental, or acquired through some damaging or disease process.

Similarities.   Deficits on the Similarities subtest reveal difficulties in concept formation. Children of poor general intelligence do quite poorly on this test. Similarities performance tends to be lowered due to neuropsychological deficits in either the left or the right hemisphere. Children who do poorly on this subtest may lack facility with verbal associations and may have poor elementary verbal concept formation. A relatively depressed Similarities score may be associated with left temporal and frontal involvement. This problem tends to appear as children move toward adolescence, and may not be as significant during earlier years.

Digit Span.   Poor performance on the Digit Span subtest may indicate that the child has poor attention span and/or is very distractible. It is a measure of immediate memory for meaningful and nonmeaningful auditory–verbal material. Serious deficits in the performance of the backward digits portion of this test suggest that the child has difficulty with the memory storage of a few bits of data for a brief period of time. This task involves mental double-tracking because memory and reversing operations must proceed simultaneously, and difficulty suggests that the brain's normal function of temporal ordering is somehow defective. This subtest is very sensitive to any kind of brain dysfunction.

Vocabulary.   The clinician must determine whether a lowered Vocabulary score represents cultural factors, educational insufficiency, previously learned material that has been "forgotten" as a result of brain disorder, or material that has never been learned. Lowered Vocabulary performance is likely to represent factors *other* than recent brain deficit. The child whose Vocabulary performance is significantly below the mean of the other WISC-R tests generally has had social deprivation, educational problems, or a long-existing left hemisphere deficit.

Coding (Digit Symbol).   In Coding, a test of psychomotor performance, intellect plays less a part than visual–motor coordination. The subtest also measures motor persistence, attention, and response speed. This test is considered the most sensitive to neuropsychological deficit, and it tends to be affected by difficulties arising in all parts of the cortex. A significant lowering of performance in this subtest ordinarily is not associated with cultural background or academic opportunity.

Picture Completion.   The Picture Completion subtest is relatively unaffected by recent brain disorder. When neuropsychological deficit is present, this is likely to be the youngster's highest Performance subtest. Picture Completion can often represent the youngster's highest level of intellectual function before neuropsychological deficit occurred. When a youngster does poorly on this test in respect to others, problems in visual acuity and visual scanning should be suspected.

Block Design.   Block Design has been considered the subtest most likely to reflect the presence of brain damage. Poor performance on Block Design represents a slowness in learning new response sets. Poor performance suggests posterior cortical deficiencies, particularly in the parietal areas. Consistent errors at the top or at the bottom of the design may suggest visual field deficits. In general, significantly lowered Block Design performance in a child suggests visual–spatial organization problems, which further suggest clumsiness, difficulty in writing and drawing, and trouble playing games that require relatively good eye–hand coordination and planning.

Picture Arrangement. Poor performance on Picture Arrangement suggests judgment and reasoning difficulties. Lack of age-related performance on this test tends to reflect a lack of social adaptation. Youngsters who do badly on this subtest tend to exhibit socially inappropriate thinking.

Object Assembly. Significantly lowered performance on Object Assembly suggests that the child has impaired ability to manipulate objects requiring visual–spatial skills commensurate with age. A child who does well on the simplest design but is unable to conceptualize the more difficult designs may have a very concrete approach to life, suggesting the presence of neuropsychological deficit. When this happens, a generally lowered intellectual level is common.

For any subtest, a lowering of 3 or more weighted scores below the child's own mean suggests a significant deficit in that particular scale. The more the weighted score falls below 3 scores from the mean, the more significant the lowering.

It must be remembered that children are difficult neuropsychological cases. Whatever the psychologist may find on one testing may simply represent part of the child's developmental cycle. When discrepancies occur, the clinician must decide whether to wait 6 months and retest to see whether development has lessened the deficit, or to continue the assessment and refer the child for complete neuropsychological evaluation. Tracking with two or more assessments is the surest way of differentiating between developmental lag and more permanent forms of neuropsychological deficiency.

Hand Dynamometer

The Hand Dynamometer, which measures grip strength, is a laboratory instrument that has been in use in psychological laboratories for almost 100 years. Grip strength increases with age, and tends to be higher in males than in females. Also, the dominant hand is ordinarily stronger than the nondominant hand.

The Hand Dynamometer measures strength in kilograms. Table 11.1 illustrates the means and standard deviations for the right and left hands of 6- to 12-year-old males and females. If an 8-year-old male pulls 11 kg with the right hand and 11 kg with the left hand, these results would not be considered highly significant because they are less than 1 *SD* below the mean for 8-year-old youngsters. The fact that it was somewhat lower, with no difference between the right and left hands, suggests mild developmental lag and possible mixed cerebral dominance. The Hand Dynamometer task is simple to administer, and children enjoy it. The youngster is given two trials with each hand, and the results are averaged. It is a simple screening test that can easily be included in any test battery.

Memory for Designs

The Memory for Designs Test consists of 15 cards. On each card is a simple or complex figure. The cards are presented to the child, one at a time, for 5 sec. The child is then asked to draw from memory when the card has been removed. Memory for Designs tests visual construction skill and memory. Each figure that is drawn is scored 0, 1, 2, or 3. Graham and Kendall (1960) developed a special scoring system using the Wechsler Full Scale IQ and chronological age to modify the raw score. They call this the *difference score*. Table 11.2 shows the correction for children's scores using chronological age and general intelligence.

To obtain the difference score, the following formula is used:

$$\text{Difference score} = \text{Raw score} - \left(\frac{\text{Intelligence}}{\text{value}} - \frac{\text{Chronological}}{\text{age value}} \right)$$

Thus, if a 9-year-old child has a raw score of 6 on the Memory for Designs test and a Full Scale IQ of 116 on the WISC-R, the formula from the above table would be as follows:

$$\text{Difference score} = 6 - (2.5 - 0) = 4$$

In calculating the formula, IQs that include decimal points are raised to the next highest whole number.

TABLE 11.2 Correction for Children's Raw Scores on the Memory for Designs Test

WISC-R Full-Scale IQ	Corrected Value	Chronological Age	Corrected Value
53–60	6.0	8.6–9.4	0.0
61–69	5.5	9.5–11.0	0.5
70–77	5.0	11.1–12.9	1.0
78–85	4.5	12.10–14.5	1.5
86–93	4.0	14.6–15.11	2.0
94–101	3.5		
102–110	3.0		
111–118	2.5		
119–125	2.0		

TABLE 11.3 Interpretation of Children's Difference
Scores on the Memory for Designs Test

Interpretation	Difference Score
Brain damage	7 and above
Borderline	2–6
Normal	1 and below

Table 11.3 illustrates a suggested interpretation for difference scores. Ninety-eight percent of normal control children attain a score of under 6; 80% obtain a score of 1 or less (Graham & Kendall, 1960; Lyle, 1968; & Walters, 1961).

The Aphasia and Sensory–Perceptual Deficits in Children Test

Developed by Reitan (1984), the Aphasia and Sensory–Perceptual Deficits in Children screening test uses a number of subtests from the Halstad–Reitan test battery to determine whether impairment exists in children from age 5 to age 14. The instrument is divided into two sections, one for older children (9–14) and the other for younger children (5–8). For the younger children, both the Aphasia and the Sensory–Perceptual subtests are given. In addition, Lateral Dominance and Hand Dynamometer examinations are given to all children, as well as the ABC Test for Ocular Dominance.

The younger children are asked to write their name, draw a square, draw a cross, and draw a triangle. They are asked to identify pictures of a baby, a clock, and a fork. They are then asked to read some numbers and letters. They are asked to print a word, count their fingers, and add single digits. A total of 22 items make up this test, plus some sensory–perceptual tests of the child's capacity to identify the location of touches on their hand. Hearing acuity, visual acuity, finger agnosia, and tactile form recognition are also tested.

Each test is weighted from a score of 0 for no errors to a score of 3 for the largest number of errors. A series of tables is available to identify whether a child falls into a "brain disordered" or "normal" category. The manual provides a table that suggests that 92 percent of normal subjects, 84 percent of brain damaged subjects, and 76 percent of learning disabled subjects are correctly identified by the examination.

This test requires a fair degree of skill, and much of the resulting behavior should be interpreted by a neuropsychologist. It is a good test for a clinician who is experienced in neuropsychological testing. This battery also provides the Aphasia Screening Test booklet, which is used in another screening test, the Indiana–Reitan, which is discussed on page 133.

Indiana–Reitan

The Indiana–Reitan is a short neuropsychological screening test that was developed from the research of Filskov (1975). Evaluating each of the subtests of the standard Halstad–Reitan Battery, Filskov found in her research that Cards 1, 2, 3, and 27 of the Aphasia Screening Booklet (cross, square, triangle, and key) could be used alone as a screening instrument. (Figure 11.1

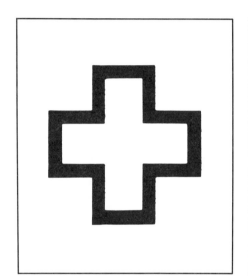

FIGURE 11.1   Indiana-Reitan Short Form Stimulus Cards

| NAME _____ | AGE _____ |

| BIRTHDATE _____ | TEST DATE _____ |

| EDUCATION _____ | PREFERRED HAND _____ |

OCCUPATION _____

CNS INCIDENTS/PATHOLOGY _____

TEST RESULTS

#	Item	Response
1	Draw square	
2	What shape called?	
3	Spell	
4	Draw cross	
5	What called?	
6	Spell	
7	Draw triangle	
8	What called?	
9	Spell	
27	What the ? (Key)	
28	Show use	
29	Draw key	

SCORING　　A. IMPAIRMENT

1 - SQUARE
4 - CROSS
7 - TRIANGLE
29 - KEY

a. Rating of 3 or more on Triangle
b. Bad 3 or more on all
c. Size prob on square & triangle
d. Unjoined lines consist.
e. Crossovers; rotations

B. RIGHT LESIONS
1. Larger size
2. Asymetry of cross
3. Unjoined lines
4. Added or missing crosspoints
5. Crossovers; rotation of figures

C. LEFT LESIONS
1. Smaller size
2. Shakiness
3. Rounded corners
4. Missing parts of key

FIGURE 11.2 Indiana-Reitan Scoring Form

shows the four figures used in this test.) The research indicated that this test was highly reliable and correctly selected 92 percent of impaired subjects, 89 percent with diffuse impairment, and 97 percent of "normal" subjects under the age of 60. Although the original research was done with adults, the instrument has been found to be useful for screening children, particularly those above the age of 7.

Each picture is presented to the child, who is asked to draw it without taking his or her pencil off the paper. The clinician records the child's responses, following the usual standardization instructions, on an answer sheet. Figure 11.2 shows the answer sheet for this test.

Not only does this test demonstrate distortions in eye–hand coordination and visual–spatial perception, but it evaluates the youngster's expressive and receptive speech. Difficulty in naming (*anomia*) is identified by difficulties shown by the child on Items 2, 5, 8, and 27 on the answer sheet. Since the child is asked to name the shape and then to spell it, dysfunction in spelling skill can also be noted. Children who cannot copy the figures with accuracy suffer *construction apraxia*. Spelling difficulties may represent *spelling apraxia*. The child who cannot demonstrate the use of a key may suffer *ideo-kinetic apraxia*.

It can be noted that, on the bottom of Figure 11.2, standards are given for scoring the degree of impairment according to the amount of distortion on the figures. Using this form, the clinician should circle the appropriate degree of distortion found in the child's drawings. The four drawings can be averaged and divided by 4. The higher the average, the higher the degree of impairment.

Below the impairment scoring, Figure 11.2 shows the kinds of distortions that are characteristic of right or left hemisphere deficiencies in the child.

Again, the screening battery can neither pinpoint the location of cortical pathology nor yield a definitive diagnosis. The purpose of any screening measure is to determine whether there is reason to believe that a child has significant neuropsychological deficit and whether to refer the child for complete neuropsychological evaluation or, in some cases, for neuropsychological assessment.

The Luria–Nebraska Neuropsychological Battery: Children's Screening Form

The Luria–Nebraska Neuropsychological Battery: Children's Screening Form was devised by Golden (1987c), who selected 15 items from the Luria–Nebraska Neuropsychological Battery: Form II and the Luria–Nebraska Neuropsychological Battery: Children's Revision (Golden, 1987a). The purpose of the screening test of 15 items is to predict overall performance on the full-length battery. The children's revision is designed for use with youngster's 8–12 years of age, whereas the adult form is designed for individuals 13 years of age and older. The screening form can be completed in less than 20 min, even by youngsters who have fairly severe neuropsychological deficits.

The tasks include number reading, paragraph reading, word reading, writing, number writing, sounding of letters, counting aloud, correctly identifying the direction of arm touches, and other tasks very similar to the Indiana–Reitan described earlier. Items are scored from 0 to 2, with the poorest performance receiving the highest score. Thus, a youngster may receive a score ranging from 0 to 45 on this test. The cutoff point recommended for children under the age of 12 would be 3 or less, which would predict a "normal" profile should the child be given the complete Luria–Nebraska Neuropsychological Battery.

For older children and adults, a cutoff score of 7 (or below) predicts a "normal" profile on the complete Luria–Nebraska Neuropsychological Battery. No effort is made to identify location or degree of impairment, although the implication is that the higher the score, the greater the impairment.

The Torque Test

The Torque Test has been available for a decade, and over 30 individual research studies have been done using the instrument. It is essentially a test of lateral dominance. Developed by Blau (1974, 1977a, 1977b), this test can be given to children or adults. Youngsters 3 years of age and older can do most of the test.

The Torque Test is a simple exercise that requires each child to do three tasks: (a) copy a simple design, (b) write his or her name, and (c) draw a circle around three Xs. Each task is to be performed by the child first with the preferred writing hand and then with the nondominant hand. Figure 11.3 shows the scoring sheet for the Torque Test.

The first two tasks are done simply to have the child become involved and to give the psychologist an opportunity to observe the youngster's ability to follow directions and to write his or her name. Only the circling of the Xs is scored. If all six of the circlings (three each with the dominant and the nondominant hand) are drawn in a counterclockwise direction, the child's performance is scored *no torque*. Any performance in which one or more circlings are observed to be done in a clockwise direction is scored *torque*. There are nine combinations of circling behavior. Table 11.4 presents the various combinations of clockwise and counterclockwise turning that may occur on the Torque Test.

Almost 100 percent of children below the age of 4½ years show some torque. Beginning at about 4½, some youngsters begin to develop solid left hemisphere dominance, and they demonstrate zero torque. Figure 11.4 shows the hypothetical baseline for the occurrence of torque based on a large sample of school children. The curve flattens out at the beginning of adolescence, with somewhere between 20 and 25 percent of children

NAME_____ DATE_____

Rt.   Lt.

Rt.   _____

Lt.   _____

Circle **X**   1. (X)   2. (X)   3. (X)

Rt.   1. **X**   2. **X**   3. **X**

Lt.   1. **X**   2. **X**   3. **X**

Torque_____   by_____

FIGURE 11.3   Torque Test Scoring Sheet

TABLE 11.4   Types of Torque Responses

	Directions of Circling	
Type	Right Hand	Left Hand
0	Counterclockwise	Counterclockwise
I	Clockwise	Counterclockwise
II	Mixed	Counterclockwise
III	Clockwise	Clockwise
IV	Counterclockwise	Clockwise
V	Mixed	Clockwise
VI	Clockwise	Mixed
VII	Counterclockwise	Mixed
VIII	Mixed	Mixed

Note: Mixed = clockwise and counterclockwise.

continuing to show some torque. Most children who do show torque after the age of 15 or 16 show Type IV.

Torque is likely to be found in youngsters who have reading problems, who have behavioral difficulties, and who frequently show attention deficit disorder. The reliability and validity of these findings have been fairly well demonstrated (Alberts & Edwards, 1983; Alberts & Tacco, 1980; Blau, 1977a; Boake, Salmon, & Carbone, 1983; Demarest & Demarest, 1980;

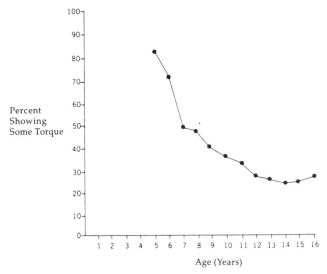

FIGURE 11.4   Base Rate for the Occurrence of Torque in Selected School Children (*N* = 1662) From Blau (1977). Copyright 1977 by the American Psychological Association. Reprinted by permission.

Jarman & Nelson, 1981; Masoth et al., 1987; Matheny, 1979; Woods & Oppenheimer, 1980; Zendel & Pihl, 1980). If torque is present, the psychologist should do a second administration on a different day. If the child continues to show torque, mixed cerebral dominance is indicated, and possibly an explanation for developmental lag. If the child shows no torque on the second administration, the clinician should consider that the child is in a developmental stage of resolving cerebral dominance.

Clinical Observation

Careful observation of the youngster walking, talking, reaching, throwing, interacting socially, working on tasks, opening doors, answering questions, and addressing the various tests that are given provides the observant psychologist with clues as to neuropsychological development. The psychologist should make careful notations of the way in which the child walks, uses expressive language, and responds to the verbal stimulation of others, and should indicate observed discrepancies (or superior performances) in any of the observed areas. Thus, the psychologist must be familiar with the literature in child growth and development and with what is to be expected of youngsters at various ages. Since developmental psychology provides one of the largest data bases in psychology, one that has been collected for over 100 years, most psychologists are well informed about ages and stages.

SUMMARIZING THE CHILD'S NEUROPSYCHOLOGICAL SCREENING

Different children will be given different screening batteries, depending upon the child's age and observed capacity to respond, as well as the psychologist's particular interests and training. Figure 11.5 presents a summary form that can be used to bring together all of the neuropsychological factors in order to form some conclusions and make recommendations in the final report.

ALBERT'S NEUROPSYCHOLOGICAL TESTS

Albert's neuropsychological screening battery consisted of his WISC-R, the Hand Dynamometer, two administrations of the Torque Test, and the Graham–Kendall Memory for Designs. Figures 11.6, 11.7, and 11.8 show the results of the first and second administrations of the Torque Test and the productions that Albert made on the Memory for Designs Test, respectively. Figure 11.9 shows the summary of all of Albert's neuropsychological tests on the single summary sheet.

NAME _____ CASE # _____

BIRTHDATE _____ AGE _____ PARENTS SES _____ GRADE _____

	WISC-R W.S.		MFD	REITAN-INDIANA	TORQUE	HAND DYNAMOMETER
Inf.	_____	R.S.	____		1. ___	R₁ ___ L₁ ___
Comp	_____	D.S.	____		2. ___	2 ___ 2 ___
Voc.	_____					
Arith	_____					
Sim	_____				Write R / L	
Dig Sp	_____				Kick R / L	
P Comp	_____				Catch R / L	
P. Arr	_____					
Bl Des	_____					
Ob Assem	____					
C.O.D	_____					

TORQUE
1. ___
2. ___

HAND DYNAMOMETER
R₁ ___   L₁ ___
2 ___   2 ___

Write R / L
Kick R / L
Catch R / L

LNNB   C.L. _____

Motor	_____	Arith	_____
Rhythm	_____	Mem	_____
Tactile	___	Intel	_____
Visual	___		
R. Sp.	_____	Path	_____
Ex Sp.	_____	LSM	_____
Writ	_____	RSM	_____
Rdg.	_____		

OBSERVATION (0 - No Deficit 1- Mild Deficit 2 - Serious Deficit)

1. Speech   0 1 2 _____
2. Vision   0 1 2 _____
3. Hearing   0 1 2 _____
4. Small Motor   0 1 2 _____
5. Large Motor   0 1 2 _____
6. Body in Space   0 1 2 _____
7. Memory   0 1 2 _____
8. Reasoning   0 1 2 _____

FIGURE 11.5   Child Neuropsychological Summary Sheet

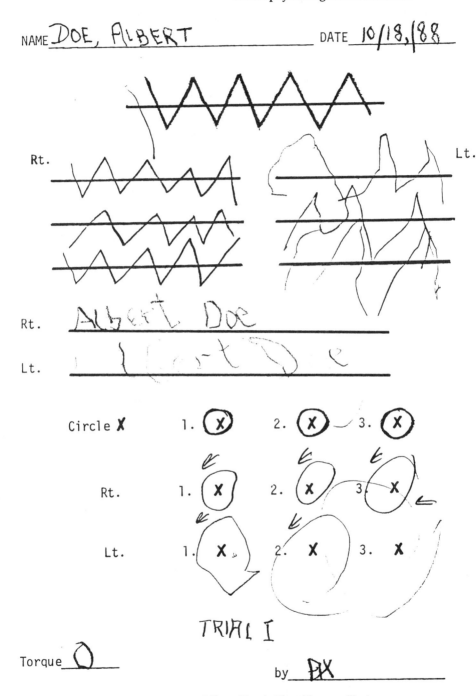

NAME DOE, ALBERT   DATE 10/18,/88

Rt.

Lt.

Rt.

Lt.

Circle X   1.   2.   3.

Rt.   1.   2.   3.

Lt.   1.   2.   3.

TRIAL I

Torque

by

FIGURE 11.6   Albert Doe's First Torque Test

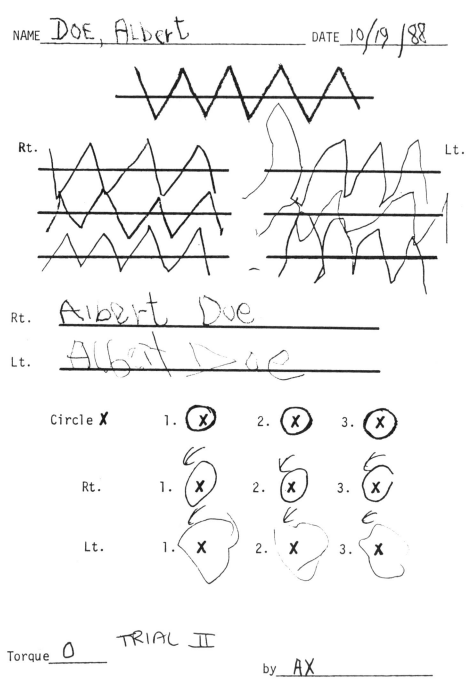

FIGURE 11.7   Albert Doe's Second Torque Test

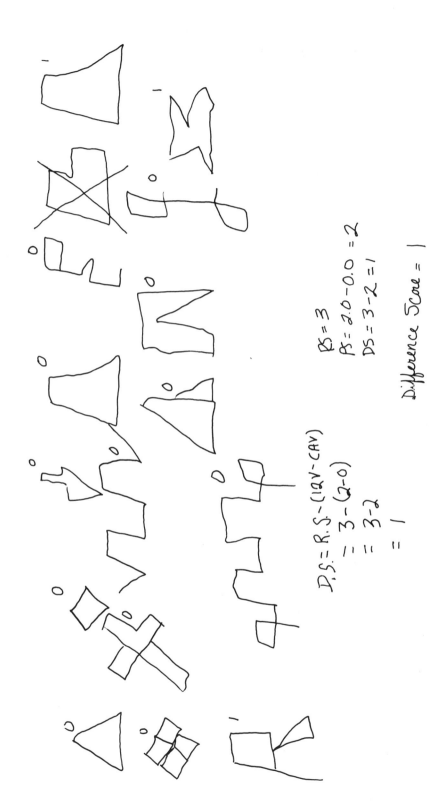

$D.S. = R.S. - (12V - CAV)$
$= 3 - (2 - 0)$
$= 3 - 2$
$= 1$

$RS = 3$
$R = 2.0 - 0.0 = 2$
$DS = 3 - 2 = 1$

Difference Score = 1

FIGURE 11.8   Albert Doe's Memory for Designs Test

143

NAME Doe, Albert   CASE # A

BIRTHDATE 7/22/81   AGE 7-3   PARENTS SES Middle   GRADE 2.2

WISC-R	MFD	REITAN-INDIANA	TORQUE	HAND DYNAMOMETER
Inf. W.S. /;/.	R.S. 3		1. 0	R₁ // L₁ //
Comp 12	D.S. /		2. 0	2 12 2 13
Voc. 10				
Arith 17				
Sim 13			Write Ⓡ L	
Dig Sp 10			Kick Ⓡ L	
P Comp 14			Catch Ⓡ L	
P. Arr 12				
Bl Des 12				
Ob Assem 14			LNNB C.L. _____	
C.O.D 16				

Motor _____   Arith _____
Rhythm _____   Mem _____
Tactile _____   Intel _____
Visual _____
R. Sp. _____   Path _____
Ex Sp. _____   LSM _____
Writ _____   RSM _____
Rdg. _____

OBSERVATION (0 - No Deficit 1- Mild Deficit 2 - Serious Deficit)

1. Speech   0 ① 2   High, crackly
2. Vision   ⓪ 1 2
3. Hearing   ⓪ 1 2
4. Small Motor   ⓪ 1 2
5. Large Motor   0 ① 2   Jumpy and impulsive
6. Body in Space   ⓪ 1 2
7. Memory   ⓪ 1 2
8. Reasoning   ⓪ 1 2

FIGURE 11.9 Albert Doe's Neuropsychological Summary Sheet

The summary sheet shows that Albert was able to pull between 11 and 12 kg with the right hand and between 11 and 13 kg with the left hand when he was examined with the Hand Dynamometer. To evaluate his score, refer to Table 11.1. Albert was approximately 7 years, 3 months, at the time he took the test. His average score of 11.5 kg for performance with the right hand is very close to the mean of 10.4 kg for 7-year-old males noted on Table 11.1. With the left hand, he pulled an average of 12 kg, which is a little more than 1 *SD* higher than the mean for 7-year-old males presented in Table 11.1.

These results would lead the clinical psychologist to wonder whether Albert has some mixed cerebral dominance, either functional or residual.

This issue is clarified by examining Albert's performance on the Torque Test. This test, given twice, a day apart, shows that Albert had Type 0 torque on both occasions. Examination of the productions with the right and the left hand strongly suggests that any mixed cerebral dominance is pretty well resolved, and Albert is right-handed and essentially left hemisphere dominant.

Examining the variation in Albert's performance on the WISC-R, the psychologist found that his lowest scores were in Vocabulary, Digit Span, and to some extent Information. This is an unusual pattern for either developmental lag or neuropsychological deficit. Such a pattern is much more frequently found in youngsters who have some cultural lag, a lack of verbal stimulation in the home, a second language spoken in the home, or attention deficits. These possibilities will be explored further in Albert's case.

Even though the Memory for Designs Test tends to be quite difficult for youngsters under 7, because of Albert's performance on the intelligence tests, the test was administered. His raw score was 3, and his difference score was 1. Clearly, Albert shows no signs of any significant neuropsychological deficit. Insofar as Albert's neuropsychological results are concerned, some effort will be made to explain some of the anomalies noted and to relate them to the history and the environmental press when the data are brought together for the report and recommendations later in the book.

CHAPTER TWELVE

Achievement Testing

THE PURPOSE OF ACHIEVEMENT TESTING IN THE BASIC PSYCHOLOGICAL EXAMINATION

Between the ages of 5 and 18 almost all children spend more time in an educational achievement setting than they spend at any other single activity. Whether this important part of the child's development is enhancing or debilitating is a question of great significance. A careful evaluation of the youngster's academic achievement in fundamental educational areas is vital to the success of the BPE. A number of specific purposes can be served through this achievement evaluation. The most important of these purposes are described in the following sections.

Level of Achievement

If a youngster is midway through the third grade, he or she supposedly has developed skills commensurate with kindergarten plus 2 1/2 years of formal academic instruction. Although the child is placed at the 3.5 grade level, the psychologist must determine whether the child is performing at grade level, or significantly below or above grade level. A standardized achievement test, properly administered, should determine the child's level of fundamental academic skills (reading, arithmetic, and language).

Academic Deficiencies

In addition to giving an objective score that indicates level of achievement, an achievement test that is carefully developed should identify specific deficiencies that the child may suffer. It is insufficient to have a total "reading" score for a child, because reading skills involve vocabulary, comprehension, word attack skills, and, for older children, speed. The achievement test should identify specific deficiencies suffered by the child so that these can be included in the psychologist's final report.

Instructional Level

The level at which a child is able to achieve on a standardized test is not the level at which the child should receive instruction. The test level is generally assumed to be the maximum performance that the child can render under ideal conditions. Although this particular level might be practical for such special educational ventures as programmed or computer-assisted instruction, for traditional classroom settings, the instructional level is approximately 6 months below the test level. This is a matter that can be conveyed to the school, giving both the teacher and the child some distinct advantages in future instruction.

Sources of Unusual Behavior

Youngsters who have social difficulties with classmates and teachers often are significantly below their classmates in academic achievement. The achievement level can give clues to the psychologist as to sources of conditions relating to a child's unacceptable behavior. Recently, poor school performance has been found to be associated with a variety of functional disturbances, including childhood depression (Rourke, 1988).

Remedial Recommendations

The achievement test results can serve as important sources for recommendations that the psychologist makes at the conclusion of his or her report. This reporting will be demonstrated in the discussion of Albert's case.

ACHIEVEMENT TESTS

Individually Administered Achievement Tests

A number of achievement tests are administered individually. In contrast to the individually administered intelligence test, which tends to be longer and more detailed than the group test, individually administered achievement tests tend to cover less material than the so-called group-administered tests. This difference has to do with the original purpose of such tests. Group-administered achievement tests were originally developed for use by the schools to determine how children were progressing and to help modify the curriculum content. As a result, these tests usually have many items and many subsections. Most individually administered achievement tests, on the other hand, were developed as screening instruments. As a result, they generally focus on a limited number of items and a limited number of areas. The following sections describe a number of the more popular individually administered achievement tests.

Wide Range Achievement Test–Revised. The Wide Range Achievement Test–Revised (WRAT-R; Jastak & Jastak, 1984) tests reading, spelling, and arithmetic skills. It was designed for use in clinical and school settings as a screening measure of academic achievement. The Reading subtest, which is actually word identification, asks the subject to pronounce each word aloud. The list includes very simple and very difficult words. A pre-reading section is provided for those who are at a very low level of reading skills. In this section, the task is to name and recognize letters. Standard scores and grade equivalents are provided in the normative tables. The test is easily administered and quickly scored. WRAT-R should be used *only* as a screening instrument to determine global achievement.

Peabody Individual Achievement Test–Revised. The Peabody Individual Achievement Test–Revised (PIAT-R; Markwardt, 1989) includes General Information, Reading Recognition, Reading Comprehension, Mathematics, Spelling, Total Reading, and Total Text subtests. An additional test measures Written Expression. Revised from the 1970 version, the 1989 revision includes more items and more contemporary item content. The achievement levels covered are from kindergarten through Grade 12. The purpose of the test is to provide a survey of a youngster's scholastic attainment. The PIAT-R was designed so that the examiner could focus his or her undivided attention on an individual subject and observe a child's levels of existing knowledge, educational strengths and weaknesses, and behavior in a testing situation. The test authors admit that, because a wide range of material is covered, the number of test items is limited so that the test is brief and simple to administer. They state that the PIAT-R is *not* designed for use as a diagnostic test in any of the content areas. Herein lies its inappropriateness for use in the BPE.

Kaufman Test of Educational Achievement. The Kaufman Test of Educational Achievement (K-TEA; Kaufman & Kaufman, 1985) was designed to measure school achievement of children in Grades 1 through 12. Two forms are available, Comprehensive and Brief. The Brief Form samples reading, mathematics, and spelling, whereas the Comprehensive Form measures reading, decoding and comprehension, mathematical applications and computation, and spelling. Norm-referenced measures are included with both forms. Criterion-referenced assessment data to analyze student errors are available for the Comprehensive Form. The authors recommend the Brief Form for testing and the Comprehensive Form for data concerning the student's strengths and weaknesses (which, this book suggests, is necessary for all children being examined). The K-TEA is a useful, carefully developed instrument. Analysis of the results and the consequent interpretation are, however, somewhat convoluted and difficult.

There are many other individually administered tests of academic achievement. Those listed here are considered to be the best available at the present time, but undoubtedly, new instruments will be developed as time goes on. The clinician must select those that are most applicable, when such individual achievement tests are appropriate. Generally, individually administered achievement tests are not recommended for use in the BPE.

Group-Administered Achievement Tests

Although originally developed to be used in the school systems and administered in groups, these are the best instruments to use as part of the BPE. Academic performance is a vital part of the child's development. The questions regarding how well the child is doing, what deficits exist, and what the relationships are between the child's academic acquisition and current level of adjustment are critical.

The group-administered achievement tests were originally developed to help educators understand the effectiveness of their teaching and make changes in the basic curriculum. Because so much time, effort, and expertise were involved in developing these tests, the format and content of such instruments tend to be carefully and thoroughly standardized.

The clinician has a wide choice of group achievement tests for evaluating the child's achievement. Several of these tests are described below.

Stanford Achievement Test, Seventh Edition.   The Stanford Achievement Test (SAT) is one of the oldest and most respected norm-referenced, objectively scored measures of school achievement; it covers mid-Grade 1 through the end of Grade 9. There are 10 levels or separate tests, each overlapping to some extent the grades of adjacent levels. The Stanford Early School Achievement Test covers kindergarten through the end of Grade 1. The Stanford Test of Academic Skills covers Grades 8–13 (first year of college).

The focus of the seventh edition of the SAT (Gardner, Rudman, Karlsen, & Merwin, 1982) is on basic skill areas: reading, listening, language, and mathematics. The Primary I and II Reading subtests are Word Study Skills, Word Reading, and Reading Comprehension. Listening subtests include Vocabulary and Listening Comprehension. Different levels measure different specific areas. For instance, the advanced forms include Mathematical Application, Social Science, and Science. Standardization was extremely well done. An optional writing test is available which assesses describing, narrating, explaining, and reasoning. About a quarter of a million students from 300 school districts were used for the standardization. There are norms for the beginning of the year and the end of the year. Scaled scores, percentile ranks, and grade equivalent scores are the most useful normative data available for the purposes of the BPE. The SAT is an excellent example of an extremely useful achievement test (Gardner et al., 1982).

California Achievement Test.   The California Achievement Test (CTB/McGraw-Hill, 1977) and its various forms are a series of norm-referenced achievement tests covering Grades K–12. There are 10 overlapping levels covering prereading, reading, spelling, language, mathematics, and reference skills. The higher the academic level measured, the more complex the test items and the more extensive the battery.

The use of this particular test, like other criterion- and norm-referenced tests of school achievement, allows for very careful diagnostic evaluation of the child's achievement, areas of difficulty, and superior academic acquisition. This is an excellent instrument to assess achievement in reading, language, and mathematics throughout the entire public school grade range.

Metropolitan Achievement Test, Fifth Edition. The Metropolitan Achievement Test (MAT; Balow, Farr, Hogan, & Prescott, 1978) is very similar to the previously described group-administered tests of academic achievement. It is designed to assess school curriculum accomplishment for children in Grades K–12. The content of the test was formulated on the basis of instructional objectives that had gone through a validation process with a sample of over 3,000 teachers.

The MAT provides an in-depth evaluation of the child's achievement of educational material and objectives. It also provides an analysis of strengths and weaknesses in the major areas. The focus is on reading, mathematics, and language at seven instructional levels (Primer: K.5–1.4; Primary I: Grades 1.5–2.4; Primary II: Grades 2.5–3.4; Elementary: Grades 3.5–4.9; Intermediate: Grades 5.0–6.9; Advanced I: Grades 7.0–9.9; and Advanced II: Grades 10.0–12.9). Administration time ranges from 98 min (Primer) to 120 min (Elementary and Intermediate); no test in the MAT takes more than 2 hr.

These tests provide a detailed, highly specific evaluation that can be used in planning instructional programs for individual students. The results also give a picture of the student's performance capabilities in major areas of the curriculum. The instructional levels provided by this test correspond very closely to the levels in the Basic Reader Series, giving an additional advantage to this particular test.

The format of the MAT is particularly attractive, and children like to take this test. At this moment in test development, it is the instrument of choice in most cases for the achievement portion of the BPE.

Although specific tests may be chosen as part of the BPE, this does not mean that they are the "best" and certainly not the "only" tests that can be used. Achievement test development in particular has produced a wide range of instruments to serve general as well as specific purposes.

Additional Achievement Testing

Although in most cases a very thorough achievement battery is likely to answer any questions about the relationship of school achievement to the child being examined, occasionally further testing is required, such as when there is a discrepancy between the child's performance on the achievement test and the reported performance in school, or when there is extreme variability in the youngster's performance. In those cases, the psychologist may wish to focus specifically on reading, arithmetic, language, or other achievement areas. The variety and applications of achievement tests for children number in the hundreds. The range of these tests, their designs, and a critique of their value can be found in *Test Critiques* (Keyser & Sweetland, 1987).

In the past, full achievement testing was not a universal part of psychological evaluations of children. One reason is that about 2 hrs are required for a complete test, plus another 1–1 1/2 hr for scoring. Since psychologists have traditionally done all of their own work, the popularity of limited screening tests of achievement has been maintained. This is unfortunate for the child, the child's family, and the school. As illustrated in Albert's case study, a complete, thorough evaluation of the youngster's achievement adds considerably to an understanding of why the youngster is having difficulty and, more particularly, what can be done about it.

ALBERT'S ACHIEVEMENT TESTING

Albert was said to have problems academically. The first choice for achievement testing of this youngster was the MAT Primer, Form JS. This test is appropriate for a youngster just starting the second grade who is said to have academic difficulties. Figure 12.1 summarizes Albert's performance on the MAT Primer form.

Examination of Figure 12.1 shows that the psychologist erred in choosing the Primer form. Albert performed so well that he only missed 2 of 37 items on Reading, 3 of 35 on Math, and 2 of 25 on Language. Only the vaguest hint of difficulty is noted in that he got no score on the Literal Global and missed 2 possible items on Listening Comprehension. Because of the psychologist's error, it was necessary to test Albert on the next highest form, the MAT Primary I. Figure 12.2 shows the results of this second achievement testing, which indicated that Albert is within expectancy for his grade level in Mathematics and Language. He has some moderate deficiency in Reading. Examination of the cluster analysis showed that Albert is deficient in Vocabulary, Literal–Specific Reading, Inferential–Specific Reading, and Inferential–Global Reading. Other deficiencies noted are appropriate for a youngster just starting the second grade.

These results are very instructive. We know from previous testing that Albert is a youngster of potentially superior intellectual capacity. His score on the Vocabulary subtest of WISC-R was significantly lower than his other subtest scores, indicating that Albert has had some difficulty in acquiring vocabulary. A lack of vocabulary skills also seems to be the most significant deficit in the MAT Reading subtest. This information will be useful in

| Metropolitan Achievement Tests | | | Primer Form JS | |
Test	Number Possible	Number Right	Grade Equivalent	Percentile Rank	(Spring-Grade 1)
Reading	37	35	2.3	80th	
Mathematics	35	32	2.4	74th	
Language	25	23	2.0	66th	
Basic Battery	97	90	1.8	60th	

Cluster Analysis
(Performance by Objective)

READING

Test	# Right
Word Reading	11/12
Rebus	5/5
Sentence Reading	5/5
Literal Specific	10/10
Literal Global	0/1
Inferential Specific	1/1
Inferential Global	1/1
Evaluative	1/1

MATHEMATICS

Test	# Right
Numeration	13/14
Geom. & Meas.	9/9
Problem Solving	4/6
Operations: Whole No.	6/6

LANGUAGE

Test	# Right
Listening Comp.	7/9
Spelling	8/8
Study Skills	8/9

FIGURE 12.1   Albert Doe's MAT-Primer Test Results

making recommendations when Albert's report is written. Important points include the following:

1. Albert has vocabulary skills that are below his grade placement and below his intellectual capacity in general.
2. In his early reading training, Albert is beginning to show difficulty in literal–specific, inferential–specific, and inferential–global reading.

Unless these issues are addressed with remedial work, it is likely that the problems will escalate. Albert's reading level will remain behind his grade placement, and continue to be the source of difficulties in future grades. Recommendations to reverse this situation will be made when the report is written.

Metropolitan Achievement Tests   Primary 1 Form JS

Test	Number Possible	Number Right	Grade Equivalent	Percentile Rank	(Fall-Grade 2)
Reading	55	31	1.9	38th	
Mathematics	40	28	2.3	52nd	
Language	40	30	1.9	46th	
Basic Battery	135	89	1.9	40th	

Cluster Analysis
(Performance by Objective)

READING

Test	# Right
Rebus	5/5
Sentence Reading	5/5
Vocabulary	0/1
Literal Specific	13/24
Literal Global	3/4
Inferential Specific	4/10
Inferential Global	1/4
Evaluative	0/2

LANGUAGE

Test	# Right
Listening Comp.	6/6
Punc. & Cap.	4/6
Usage	3/5
Grammar & Syntax	7/7
Spelling	7/9
Study Skills	3/4

MATHEMATICS

Test	# Right
Numeration	9/10
Geom. & Meas.	5/9
Problem Solving	8/9
Operations: Whole No.	6/12

FIGURE 12.2   Albert Doe's MAT-Primary I Test Results

CHAPTER THIRTEEN

Personality Assessment

Of the kinds of assessment that we do with children, the personality assessment is the most frequently neglected, even perhaps avoided. In the most respected texts on the assessment of children, the evaluation of personality is all but omitted (Sattler, 1988). In those texts that do present methods of evaluating personality, the focus is almost entirely upon severe disturbances (Sattler, 1982; Simeonsson, 1986). This unfortunate state of affairs seems to have emerged from following the medical or pathological model in clinical psychology. Personality testing has focused on the pathological, the abnormal, and the unacceptable. In the development of psychological instruments measuring intelligence, development, and academic skills, however, traditional behavioral science methods have been followed, and base rates are relatively well known.

Psychologists who have studied personality development in children have tended to follow psychiatric nomenclature and very traditional definitions and descriptions of abnormal behavior. Almost 40 years ago these kinds of classifications and symptom descriptions were demonstrated to be relatively useless in understanding children at various stages of development. It has been almost half a century since base rate studies have shown that the so-called *neuropathic traits* of children are in reality behaviors that occur among children who are quite normal (MacFarlane et al., 1954). In their longitudinal study, MacFarlane et al. demonstrated very clearly that bedwetting, irritability, sibling rivalry, sleep disturbances, rebellion, and a host of other behaviors occur in relation to age, sibling position, and sex in the normal development of children.

These early studies were replicated 30 years later (Byar, 1983). Thus, one should be extremely wary of any sort of neuropathic diagnostic label that is placed upon a child. In viewing any kind of personality response or behavior anomaly presented by a child, the significant questions that should be asked are:

1. What is the child's age?
2. What is the child's sex?

3. What is the child's sibling position?
4. How long has the symptom occurred and with what frequency?

Table 13.1 presents the data from the studies of MacFarlane et al. (1954). Symptoms that at one time or another have been considered "pathological," and their occurrence by age and sex, are presented. The table demonstrates that whether a symptom occurs might be a function of age or sex. Table 13.2 presents problem incidents among first-born and non–first-born children by age and by sex.

The information in these two tables is extremely valuable for the clinician in assessing the importance of behavior described by the parents, school personnel, or other significant adults in the child's life. Being unaware of these base rates, the individual who reports the "problem" may be seeing a behavior that tends to disappear with time. Instead of helping, focusing attention on the behavior may enhance the behavior's continuance.

"Behavior Problems of Normal Children Form," Figure 6.6 on page 58, was developed to enable the clinician to graphically depict the kinds of problems described by the adults in the child's environment. These data should be compared with those in Tables 13.1 and 13.2 to determine whether indeed these behaviors represent significant behavioral anomalies. A good example of the importance of base rates can be seen in the case of Albert. In Figure 8.5, the psychologist recorded that Albert's parents reported temper tantrums for most of Albert's life. According to Table 13.1, however, half or more of normal boys exhibit this behavior during the first 9 years of development.

PURPOSES OF PERSONALITY ASSESSMENT

For the purposes of the BPE, the personality assessment of the child should consist of various psychological tests that enable the clinician to learn about the child's past and the factors that influence the way the child sees the world, makes choices, and takes action. This portion of the personality assessment should provide a picture for everybody who may be involved in working with the child, helping the child, or providing opportunity for the child. These people will benefit by knowing how the youngster reacts to a variety of situations; understanding the degree to which the affective factors influence the youngster's capacity to deal with stress, resolve fears, and identify opportunities; learning ways to utilize emotional and intellectual energies to make choices that are in the best interests of the child; and discovering ways to influence future opportunities as the child becomes old enough to attain various levels of independence. In essence, the goal is to understand how this child sees the world and how the child reacts to the world.

TABLE 13.1 Percentage of Problem Incidence of Boys and Girls at Successive Ages

									Age in years							Average (in percent)
		1¾	3	3½	4	5	6	7	8	9	10	11	12	13	14	
Sex	Sex							Number								
Boys		56	49	41	45	39	34	35	32	35	27	27	23	24	18	
Girls		60	49	47	49	52	49	48	43	43	34	38	42	34	23	
Problem	Sex							Percentage of problem incidence								
Sleep																
Disturbing dreams	B	16	29	22	24	20	24	26	22	29	33	26	9*	4	6	20.7
	G	13	29	28	22	29	35	23	23	28	47	42	26	15	4	26.0
Restlessness in sleep	B	38	18	5	2	8	12	11	9	14	22	22	13	0	11	13.2
	G	27	22	4	2	10	2	10	12	5	15	16	17	9	0	10.8
Elimination																
Diurnal enuresis	B	62*	6	2	0	3	0	0	0	0	0	0	0	0	0	5.2
	G	43	2	4	2	0	2	2	0	0	0	0	0	0	0	3.9
Nocturnal enuresis	B	75	18	17	13	8	9	17	12	11	11	15	9	8	11	16.7
	G	73	31	30	20	10	10	8	14	9	6	10	7	0	0	16.3
Soiling	B	32	4	0	0	3	0	0	0	0	0	0	0	0	0	2.8
	G	20	0	4	2	0	0	0	0	0	0	0	0	0	0	1.9
Eating																
Insufficient appetite	B	7	2	17	31	23	29	23	16	6	7	7	9	8	0	13.2
	G	10	6	17	29	31	37	19	21	9	9	13	14	0	0	15.4
Food finickiness	B	30	37	32	31	28	29*	17	12	6	4	11	17	4	6	18.9
	G	37	43	36	31	31	51	15	16	14	9	10	24	3	4	23.1
Sex																
Excessive modesty	B	0	8*	7*	16	20	12	6	22*	17	15	30	17	8	22	14.3
	G	5	22	26	24	25	16	12	5	16	26	13	21	18	17	17.6
Exhibitionism	B	0	0	0	0	0	0	0	0	0	0	0	0	0	0	—
	G	0	0	0	0	0	0	0	0	0	0	0	0	0	0	—
Masturbation	B	9	8	7	16	8	6	3	6	3	4	4	4	4	0	—
	G	8	4	6	8	6	2	4	2	0	0	0	0	0	0	—
Unusual sex interest	B	—	—	—	—	—	—	0	0	0	0	4	0	0	0	—
	G	—	—	—	—	—	—	0	0	0	0	0	0	3	0	—

Motor Habits

Tics and mannerisms	B	0	0	5	4	5	3	11	3	3	0	4	0	0	0	2.7
	G	3	4	4	2	6	10	4	5	5	0	0	0	0	0	3.1
Nail biting	B	5	8	7	9	8	12	23	16	20	18	30	22	33	33	17.4
	G	3	10	17	14	17	20	27	23	35	32	40	31	26	22	22.6
Thumb sucking	B	21	18	12	7**	5*	6	3	3	0	0	4	0	0	0	5.6
	G	33	35	28	27	19	16	12	12	5	6	3	2	0	0	14.1
Excessive activity	B	29	37	37	44	46	32	40	38*	34	26	30	26**	17*	11	31.9
	G	17	33	34	35	35	29	23	16	19	15	16	2	0	0	19.6
Speech problems	B	30	24	17	16	18	12	6	6	6	11	7	9	8	0	12.1
	G	17	18	17	10	8	8	6	12	9	3	5	5	0	4	8.7

Social standards

Lying	B	0	14	37	33	49	53	26	41*	31	15	11*	9*	8	6	23.8
	G	0	12	36	49	42	49	12	19	21	12	0	0	0	0	18.0
Truancy from home	B	0	2	7	9	10	6	0	0	0	0	0	0	0	0	2.4
	G	0	0	8	6	2	4	0	0	0	0	0	0	0	0	1.4
Stealing	B	7	12	10	11	10	6	9*	9	6	4	0	0	0	0	6.0
	G	3	18	2	6	4	0	0	5	0	0	0	0	0	0	2.7
Destructiveness	B	14	20	10	20	28	24	17	22	11	11	7	4	0	0	13.4
	G	2	20	13	12	10	8	6	5	5	6	0	2	0	0	6.4
Selfishness in sharing	B	—	—	—	—	—	—	6	22	17	18	18	9	12*	0	12.8
	G	—	—	—	—	—	—	12	12	5	9	5	7	0	4	6.8
Quarrelsomeness	B	—	—	—	—	—	—	9	6	9	7	7	4	4	0	5.8
	G	—	—	—	—	—	—	2	5	2	12	5	7	3	0	4.5

Personality characteristics

Excessive emotional dependence	B	21*	14	24	27	13	18	3**	3	11	15	11	13	4	11	13.4
	G	8	14	13	14	21	20	27	7	16	21	24	17	9	9	15.7
Excessive demanding of attention	B	20	20	24	27	10	9	11	22	23*	26	18**	13	8	0	16.5
	G	27	26	15	18	15	18	19	14	7	12	0	5	3	0	12.8
Oversensitiveness	B	9	29	34	42	46	32*	37	50	51	59	59	39	21	17	37.5
	G	18	31	47	51	52	53	50	49	46	38	45	48	41	52	44.4
Physical timidity	B	23	31	24	16	15*	18	26	16	23	30	26	4*	0	0	18.0
	G	25	24	38	24	35	31	23	30	30	24	21	21	12	13	25.1

157

TABLE 13.1 (continued)

Problem	Sex	Age in years														Average (in percent)
		1¾	3	3½	4	5	6	7	8	9	10	11	12	13	14	
		Number														
Boys	B	56	49	41	45	39	34	35	32	35	27	27	23	24	18	
Girls	G	60	49	47	49	52	49	48	43	43	34	38	42	34	23	
		Percentage of problem incidence														
Shyness	B	—	—	—	—	—	—	9*	16	3**	18	15*	22	8	0	11.4
	G	—	—	—	—	—	—	25	21	21	24	37	21	18	26	24.1
Specific fears	B	30	43*	56	47	46	38	37	34	40	22	52	17	4*	6	33.7
	G	33	67	60	45	36	41	33	35	21	26	40	21	21	17	25.4
Mood swings	B	9	18	24	24	8	6*	—	—	—	37	41	22	33	22	22.2
	G	8	12	22	16	12	22	—	—	—	32	40	24	26	30	22.2
Somberness	B	0	0	5	16	36	26	11	16	9*	18	30	26	12	6	15.1
	G	0	0	8	14	26	33	8	19	26	21	26	29	15	22	17.6
Negativism	B	18	29	42	20	33	26	11	19	11	22	22	9	17	11	20.7
	G	18	26	23	37	19	29	10	9	5	9	10	10	12	9	16.1
Irritability	B	16*	10	24	18	10	9	6	9	14	15	18	13	12	11	13.2
	G	3	8	17	24	4	16	4	7	5	12	13	10	9	4	9.7
Temper tantrums	B	59	69	66	53	59*	59	57	53*	51	44	44	39	33	22	50.6
	G	43	63	51	47	38	51	56	28	30	32	34	29	15	9	37.6
Jealousy	B	30	29	27	29	36	24	29	44	34	41	48*	44	33	22	33.6
	G	20	29	40	22	38	26	33	28	28	35	24	31	29	22	28.9
Excessive competitiveness	B	—	—	—	—	—	—	11	19	9	11	11*	4	0	0	8.1
	G	—	—	—	—	—	—	19	12	5	3	0	2	0	0	5.1
Excessive reserve	B	—	—	—	—	41	41	20*	19*	26	22**	52	39	25	17	30.2
	G	—	—	—	—	38	47	40	42	37	59	47	38	24	35	40.7
Unself-reliance	B	—	—	—	—	—	—	23	25	26	22	4	17	12	11	17.5
	G	—	—	—	—	—	—	29	21	14	6	5	7	3	4	11.1

*Sex differences significant at the 5% level.
**Sex differences significant at the 1% level.
Source: MacFarlane, J. W., Allen, L., & Houzik, M. P. (1954). A developmental study of the behavior problems of normal children between twenty-one months and fourteen years. Berkeley/Los Angeles: University of California Press.

158

TABLE 13.2 Problem Incidence Among First-Born and Non–First-Born Children

						Age in years							
Sib order	1¾	3	4	5	6	7	8	9	10	11	12	13	Average (in percent)
						Number							
First-born boys	24	19	18	13	14	14	14	15	15	12	8	10	
Non-first-born boys	32	30	27	26	20	21	18	20	12	15	15	14	
First-born girls	28	24	27	27	26	24	24	25	18	20	21	17	
Non-first-born girls	32	25	22	25	23	24	19	18	16	18	21	17	
Problem, sib order, and sex					Percentage of problem incidence								
Sleep													
Disturbing dreams													
First-born boys	8	42	39	23	36	36	29	47*	47	25	25*	10	30.6
Non–first-born boys	22	20	15	19	15	19	17	15	17	27	0	0	15.5
First-born girls	18	33	30	33	38	12	21	24	50	40	24	18	28.4
Non–first-born girls	9	24	14	24	30	33	26	33	44	44	29	12	26.8
Restlessness in sleep													
First-born boys	29	11	6	8	14	7	21*	13	27	25	38**	0	16.6
Non–first-born boys	44	23	0	8	10	14	0	15	17	20	0	0	12.6
First-born girls	32	29	4	11	4	8	21*	8	28*	20	33**	6	17.0
Non–first-born girls	22	16	0	8	0	12	0	0	0	11	0	12	6.8
Elimination													
Diurnal enuresis													
First-born boys	50	5	0	0	0	0	0	0	0	0	0	0	4.6
Non–first-born boys	72	7	0	4	0	0	0	0	0	0	0	0	6.9
First-born girls	43	4	4	0	4	4	0	0	0	0	0	0	4.9
Non–first-born girls	44	0	0	0	0	0	0	0	0	0	0	0	3.7
Nocturnal enuresis													
First-born boys	71	11	11	8	7	21	21	7	7	17	0	0	15.1
Non–first-born boys	78	23	15	8	10	14	6	15	17	13	13	14	18.8
First-born girls	71	38	26	7	12	8	8	8	11	15	10	0	17.8
Non–first-born girls	75	24	14	12	9	8	21	11	0	6	5	0	15.4

TABLE 13.2 (*continued*)

	Age in years												Average (in percent)
Sib order	Number												
	1¾	3	4	5	6	7	8	9	10	11	12	13	
First-born boys	24	19	18	13	14	14	14	15	15	12	8	10	
Non–first-born boys	32	30	27	26	20	21	18	20	12	15	15	14	
First-born girls	28	24	27	27	26	24	24	25	18	20	21	17	
Non–first-born girls	32	25	22	25	23	24	19	18	16	18	21	17	
Problem, sib order, and sex	Percentage of problem incidence												
Eating													
Insufficient appetite													
First-born boys	4	0	22	23	36	7	7	0	0	8	0	10	9.8
Non–first-born boys	9	3	37	23	25	33	22	10	17	7	13	7	17.2
First-born girls	7	4	33	26	42	21	21	8	11	20	14	0	7.2
Non–first-born girls	12	8	23	36	30	17	21	11	6	6	14	0	15.3
Food finickiness													
First-born boys	21	26	33	15	14	0*	0	0	0	8	12	0	10.8
Non–first-born boys	38	43	30	35	40	29	22	10	8	13	20	7	24.6
First-born girls	43	46	26	26	42	12	17	20	17	10	29	6	24.5
Non–first-born girls	31	40	36	36	61	17	16	6	0	11	19	0	22.8
Sex													
Excessive modesty													
First-born boys	0	11	6	8	14	14	21	20	13	25	12	0	12.0
Non–first-born boys	0	7	22	27	10	0	22	15	17	33	20	14	15.6
First-born girls	4	17	30	26	19	12	8	12	22	15	24	18	17.2
Non–first-born girls	6	28	18	24	13	12	0	22	31	11	19	18	16.8
Exhibitionism													
First-born boys	0	0	0	0	0	0	0	0	0	0	0	0	—
Non–first-born boys	0	0	0	0	0	0	0	0	0	0	0	0	—
First-born girls	0	0	7	0	0	0	0	0	0	0	0	0	—
Non–first-born girls	0	0	0	0	0	0	0	0	0	0	0	0	—

													%
Masturbation													
First-born boys	8	16	22	8	7	7	7	0	0	0	0	0	—
Non–first-born boys	9	3	11	8	5	0	6	5	8	7	7	7	—
First-born girls	11	8	11	4	4	4	4	0	0	0	0	0	—
Non–first-born girls	6	0	5	8	0	4	0	0	0	0	0	0	—
Unusual sex interest													
First-born boys	—	—	—	—	—	0	0	0	0	0	0	0	—
Non–first-born boys	—	—	—	—	—	0	0	0	0	7	0	0	—
First-born girls	—	—	—	—	—	0	0	0	0	0	0	6	—
Non–first-born girls	—	—	—	—	—	0	0	0	0	0	0	0	—
Motor habits													
Tics and mannerisms													
First-born boys	0	0	6	0	0	14	7	0	0	0	0	0	2.2
Non–first-born boys	0	0	4	8	5	10	0	5	0	7	0	0	3.2
First-born girls	0	4	4	7	19*	8	8	4	0	0	0	0	4.5
Non–first-born girls	6	4	0	4	0	0	0	6	0	0	0	0	1.7
Nail biting													
First-born boys	4	5	11	8	21	29	7	13	13	33	12	30	15.5
Non–first-born boys	6	10	7	8	5	19	22	25	25	27	27	36	18.1
First-born girls	7	8	22	26	27	33	33	48	39	40	43	29	29.6
Non–first-born girls	0	12	5	8	13	21	11	17	25	39	19	24	16.2
Thumb sucking													
First-born boys	21	11	6	8	0	0	0	0	0	8	0	0	4.5
Non–first-born boys	22	23	7	4	10	5	6	0	0	0	0	0	6.4
First-born girls	32	25	22	19	12	4	4	4	0	0	0	0	10.2
Non–first-born girls	38	44	32	20	22	21	21	6	12	6	5	0	18.9
Overactivity													
First-born boys	33	37	50	31	29	36	21	33	20	8*	25	10	27.8
Non–first-born boys	25	37	41	54	35	43	50	35	33	47	27	21	37.3
First-born girls	14	38	37	52**	46**	25	21	16	17	15	5	0	23.8
Non–first-born girls	19	28	36	16	9	21	11	22	12	17	0	0	15.9
Speech problems													
First-born boys	17	11	6	8	0	7	0	0	0*	0	0	0	4.1
Non–first-born boys	41	33	22	23	20	5	11	15	25	13	13	14	19.6

TABLE 13.2 (continued)

Sib order	Age in years													Average (in percent)
	1¾	3	4	5	6	7	8	9	10	11	12	13	
	Number													
First-born boys	24	19	18	13	14	14	14	15	15	12	8	10	
Non-first-born boys	32	30	27	26	20	21	18	20	12	15	15	14	
First-born girls	28	24	27	27	26	24	24	25	18	20	21	17	
Non-first-born girls	32	25	22	25	23	24	19	18	16	18	21	17	

Problem, sib order, and sex	1¾	3	4	5	6	7	8	9	10	11	12	13	Average (in percent)
	Percentage of problem incidence												
First-born girls	14	21	15	7	15	12	17	12	6	10	10	0	11.6
Non-first-born girls	19	16	5	8	0	0	5	6	0	0	0	0	4.9
Social standards													
Lying													
First-born boys	0	11	22	69	43	21	36	33	13	0	0	10	21.5
Non-first-born boys	0	17	41	38	60	29	44	30	17	20	13	7	26.3
First-born girls	0	12	44	48	46	8	17	32*	17	0	0	0	18.7
Non-first-born girls	0	12	55	36	52	17	21	6	6	0	0	0	17.1
Truancy from home													
First-born boys	0	0	6	0	14	0	0	0	0	0	0	0	1.7
Non-first-born boys	0	3	11	15	0	0	0	0	0	0	0	0	2.4
First-born girls	0	0	7	4	4	0	0	0	0	0	0	0	1.2
Non-first-born girls	0	0	5	0	4	0	0	0	0	0	0	0	0.7
Stealing													
First-born boys	0	16	6	8	0	14	0	0	0	0	0	0	3.7
Non-first-born boys	12	10	15	12	10	5	17	10	8	0	0	0	8.2
First-born girls	4	17	7	4	0	0	0	0	0	0	0	0	2.7
Non-first-born girls	3	20	5	4	0	0	11	0	0	0	0	0	3.6
Destructiveness													
First-born boys	4	16	6*	23	21	7	21	20	13	0	12	0	11.9
Non-first-born boys	22	23	30	31	25	24	22	5	8	13	0	0	16.9
First-born girls	4	25	15	7	12	12	8	8	11	0	5	0	8.9
Non-first-born girls	0	16	9	12	4	0	0	0	0	0	0	0	3.4

Selfishness in sharing												
First-born boys	—	—	—	—	14	21	27	13	8	0	0	11.9
Non–first-born boys	—	—	—	—	0	22	10	25	27	13	21	18.3
First-born girls	—	—	—	—	17	17	4	11	10	14	0	10.4
Non–first-born girls	—	—	—	—	8	5	6	6	0	0	0	3.6
Quarrelsomeness												
First-born boys	—	—	—	—	7	0	13	7	0	0	0	3.9
Non–first-born boys	—	—	—	—	10	11	5	8	13	7	7	8.7
First-born girls	—	—	—	—	4	8	4	17	10	14	0	8.2
Non–first-born girls	—	—	—	—	0	0	0	6	0	0	6	1.7
Personality characteristics												
Excessive emotional dependence												
First-born boys	16	17	8	14	7	7	13	7	8	0	0	9.5
Non–first-born boys	13	33	15	20	0	0	10	25	13	20	7	15.1
First-born girls	17	15	26	27	38	12	16	28	35	24	12	21.4
Non–first-born girls	12	14	16	13	17	0	17	12	11	10	6	11.4
Excessive demanding of attention												
First-born boys	26	17	23	7	57*	29	40*	27	17	25	10	20.2
Non–first-born boys	17	33	4	14	24	17	10	25	20	7	7	15.7
First-born girls	42*	22	22	25	50	25*	12	11	0	10	6	19.8
Non–first-born girls	12	14	8	13	50	0	0	12	0	0	0	7.2
Oversensitiveness												
First-born boys	32	33	46	36	36	57	67	60	67	38	20	44.5
Non–first-born boys	27	48	46	30	19	44	40	58	53	40	21	35.9
First-born girls	21	37*	56	50	25	50	40	33	50	48	29	40.2
Non–first-born girls	40	68	48	57	21	47	56	44	39	48	53	47.2
Physical timidity												
First-born boys	32	11	8	21		29	47**	33	33	0	0	22.6
Non–first-born boys	30	19	19	15		6	5	25	20	7	0	15.8
First-born girls	33	19	37	35		29	28	22	35*	19	6	25.5
Non–first-born girls	16	32	32	26		32	33	25	6	24	18	24.7
Shyness												
First-born boys	—	—	—	—	14	7	0	7	0	12	0	5.7
Non–first-born boys	—	—	—	—	5	22	5	33	27	27	14	19.0

TABLE 13.2 (continued)

	Age in years												Average (in percent)
Sib order	1¾	3	4	5	6	7	8	9	10	11	12	13	
	Number												
First-born boys	24	19	18	13	14	14	14	15	15	12	8	10	
Non–first-born boys	32	30	27	26	20	21	18	20	12	15	15	14	
First-born girls	28	24	27	27	26	24	24	25	18	20	21	17	
Non–first-born girls	32	25	22	25	23	24	19	18	16	18	21	17	
Problem, sib order, and sex													
	Percentage of problem incidence												
First-born girls	—	—	—	—	—	42**	25	28	33	55*	24	24	33.0
Non–first-born girls	—	—	—	—	—	8	16	11	12	17	19	12	13.6
Specific fears													
First-born boys	29	47	50	38	50	43	29	47	27	58	12	10	36.7
Non–first-born boys	31	40	44	50	30	33	39	35	17	47	20	0	32.2
First-born girls	18*	67	44	41	46	42	46	20	28	50	19	24	37.1
Non–first-born girls	47	68	45	32	35	25	21	22	25	28	24	18	32.5
Mood swings													
First-born boys	4	21	22	15	0	0	—	0	47	42	25	40	24.0
Non–first-born boys	12	17	26	4	10	0	—	0	25	40	20	29	20.3
First-born girls	4	21	22	19	27	0	—	0	44	65**	38*	24	29.3
Non–first-born girls	12	4	9	4	17	0	—	0	19	11	10	29	12.8
Somberness													
First-born boys	0	0	11	46	21	7	7	13	7	25	12	0	15.3
Non–first-born boys	0	0	19	31	30	14	22	5	33	33	33	21	24.7
First-born girls	0	0	11	30	27	12	29*	40*	33	40*	33	18	29.1
Non–first-born girls	0	0	18	24	39	4	5	6	6	11	24	12	14.6
Negativism													
First-born boys	12	21	17	31	21	14	21	13	20	17	0	10	16.4
Non–first-born boys	22	33	22	35	30	10	17	10	25	27	13	21	22.1
First-born girls	21	33	44	15	31	17	17	8	11	20*	19*	12	20.7
Non–first-born girls	19	20	27	24	26	4	0	0	6	0	0	12	11.5

164

Irritability													
First-born boys	4*	16	11	8	7	7	7	20	13	8	12	10	10.2
Non–first-born boys	25	7	22	12	10	5	11	10	17	27	13	14	14.4
First-born girls	7	12	33	7	27*	8	12	8	17	25*	14	12	15.2
Non–first-born girls	0	4	14	0	4	0	0	0	6	0	5	6	3.2
Temper tantrums													
First-born boys	62	74	50	69	43	50	43	47	33	42	38	10*	46.8
Non–first-born boys	56	67	56	54	70	62	61	55	58	47	40	50	56.3
First-born girls	39	75	48	44	50	67	42*	40	28	50*	38	18	44.9
Non–first-born girls	47	52	45	32	52	46	11	17	38	17	19	12	32.3
Jealousy													
First-born boys	4**	37	22	46	29	36	43	40	47	42	38	30	34.5
Non–first-born boys	50	23	33	31	20	24	44	30	33	53	47	43	35.9
First-born girls	11	38	26	44	31	46	33	24	39	30	38	35	32.9
Non–first-born girls	28	20	18	32	22	21	21	33	31	17	24	24	24.2
Excessive competitiveness													
First-born boys	—	—	—	—	—	0	0*	13	13	0	12	0	5.4
Non–first-born boys	—	—	—	—	—	19	33	5	8	20	0	0	12.2
First-born girls	—	—	—	—	—	21	12	4	0	0	5	0	6.0
Non–first-born girls	—	—	—	—	—	17	11	6	6	0	0	0	5.7
Unself-reliance													
First-born boys	—	—	—	—	—	36	29	20	13	0	12	10	17.2
Non–first-born boys	—	—	—	—	—	14	22	30	33	7	20	14	20.0
First-born girls	—	—	—	—	—	29	29	12	11	10	14	6	15.8
Non–first-born girls	—	—	—	—	—	29	11	17	0	0	0	0	8.1
Excessive reserve													
First-born boys	—	—	—	62	36	14	14	40	13	50	25	30	31.6
Non–first-born boys	—	—	—	31	45	24	22	15	33	53	47	21	32.3
First-born girls	—	—	—	30	46	46	46	52*	61	50	43	24	44.2
Non–first-born girls	—	—	—	48	48	33	37	17	56	44	33	24	37.8

*Differences in incidence between first and non–first children significant at the 5% level.
**Differences in incidence between first and non–first children significant at the 1% level.

Source: MacFarlane, J. W., Allen, L., & Houzik, M. P. (1954). A developmental study of the behavior problems of normal children between twenty-one months and fourteen years. Berkeley/Los Angeles: University of California Press.

The personality assessment should provide rich material about any child brought to the attention of the psychologist, whether he or she is of superior intellect, emotionally disturbed, functionally successful, disabled, or so forth. A simple finding of "no pathology" is unacceptable in the comprehensive evaluation of the child.

PERSONALITY TESTS FOR CHILDREN

Objective Personality Measures

Objective tests of personality are generally the so-called paper-and-pencil tests. In these tests, the individual is asked to make a choice, often true or false, in respect to each item. Children's personality tests are more frequently rating scales that are filled out by the parents rather than measures made directly with the child. In some cases these scales are completed by the examiner. A number of these measures are described below.

Burks Behavior Rating Scales.   Like most psychological measurements of personality, the Burks Behavior Rating Scales (Burks, 1977) were developed to measure behavior problems. The instrument consists of 110 items that are answered by parents or teachers. The scale does not assess the inner experiences of the child. It is mainly for use with children in Grades 1–9 who already have presenting problems. A preschool and kindergarten form is also available. Ratings are available for excessive self-blame, excessive anxiety, excessive withdrawal, excessive dependency, poor ego strength, poor physical strength, poor coordination, poor intellectuality, poor academics, poor attention, poor impulse control, poor reality contact, poor sense of identity, excessive suffering, poor anger control, excessive sense of persecution, excessive aggressiveness, excessive resistance, and poor social conformity. Essentially, this instrument is built to gauge the severity of negative symptoms presented by the child. It has no focus on positive aspects of a child's personality.

Child and Adolescent Adjustment Profile.   The Child and Adolescent Adjustment Profile (Ellsworth, 1981) measures a child's or adolescent's adjustments in the areas of peer relations, dependency, hostility, productivity, and withdrawal. The ratings are filled out by teachers, parents, or any adults who may have close association with the child. This instrument, like the others, focuses on pathology and provides no real picture of a normal child or certainly not of an accomplishing or accomplished child. Children are rated on a total of 20 items.

Child Assessment Schedule.   The Child Assessment Schedule (Hodges, 1985) is essentially a structured interview designed to evaluate psychological disorders in children between the ages of 7 and 12. The first of three sections is a series of open-ended questions regarding school, friends, and activities. The second asks about family, fears, worries, self-images, mood, somatic concerns, and anger. A third section covers symptoms of thought disturbance. Any item can be scored *yes, no, ambiguous,* or *not applicable.* Part of the information gathering enables the clinician to generate a DSM-III diagnosis (*Diagnostic and Statistical Manual of Mental Disorders,* 3rd ed., the American Psychiatric Association, 1980). This instrument also focuses on dysfunctional behaviors. A parent form provides a comparison of the parent's view of the child with what the child thinks of himself or herself.

Children's Personality Questionnaire. Developed by Porter and Cattell (1975), the Children's Personality Questionnaire is one of the instruments generated through factor analytic studies of personality. The questionnaire that the child fills out assumes a certain reading capacity. Younger children may have difficulty understanding the items. Fourteen source traits are scored: coolness versus warmth, concrete thinking versus abstract thinking, affected by feeling versus emotionally stable, phlegmatic versus excitable, obedient versus dominant, sober versus enthusiastic, expedient versus conscientious, shy versus bold, tough-minded versus tender-minded, vigorous versus guarded, forthright versus shrewd, self-assured versus apprehensive, undisciplined self-conflict versus control, and relaxed versus tense. In addition, there are second-order factors of extroversion, anxiety, tough poise, and independence.

The factors developed from this questionnaire are extremely useful in describing a youngster's presentation of self. The greatest difficulty with this test is the reading level required: A sixth-grade reading level should produce valid results. The questionnaire generally yields important data, and it certainly goes beyond the study of pathology. Validity studies are unfortunately lacking in this instrument, which otherwise shows a lot of promise.

Many more behavior rating scales and paper-and-pencil tests are available to measure children's personalities. Most of them suffer from the problems noted above. More detailed descriptions can be found in *Test Critiques* (Keyser & Sweetland, 1987).

Projective Techniques

Children's personalities have been measured through the use of projective techniques, mostly projective drawings, for over half a century. In the hands of an expert, the projective technique is quite valuable in demonstrating the child's usual presentation of self to the world, as well as the nature of the child's inner personality. Unfortunately, these tests are rarely taught in depth in graduate school, and the clinical psychologist must acquire these skills through reading, continuing education workshops, or special courses taken during or after graduate school. Palmer (1983) and Knoff (1986) provided summaries of interpretation styles and methods.

Teaching these tests presents certain difficulties. Many professors of psychology have had little training or experience in administering these tests, and tend to fall back on the concept that such instruments are not sufficiently standardized. To some extent this is true, but the absence of standardization (or the absence of any kind of research) demonstrates nothing. Hopefully, in the future, more research will be done on those factors that represent common interpretive styles for projective techniques. A number of commonly used projective techniques are considered below.

Thematic Apperception Test.   The Thematic Apperception Test (TAT) is one of the most widely used personality tests for both children and adults worldwide. Originally developed by Henry Murray (1938, 1943), the TAT consists of a series of pictures that are of relatively ambiguous structure. The youngster is asked to make up a story or a fantasy concerning what is happening, what led up to the scene in the picture, and what will happen in the future. The skillful clinician also asks the child what sorts of thoughts and feelings he or she has about each character depicted. The youngster's productions are used in constructing a picture of the child's current needs, motives, emotions, and conflicts.

Although originally developed for adults, the TAT is extremely useful for children. It may be the most powerful projective technique for eliciting the way a child feels about himself or herself, about the adults who are significant in his or her life, and about the world and its expectations. It is assumed that the youngster will project motives, emotions, and attitudes in response to the stimulus cards (Peterson & Schilling, 1983).

Not all of the 20 pictures in the TAT set are used with every subject. Originally, the cards were identified as being appropriate for adult males, adult females, boys, and/or girls. The use of the code "3BM" would indicate that Card 3 is particularly useful for male youngsters and adults.

An important concept involved in the use of the TAT, as well as other projective stimuli, is the degree to which the material will "pull." Some of this pull is based on the quality of the material itself, but a great deal depends upon the skill of the clinician in creating a setting in which the child can be comfortable enough to project a broad range of feelings and perceptions. For use with children, in order to increase the pull, some form of the following directions is recommended when using the TAT:

> I'm going to show you a card. There's a picture on the card. It may be hard to see what the picture is, but that's all right. I want you to make believe that you're watching a very interesting television show. Look at each picture and make believe that the show has stopped at a very important point where something very exciting is happening. When you look at the card, I want you

to tell me what is happening in the story. Tell me who the people are. I'd like you to also make up what they're thinking.

After the child makes the initial presentation, the clinician should move on to the second phase of the inquiry, as follows:

That was very good! I'd like you to tell me what led up to this. What happened before this scene in the television show? What was going on before [*state the general theme that the child presented*] happened? Tell me everything you can think of about this. You're doing well. Keep it up.

After the child has said what led up to the current scene, the clinician should say the following:

That was very good. Tell me now what's going to happen to the people in this picture. In your story, so far, you've said [*repeat what led up to the scene and the scene itself*]. Now what's going to happen? Make it up as you go along. You're doing very well!

After the child has said what seems to be all that he or she sees in the picture for the past, the present, and the future, the clinician may ask a series of questions, which might include:

- What is he/she afraid of?
- What is his/her mother like?
- Tell me about his/her father.
- What does he/she want most of all?
- What does he/she do that people don't like?

The number of questions that may be asked is almost endless. The skill and sensitivity of the psychologist in understanding what directions to take in the inquiry will determine the richness that emerges from this particular technique. Some clinicians do an inquiry after all of the tests are finished. The child's responses should be recorded verbatim.

Murray's (1938, 1943) original concepts of *needs* and *presses* are valuable in interpreting the stories that emerge. The 36 needs can be rated by the examiner on a scale of 1–5 in terms of the intensity and/or the centrality of their expression within a story. The same can be done with the presses. It would behoove the clinician to study Murray's original work to understand how directly the children's expressions can demonstrate their identification, fears, mechanisms of defense, and hopes.

After Murray developed the TAT, other clinicians used it in a variety of ways. The test is fairly consistently viewed as being extremely useful for understanding the child's personality structure. Most clinicians focus on content analysis, as opposed to formal considerations. The primary focus for interpretation is Murray's concept of the "hero." One can assume that the hero—the protagonist of the youngster's story—is one of the child's parents, or another significant adult in the child's life. The description may include the child's own life experiences and attitudes toward adult figures. The child's confusions and conflicts emerge very directly in the descriptions of confusion and conflict occurring within the pictures themselves.

To successfully interpret the TAT, as well as any personality test of similar structure, the clinician should become familiar with literature in this area (Bellak, 1975; Campus, 1976; Dana, 1982; Goldfried & Zax, 1965; Rapaport, Gill, & Schafer, 1968; Stein, 1981; Tomkins, 1947).

House–Tree–Person Technique. Buck (1948) proposed using the House–Tree–Person Technique, used by many psychologists as an intelligence test, as a personality test. His original efforts included some attempts at standardization of this test as a measure of intelligence. In his version, the child is asked to draw a house, a tree, and a person on the same sheet of paper. Many clinicians prefer to separate the person from the house and tree.

Most clinicians ask the child to tell a story after making each of the drawings (Diamond, 1954). In the House–Tree Technique, the child may be asked the following while being presented with a blank sheet of paper and a soft-lead pencil:

> Here is a blank piece of paper. I want you to draw a house, and a tree. You can draw any kind of house and any kind of tree. Take your time. Draw this any way you want.

When the house and tree are drawn separately from the person, the drawing of the person may be more formalized by putting it in a booklet. For the first page, the child is told the following:

> Draw a person. Draw any kind of a person you would like. This is not a test of drawing skill. Be sure you draw the whole person, top to bottom. Take your time.

The child may ask, "What kind of a person," but the clinician should tell the child to make the decision.

On the second page of the booklet, the child may be told the following:

> That was very good. Now I'd like you to draw another person on this page. Make this person different from the first one. If the first person you drew was a man or a boy, now draw a girl or a woman. If the first person you drew was a girl or a woman, draw a man or a boy. Do the best you can. Take your time. Make sure you draw the whole person from top to bottom.

Most clinicians ask the youngster to tell a story about each figure that has been drawn. Some children have difficulty in producing a spontaneous story, and the clinician may wish to ask a series of questions about the figures:

- How old is this person?
- What does this person do for a living?
- Does this person like children?
- Does this person like boys better than girls or girls better than boys?
- What makes this person angry?
- What does this person do when he or she is angry?
- What do children think about this person?
- What is the best thing about this person?
- What is the worst thing about this person?

These questions given here are not all-inclusive, and the experienced clinician may develop other questions pertinent to the information already obtained about the child.

There are a number of variations to these drawing tests. A commonly used form is the Draw-a-Family test (Hammer, 1978). The child is asked to draw all members of his or her family on a blank sheet of paper. The drawings are used to test the individual's perception of his or her place in the family interaction, as well as the interaction of parent and sibling figures.

Drawings are fairly standard techniques used by clinical child psychologists. It is generally believed that using drawings to introduce the youngster to the test battery minimizes the threat and strangeness of the testing situation.

Some psychologists believe that the child's drawings present a deeper, more conflict-oriented picture of the child's personality than material that is obtained from objective tests (Wyatt, 1949). Some feel that drawings are useful as a screening tool for detecting the onset of psychopathology (Hammer, 1978; Zucker, 1948). Most clinicians believe that instruments such as the Rorschach are better indicators of deep psychopathology than are other techniques.

To interpret the drawings of a child, the clinician must be thoroughly schooled in ages and stages of development and the kinds of drawings that can be expected of a child at various developmental levels. The use of drawing techniques with children who are neurologically impaired or developmentally disabled poses complexities that should be taken into consideration whenever these tests are used with such children.

Although some scoring techniques have been developed for use with drawings, scoring remains a subjective technique dependent on the skills and experience of the psychologist. An extensive early description of how to interpret the various aspects of drawings was originally developed by Machover (1949), and some more recent work has been done in providing catalogs of interpretation for scoring drawings (Jolles, 1983; Wenck, 1984).

In using projective drawings, the clinician must understand that the interpretations of these productions must conform to the results of other tests. Drawings should not be used as the sole basis for personality descriptions of children.

Sentence Completion Tests.   The Sentence Completion Test is a frequently used projective test in which the child is asked to finish a sentence. The subjects that are presented in the incomplete sentences are stimuli to which the child is asked to respond from his or her own experience. The test has a good deal of face validity, as do all projective techniques, but the psychometric properties of the instrument leave much to be desired.

The test does not seem to distress subjects. As with many such instruments, the administration is very simple and can be done by a psychological assistant. Although objective scoring systems are available, most clinicians prefer to interpret the test according to their own concept of psychodynamics and their own particular theoretical orientation for the interpretation of projective tests (Goldberg, 1965; Turnbow & Dana, 1981).

The stimulus sentences used for children differ considerably from those used with adolescents and adults.

The Rorschach Test.   Developed originally by Herman Rorschach in 1929 (Rorschach, 1942), the Rorschach test is the projective technique used most often by clinical psychologists throughout the world. The test comprises 10 cards, each having a colored or black figure. The amount of research attention that this technique has received is legion. The test was interpreted according to a variety of scoring systems focusing on the content, form, and use of portions of the blot, until Exner (1974) developed a comprehensive scoring and interpretation system that has become standard in the field for adults (Exner, 1974, 1978).

Exner suggested that human movement responses and color responses, compared with the sum of nonhuman movement, shading, and gray–black responses, tend to stabilize during development and achieve permanence by adulthood. The problems of using this adult instrument with children is similar to the problems of using adult neuropsychological tests with children. Since children develop at different rates, what may appear to be a pathological sign may simply be a picture of the child at that particular moment in development. A relatively small number of clinical psychologists use the Rorschach with young children. A good deal more experience is necessary in using this instrument with children than if it is used only with adults (Rogolsky, 1968; Tolpin & Kohut, 1978).

The projective tests described above represent the more commonly used techniques with children. Each clinician, based on training, experience, and personal preference, must choose the kinds of projective techniques to be used with children. As more objective forms of personality testing with children are developed, the psychologist's need to become proficient through extensive study, supervision, and experience may lessen. At the present time, however, a comprehensive psychological examination of the child should include several projective techniques that are interpreted in a thorough, expert manner.

PERSONALITY EVALUATION AND THE YOUNGER CHILD

The projective techniques are most applicable to youngsters 4 years of age and older. Children under 4 are rarely brought for a thorough psychological examination. When they are, the same general format used for older children should be followed. In respect to personality analysis, however, the clinical psychologist must depend on environmental reports and behavior scale ratings, as well as clinical observation. For most of the personality tests to be effective with children, a relatively high degree of neuropsychological development in the child is necessary. Expressive speech, receptive speech, visual–motor coordination, and conceptualization ability are required simply to perform the tasks inherent in projective testing.

One approach to evaluating the personalities of younger children is the analysis of pathological responses, which is the approach taken with testing children who are diagnosed as autistic or as childhood schizophrenics (Sattler, 1982). However, such pathology is the exception rather than the rule. Examining the personalities of most children under 4 years of age is more difficult than assessing youngsters with very severe pathology. Traditionally, young children raise parental concern when they exhibit anxiety, sleep disturbances, resistance to going to sleep, phobias, hysteria, obsessions, and tantrums (Kessler, 1966).

A careful study of the personalities of young, normal children and of children whose growth and development is a cause for concern to the parents, requires the use of behavior-based measures. These checklists or rating scales require that the child be observed by the examiner in a variety of situations, or that the parents and/or teachers fill out such rating scales on the basis of their long-term observation of the child. Many technical difficulties are involved in the interpretation of such observations, even where the psychologist makes a home visit and attempts to very objectively record observations on standardized checklists (Drotar & Crawford, 1987).

The lack of validity of such behavioral observations was well illustrated by MacFarlane et al. (1954), as discussed earlier in this book. Observations of so-called "atypical" infants at an early age were found to be poor predictors of later levels of adjustment (Field, 1987). There are indications that as the child reaches 3, behavioral observations are more useful in predicting short-term adjustment. The social behavior of 3-year-olds in a free-play situation in September apparently predicts teachers' evaluations of emotional, social, and learning functioning 8 months later. Behavior such as wandering around unoccupied, deficiencies in verbal initiation, difficulties in sustaining social contact, physical aggression, reduced positive affect, and tendency to be onlookers were factors that significantly predicted teachers' ratings of poor adjustment. A review of behavior-based measures for young children can be found in Goldman et al. (1983).

It is probably impossible to accurately assess the personalities of children under the age of 4. The focus of attention at these early ages would be in terms of the youngster's risk potential. Sufficient research suggests that young children who have anomalies of development, whether caused by neuropsychological deficits, brain damage, failure to thrive, or lack of stimulation, cannot be diagnosed with any degree of accuracy. Analysis of the personalities of children at risk during the earlier ages tends to focus on child-based factors, nuclear family factors, and environmental factors (Lewis, Dlugokinski, Caputo, & Griffin, 1988). Because the BPE usually is done with children above the age of 4, these issues are not of broad significance. It behooves the clinical psychologist who will examine children under the age of 4 to become very familiar with modes of thinking in young children. Creativity and interactional skills are very important in identifying the degree to which the young child's development is within normal expectation (Wallach & Kogan, 1965).

A particular concern regarding the observational evaluation of young children (and older children, for that matter) is the traditional thought that fantasy predicts later maladjustment. In fact, current research indicates that the tendency of children, younger and older, to be able to produce fantasies in no way predicts psychological problems or pathological behavior (Rhue & Lynn, 1987). It is more likely that the more intelligent the child, the more extensive the fantasy proneness, given an open family setting and a flexible social environment.

None of this commentary should be construed to mean that children under the age of 4 do not sometimes suffer personality disturbances. These cautionary remarks are based on long clinical experience which suggests that great harm can be done in misinterpreting that which is part of children's fluctuating development as predictive of psychopathology.

The importance of personality assessment of children is not at issue. Psychologists generally agree that this is a critical area for assessment. Because of a paucity of available literature in this area, however, the personality assessment of young children is rarely taught in graduate school. Even in clinical psychology internships, 48% of general internships and 35% of child clinical specialty internships do not provide seminars or didactic training in child personality assessment (Elbert & Holden, 1987).

Clearly, even after school and internships, clinical child psychologists remain deficient in the assessment of children's personality. Hopefully, new methods will be developed for such assessment, which will gradually drift into the education and training sectors. Because personality is such an important part of clinical psychology, and because there is general agreement that early childhood experience is extremely important in the formation of later personality structure, increased attention in both research and practice to the area of child personality assessment is warranted.

DESCRIBING THE CHILD'S PERSONALITY

When clinical psychologists learn to write reports, they have little difficulty in describing intelligence, neuropsychological factors, or achievement. The ways and means of describing such behavior are carefully taught and well known. In the area of personality assessment, however, guidelines are rare. This may be the central reason as to why there is such difficulty in developing standardized teaching and training methods in the personality assessment of children.

For the purposes of the BPE, the analysis of the child's personality is as important as any other part of the examination. Each part provides information that can be helpful in promoting the best interests of the child. For the psychologist to accomplish the worthy goal of helping the child, information about personality must be meaningful and, most importantly, must be communicated to those who have the most significant influence on the child's development. The psychologist should bear in mind that any information that is conveyed to the significant adult figures in the child's environment should be very understandable and should lead to useful recommendations. Diagnostic labels and generalized descriptions are relatively worthless. Regardless of what personality assessment techniques are used, the psychologist should organize the results of these techniques, as well as the results of observations and environmental information, in a sensible, purposeful manner. To this end, a *quadrant analysis* is recommended.

QUADRANT ANALYSIS

The quadrant analysis method of analyzing and presenting personality assessment results is not restricted to any specific tests. It is a format within which the results of any series of personality tests may be assigned. Each of the four quadrants presents a different aspect of the child's affective and motivational life. The richness and the depth of the quadrant analysis depends, of course, on the richness and depth of the analysis of personality tests.

The sources of the material presented in any quadrant analysis can vary. The clinician may emphasize observations of the parents, school reports, and observations of the child in a clinical or play setting. Descriptive materials from any source, as well as the results of psychological tests done directly with the child, provide information of value. The philosophy behind the quadrant analysis suggests that if the psychologist uses multiple sources to determine information about the child's personality, any so-derived aspect of the personality should be observed from different sources. An aspect of the child's personality that appears in only one setting or one observation should be held suspect. Thus, if the child appears to have a high level of aspiration according to the mother, but presents a Thematic Apperception Test story on Card 1 that reflects pessimism and a low level of aspiration, further test or observational data must be obtained to clarify this difference. The final presentation in the quadrant analysis should reflect clinical judgment as to the degree to which the description truly defines the child. Discrepancies between parental descriptions and personality descriptors emerging from test analysis can provide helpful clinical information about intrafamily communication. A detailed description of each of the quadrants follows in the sections below.

Interpersonal Activity

This first quadrant should reflect the child's presentation of self in everyday life. Statements in this quadrant should indicate how this child generally appears to adults during everyday interaction, for example, "tends to become shy and withdrawn when meeting a new adult figure." Other statements describe the way in which the child interacts with peers, for example, "frequently acts in an aggressive, bullying manner with those his age or younger." Also in this quadrant should be some description of the child's communication style. Such a description, which might come from the Sentence Completion Test or other thematic-expressive test, might be "is very articulate for her age." The level of the child's expressed or functional intellect and any observations relating to unusual or creative style, such as "seems to function at a level below measured intellectual capacity," also should be included.

The older the child, the more likely the clinician will be able to say something in this section about the youngster's level of aspiration. This might include such statements as "seems to generally expect very little out of situations" or "approaches new situations with enthusiasm and energy." These factors, of course, are not pure, and this quadrant might include the degree to which the child seems to have self-esteem and confidence. Statements relating to the child's general responsiveness also are useful in this section. Such an item might be "seems to enjoy challenge, and responds with energy" or "seems shy and timid, often not responding when one can be fairly sure he knows the answer."

This is the section in which the clinician would present the absence or presence of related social skills demonstrated by observations or described in behavioral rating scales that were completed by parents or teachers. Thus, interpersonal activity is the quadrant that describes how the child is likely to appear to an individual who comes to know the youngster. It should be an accurate description of the child's socialization and interactional style and capacity.

Early Identifications

The second quadrant should present a picture of the most significant adults who have influenced the child's life. Three elements that can be presented in almost all cases are the mother figure (or figures), the father figure (or figures), and the interaction between or among these important adults. In most instances, the significant figures that represent love object and identification object are the child's biological parents. With the current frequency of divorce and separation, as well as alternate living styles, the child may be exposed to more, sometimes many more, than two parental figures. Nevertheless, most children perceive themselves as part of a nuclear family, with a mother, a father, and children. Even when this situation does not exist, children can conceptualize themselves in this interaction (Elkin, 1960; Piaget, 1962).

The clinical child psychologist's job is to produce a picture of how the child sees significant males and females in his or her life. To this purpose, the quadrant on early identification should focus on how the child views mother and father figures: as love objects, as identification objects, or as objects of mixed affective attachment and identification.

Given the materials that are recommended for inclusion in the BPE, the clinician should have access to projective techniques, objective rating scales, observations, interviews with the parents, and other materials from which to glean a picture of the child–adult interactions of significance. The following are common things that can be included in the youngster's early identifications quadrant:

- Indications of which parent is being imitated (identification object) and which parent is sought for closeness and affection (love object)
- The communication style of each parent
- Each parent's usual response style to stress
- Any anxieties that seem consistently attributed to the parents
- The degree of closeness and availability of the parents
- The parental attitudes toward such things as sexuality, religion, social expectations, and family opportunities
- Each parent's level of aspiration
- The degree to which each parent has self-esteem and is able to encourage it in the child
- Each parent's attitude toward control, mastery, punitiveness, and tolerance
- Each parent's concept of work and the degree to which each is involved in work pursuits.

In this quadrant, perhaps more than in any other quadrant, the range of material available to the psychologist for interpretation varies considerably.

This is also the quadrant in which the psychologist must be most careful not to include his or her own prejudices and tunnel vision. There is almost a tradition of parent blaming in mental health work that must be avoided in a proper BPE.

Anxiety Structure

Anxiety reactions or responses may range from mild uneasiness on the part of the child to panic and terror. The material in this quadrant should reflect information that the psychologist has gleaned from various sources in the BPE that reflect the child's response propensities in this range. The most common descriptions that would be put into this quadrant include the following:

- Anticipations of the future with discomfort or negative feelings
- Fears in respect to interaction or lack of interaction with the mother
- Fears in respect to interaction with the father or the absence of the father
- Fears in relation to siblings
- Fears regarding the integrity of the family
- Fears regarding spontaneity (usually sensuality, anger, or creativity)
- Unsureness or anxiety regarding future expectations (of the self or of others)
- Concerns about performance
- Concerns or ambivalence regarding dependence and independence
- Worries about his or her own intrinsic worth
- Guilt responses regarding current or past interaction, fantasized or real.

The clinician's awareness of the child's anxiety responses may come from almost any source. The intensity of the reaction is to some degree demonstrated by the variety of places in which the reaction is found. Attributions of intensity or pervasiveness of anxiety are demonstrated in the case material presented later.

Some statements that are frequently gleaned from psychological testing and are appropriate for the anxiety structure quadrant include the following:

- "He is fearful of new situations."
- "She tends to be frightened of not meeting parental expectations."
- "He is fearful of expressing his angry thoughts."
- "She anticipates moving into early adulthood with fear and trepidation."

- "He is fearful that he will lose either his mother or father or both as the result of the divorce action."
- "She is aware of her poor school performance and dreads each next experience of failure."
- "He sees himself as lesser than others. His idea of his own worth is that he's not very good."
- "She feels that she is responsible for the conflict between her mother and father."

This quadrant should present a picture of the kinds of emotional stimuli that press the child to "do something" in order to be relieved of the discomfort brought on by the anxiety.

The psychologist should be extremely cautious not to overlabel anxiety as "bad." Students who perform extremely well in school undoubtedly suffer a moderate level of anxiety about their performance which ensures that homework gets done and preparation for examinations is accomplished. Certainly, some kinds and levels of anxiety are debilitating. The simple presence of anxiety, however, must be viewed within the context of the child's life and the manner in which the child channels this anxiety. Thus, the anxiety structure quadrant must be viewed in concordance with the *outlets and defenses* quadrant.

Outlets and Defenses

In the fourth quadrant, the psychologist should note the child's coping mechanisms. Children adapt to the pressures in their environments in a wide variety of ways. In some cases the child's responses are defenses against anxiety, and in other cases the child channelizes energies that then operate in the child's best interests. Unfortunately, the child may develop outlets or defenses that are not in his or her best interests. Thus, the fourth quadrant should show us what the child does with the energies generated and demonstrated in the third quadrant.

Outlets and defenses can be split roughly into intellectual defenses and spontaneous or labile outlets. The intellectual outlets include those things about which the child is relatively aware. Thus, children who have learned to channelize anxiety through the mechanism of denial say "fine" when asked how they feel even though they may feel poorly.

The child who gets much relief of tension and a sense of pleasure and accomplishment through free play, running and jumping, yelling on the playground, or other forms of physical expression, relieves anxieties through nonintellectual outlets. This kind of behavior might be represented by a statement such as, "Much tension is relieved through spontaneous physical activity in game playing."

The fourth quadrant is the place where the psychologist identifies the ways in which the child achieves emotional homeostasis, or balance, in dealing with everyday stresses and tensions. The following are some common statements that are appropriate for this quadrant:

- "He tends to obsess about minor concerns."
- "She is very energetic and goal oriented."
- "He tends to be very obedient to authority figures."
- "She avoids expressing any form of anger or resentment."
- "He frequently tells lies to gain attention."
- "She has good social skills, beyond her developmental age."
- "He frequently denies knowing the answer to a question in order to avoid interaction."
- "She becomes overly emotional and cries easily in the face of minimal stimuli."
- "He tends to internalize stress and suffer somatic complaints."
- "When under pressure she tends to drift away and to withdraw."

This quadrant should provide a fairly clear picture of how the child balances the emotional pressures in his or her life. The quadrant should express fairly clearly the degree to which the child's outlets and/or defenses work in the child's best interests, are acceptable to the child's environment, or are the sources of conflict and difficulty.

Figure 13.1 shows a quadrant analysis worksheet. As the clinician works with the material from the BPE, brief descriptors should be entered into the appropriate quadrant of the quadrant analysis worksheet. The worksheet is then used to construct the personality section of the report, as well as the recommendations. The clinician uses the area at the bottom of the sheet to write any recommendations that seem appropriate from material presented from the initial contact with the parents through the final testing of the child.

RECOMMENDATIONS

The end result of the work done during the BPE is a set of recommendations that can be given to all appropriate parties, to serve the best interests of the child. The clinician should, from the very beginning of the BPE, be concerned with outcomes. It is easy to fall into the trap of focusing on the process of giving the tests and collecting the interviews, and relegating recommendations to a secondary role. The clinician must keep in mind throughout the process that the recommendations that are going to be made to ease stresses, resolve problems, and enhance the youngster's developmental experience represent the primary focus of the entire process.

QUADRANT ANALYSIS

NAME _____   DATE _____

INTERPERSONAL ACTIVITY	EARLY IDENTIFICATIONS
ANXIETY STRUCTURE	OUTLETS AND DEFENSES

RECOMMENDATIONS

FIGURE 13.1   Quadrant Analysis Worksheet

Several general concerns should be kept in mind in making recommendations:

1. The needs of the child
2. The needs and expectations of the parents
3. The expectations of society and the child's environment.

In preparing to advise and counsel all parties involved in the BPE, the clinician should focus his or her attention on these concerns in the order noted.

The implementation of recommendations is a complex process. Implementation should not be a concern of the clinician at the end of the process, but from the very beginning. The *practicality* of recommendations is going to be the key factor in whether they will ever take place or indeed be in the child's best interests. As the clinician goes through the BPE and considers recommendations that might be useful, implementation factors that must always be kept in mind and considered include those listed in the following sections.

The Parents' Resources and Limits

In considering recommendations that may be useful, the clinician must consider the capabilities of the parents or the surrogate parents in carrying out the recommendations. The following are some of the basic elements that must be considered in making practical recommendations:

- The level of each parent's intelligence
- The parents' cultural backgrounds and limitations
- The parents' level of cooperation versus conflict with each other
- The degree to which the parents are available to the child in terms of time, marital stability, home conditions, and personal interest in the child
- The number of other children in the family.

The clinician should always judge whether the recommendations being considered can be implemented with a reasonable degree of certainty, considering these and other factors.

The Child's Resources and Limits

Throughout the BPE, the clinician will become more and more aware of the child's resources and limitations. In selecting recommendations, the clinician must constantly be concerned with the following:

- The child's intellectual function and potential
- The child's level of development in all spheres
- The educational circumstances of the child
- The child's physical health
- Any special handicaps or disabilities
- The child's current personality structure and limitations.

The Community's Resources and Limits

The clinical child psychologist is most effective when he or she is thoroughly familiar with the community in which the child and family live. Larger communities often have greater facilities available for helping children, but these facilities are frequently crowded. In making recommendations, the clinician should keep some of the following considerations in mind:

- The child's neighborhood
- The safety of the streets in which the child plays
- The community recreational resources
- Club and social activities sponsored by the community
- Available social services
- Private professional services and their reputation
- Health, weather, and geographic aspects of the community.

School Resources and Limits

As noted previously, many children spend a large number of hours per week in an academic setting. Schools vary, not only from state to state, but even within the same community. The psychologist should be knowledgeable about schools in the child's community. Concerns include the following:

- The size of the school and its facilities
- The number of children in the child's classroom
- The opportunity for special classroom placement
- The opportunity for tutoring or special attention
- The safety and security of the school and its playgrounds
- The degree of acceptance and concern on the part of the principal and the teachers in respect to the special needs of the individual child
- The flexibility of the school and its personnel in accepting recommendations and support from an external professional source.

It behooves the clinical child psychologist to establish the best possible relationships with principals and teachers in the elementary schools of the children served.

Professional Resources and Limitations

Recommendations for special services are only as good as the availability of such services. A large number of children are found, upon examination, to need remedial reading of one sort or another, particularly children between Grades 2 and 7. If the community has no public facilities to offer remedial reading, and no private specialists are available, a recommendation of remedial reading is relatively useless. The psychologist then has to engineer some solutions that may involve student tutors, parents as surrogate teachers, or special programmed instructional materials to help the child improve skills.

Iatrogenic Pitfalls

The overly enthusiastic psychologist may have a tendency to generalize in making recommendations. Psychotherapy, Ritalin, and family group therapy may or may not be appropriate kinds of recommendations. The clinician must consider all of the implications and factors that may be involved, and must remain constantly concerned with recommendations which may have negative or *iatrogenic* effects. This can be true for medication, therapeutic interventions, or school placements.

The complexity of the collection of data, the analysis of data, and the making of a report and recommendations are illustrated in the case materials that follow.

ANALYSIS OF ALBERT'S PERSONALITY TESTING

Figure 8.6 lists the specific tests that were used for Albert. These included the Thematic Apperception Test, the House–Tree Technique, the Draw-a-Person Series, the Child Sentence Completion Test, Family Drawing, and Drawing of Choice.

Albert's House–Tree Test

Albert's house and tree reproductions can be seen in Figure 9.4. Examining the drawing, we can see that the figures are drawn low on the paper, suggesting a low level of aspiration. The house is simplistic and has little elaboration, suggesting that the mother is relatively traditional. The house is centered, suggesting that the mother has been the primary available parent during the growing years. The drawing of the tree exhibits a hole in the center with an object inside, which is frequently characteristic of children whose fathers sometimes take on mothering tasks. The very limited foliage in the upper portion of the drawing suggests that the father has never been much involved in the details of child rearing. The level of the drawings is age appropriate.

Albert's Draw-a-Person Test

Figures 13.2 and 13.3 represent Albert's first and second drawings of persons. The importance of this particular instrument has been confirmed in studies over the years (Yama, 1990).

Figure 13.2 shows Albert's first choice in a drawing. It is identified as a male figure. Albert's drawing is somewhat primitive for a bright 7-year-old, but consistent with a youngster who is having developmental lag. He placed the figure in the lower left-hand corner of the page, which suggests a relatively low level of aspiration. It should be noted that one of the shoes has laces that are tied, but the other shoe shows no shoelace; this sometimes indicates a person who is sometimes stable and sometimes unstable. The finely outlined hands (at Albert's age) are often characteristic of the child seeing the figure (the father probably) as a person who accomplishes things.

Figure 13.3 is Albert's second drawing. It is clearly identified as a female figure. Again, Albert drew the figure in the lower left-hand corner. Some analysts believe that the left side of the page represents socialization skills and the right side represents withdrawal. If this is so, Albert sees both of his parents as fairly sociable. The drawing of the female differs from that of the male in that both feet are firmly laced in shoelaces. This difference suggests that the mother is the more stable or consistent member of the family. The treatment of the hands suggests that the child sees the mother figure as not much of a "doer" and as someone who may be frustrated in accomplishing things. The significantly longer separation of the head from the body on the female compared with the male suggests that the father would tend to be more impulsive, whereas the mother is likely to be more controlled. The treatment of the eyes on the male figure suggests that Albert sees the father figure as more insightful and able to see the emotional needs of those with whom he is close, whereas the treatment of the eyes on the female figure suggests that the mother figure tends to have trouble seeing the emotional needs of those with whom she is close. The frilly treatment of the girl's skirt suggests that Albert sees the mother as quite feminine and is beginning to be aware of masculinity–femininity differences.

When asked to make up a short story about the man he drew, and to describe his age, his job, his family, the kind of person he is, his good points, and his bad points, Albert responded as follows:

> He's dumb. He don't like anything. He don't do good in school. He's good at school. (*How old do you think he might be?*) A hundred years old. His whole family is dumb. (Pause.) Actually and stupid too.

NAME Albert   DATE   10/18/88

DIRECTIONS

IN THE BLANK SPACE BELOW DRAW A PERSON. ANY KIND OF PERSON WILL DO. BE SURE TO DRAW
A WHOLE PERSON. THIS IS NOT A TEST OF DRAWING SKILL. JUST DRAW A PERSON THE BEST
YOU CAN.

Now turn to the next page

FIGURE 13.2   Albert Doe's Draw-A-Person Test

DIRECTIONS

NOW WE WANT YOU TO DRAW ANOTHER PERSON. THIS ONE SHOULD BE DIFFERENT FROM YOUR
FIRST DRAWING. IF YOU DREW A MAN FIRST, NOW DRAW A LADY. IF YOU DREW A LADY
FIRST, NOW DRAW A MAN.

Now turn to the next page

FIGURE 13.3   Albert Doe's Draw-A-Person Test

This story describes the way Albert sees himself and perhaps the way Albert's father sees himself. It suggests that the father is not very intellectual. There are indications that Albert is discouraged about his own academic progress, and is quite worried about it. The anger that this boy is experiencing from his frustration emerges clearly in this story.

When asked a similar series of questions about the female figure that he drew, Albert presented the following story:

> She's dumb. Her family is dumb also. She's stupid and she doesn't like school and she's bad at school and she's good at home. (*Anything else?*) Well, and she freaks out. (*What does this person worry a lot about?*) She worries about frogs in her bed.

In this story, Albert again demonstrates his anger and his concern about smartness. The absence of any statement involving nourishment or mothering, as well as the structure of the pictures that he drew, suggests that the mother is not a particularly strong nourisher.

Seven-year-olds generally give relatively short stories for their drawings. Most clinicians prefer not to press strongly on any particular projective technique, so as to maintain the sanctuary and security of the test session. Albert's stories were accepted as given.

As part of the Draw-a-Person procedures, Albert was asked some projective questions. He was asked to imagine that he could have three wishes, and to tell the three things that he would want the most. Albert answered as follows:

1. "Everybody to be dead."
2. "Everybody likes to play."
3. "My favorite ice cream is chocolate."

These responses support the original hypothesis that Albert is a very angry youngster, but also very oral dependent and childlike. Albert was then asked to state what he would consider the most pleasant idea. To this he responded, "Having your birthday every day." When asked about the most unpleasant idea that he could think of, he answered "Barf city. Slime all over your face." Again, he made an impulsive, angry, assertive response. He was asked what kind of an animal would be most like him, and he answered "I don't know—a dinosaur, I guess." The final question was whom he would like to be if he could be anyone who ever lived. Albert answered simply, "God."

The results of the Draw-a-Person and the questions suggest a number of concepts that started to emerge during the history taking, during the observations, and in the House–Tree Test. No attempt is made at this point to integrate or summarize the interpretations, since this is essentially the purpose of the quadrant analysis.

Albert's Sentence Completion Test

The Child Sentence Completion Test that was used with Albert is illustrated in Figure 13.4.

Twenty-three subject clauses were presented to Albert to be completed. Based on his response to Item 1, we can see that Albert sees himself as relatively small and insignificant in respect to those around him. (Both his parents and his stepparents are quite tall.) In Item 2 we see the continuance of his aggressive concerns. Item 3 suggests that his mother is sometimes nourishing, which contradicts some previous interpretations. This response is a more powerful indicator of nourishment than the absence of breasts on the female figure is an indicator of an absence of nourishment. The response in Item 4 continues the tendency that we see in Albert to focus on play and the obvious relief and pleasure he receives from it. Item 5 shows that he has made an attachment to the female psychological examiner, and exhibits his impulsive negative response pattern. Item 6 suggests that Albert has a positive relationship with his father in the area of play. The oral dependency is again illustrated in Item 7. Item 8 again represents Albert's preoccupation with aggression. Albert's doubts about his own esteem are illustrated in Item 9. Item 10 supports the growing picture of the mother as nourishing. Item 11 suggests that sibling rivalry is not intense. Item 12 implies that Albert has periods of loneliness. Item 13 is quite a common response for youngsters of 7 years. Albert's strong and extreme opinions are represented by Item 14, unless the response represents identification with one of the parents. Item 15 repeats the play theme. Item 16 suggests that Albert has developed some capacity to restrain himself. Item 17 indicates a capacity for creative fantasy. Item 18 might give an inexperienced clinician some feelings of anxiety about the possibility of child abuse, but the response should be viewed in light of Albert's tendency to be preoccupied with aggression and to be quite impulsive. Item 19 again suggests that he is concerned with restraint and social values, as does Item 20. Item 21 gives us a clue as to Albert's situation in school: Although he is very worried about performance, he indicates that it may be that he is insufficiently stimulated. Item 22 again indicates the restraint concerns, and Item 23 suggests that Albert takes a relatively positive view toward life in the long run.

Albert's Family Drawing

As seen in Figure 13.5, Albert drew his family in the lower left-hand corner of the paper. He placed himself between the mother and a figure he describes as both "dad" and "stepdad." He separated the baby in the crib from the rest of the family, suggesting his true feelings about the new infant brother.

Albert presented everyone with smiles, and placed himself in a cherished family position. His identifying the male figure as both parent and

NAME _Albert_   DATE _10/18/88_

DIRECTIONS

Look down. You will see some sentences that are not finished. Make up some words to finish the sentence. It can be long or short. Write the first thing you think of.

1. Most people are _Big_
2. The worst thing is _being punched. - socked in the mouth_
3. Mother always _cooks_
4. Boys are _fun to play with_
5. Girls are _wierd - except big girls like you_
6. Father is _fun to play_
7. The best thing is _ice-cream_
8. I am unhappy when _I get socked in the mouth_
9. Sometimes I am _wierd_
10. Mother is _a good mother_
11. Brothers or sisters can _be fun to play w/_
12. Sometimes I want to _play w/ somebody who's not home_
13. I am afraid of _the dark_
14. I hate _Italian food_
15. Some children are _fun to play w/_
16. When you hate somebody _you just walk away_
17. If I could _have a fridgidaire that had buttons - like if you wanted coke - you'd just push the button_
18. The trouble with parents _is when the whip you to smithereens - like black & blue_
19. It is best to be _good_
20. If you make a mistake _say the truth_
21. School is _boreing & dumb & stupid_
22. When somebody is unfair _you just walk away_
23. Most of all _you have fun_

FIGURE 13.4   Albert Doe's Sentence Completion Test

FIGURE 13.5 Albert Doe's Family Drawing

FIGURE 13.6 Albert Doe's Extra Drawing

stepparent but not doing so with the female figure suggests that he may still have some reservations about his stepmother as a mother figure (she is relatively new on the scene).

Albert asked to make an extra drawing. Figure 13.6 shows what he drew on the day following his doing the Draw-a-Person and other drawings. Again, he drew on the lower left-hand portion of the page. He drew an automobile. He exhibited some of his aggressive needs in drawing the gases emerging from the exhaust. Clearly, Albert seeks power, is assertive, and is showing a preadolescent interest in powerful vehicles, which is much more common today than in past generations. Playing with powerful automobiles in model form or with electric-powered cars is quite common for 7-, 8-, and 9-year-old youngsters.

Albert's Thematic Apperception Test

Albert was presented with seven cards of the Thematic Apperception Test. He was given the standard introductions, stated previously in this chapter. His responses were as follows:

Card Number 1. He's looking at an instrument and he's bored with the paper in it. His hands are on his head. He has paper under the instrument and it's on the desk. The end. (*What happened before what's going on in the picture?*) He started playing it but he got bored. (*Why did he begin to play?*) Because he thinks it would be fun. (*What will happen in the end?*) He broke it and he was sad that he couldn't play it anymore. (*Who wanted him to play?*) His mom. (*How did he feel about all of this?*) Real, real, real happy. (*Title?*) THE INSTRUMENT.

Card Number 3BM. The guy's dying—on his chair. He's got his nightgown on and his wife is already dead. (*What happened?*) He was real happy that his wife was alive but then she died. (*What happened to her?*) She died in her sleep. (*What happened to the man?*) He got real sick and died. It seems like all my stories are where they die. (*Title?*) THE WOMAN AND MAN WHO DIED.

Card Number 4. The guy is looking at something and the woman is holding him. (*What might he be looking at?*) Another person. There is a picture on the wall. The lady wants to kiss him. The end. (*What led up to this?*) The woman ran up to him. (*How did they know each other?*) They married each other. (*Tell me how the man feels about the woman.*) He's mad. She told a lie. (*What was that?*) That she loved him—but she didn't. (*What will happen in the end?*) He dies. (*What will happen to the lady?*) She got shot and she died. (*Who did this?*) A dumb old fartin' guy. (*Title?*) THE LOVING PEOPLE.

Card Number 6BM. There is a dining room table over there, and she's looking at it and she wished that she would have a good time . . . but she wasn't very hungry and the guy is looking at her. She's very sad. (*Why is this?*) Because she didn't get to go in. He thought that they wouldn't let her go in. That's why he's sad. But she wasn't very hungry. Then the guy got very, very mad 'cause she said that they wouldn't let her in. But then she told the truth and said that she wasn't very hungry, and he got very, very mad. (*How do the people know each other?*) That's the grandson and that's the grandma. (*Title?*) THE WOMAN WHO WASN'T HUNGRY.

Card Number 8BM. The boy is looking at something. The boy's on the bed. The guy has a pen or something. He's looking at his belly button and there's a light. The end. I'm not telling any more. The man is . . . the guy . . . the boy got really, really sick. The end. (*How did it end?*) The boy was alive and he went back home. (Pause.) In the beginning, they were happily and the boy got shot and he got wounded and he went to the hospital and the boy was getting sicker. His mother and dad were worried that he would die. He was safe and he was alive and he went back home and his Mom and Dad were glad that he was alive. (*How did the mother feel about the boy?*) I told you—happy, he was alive. (*Title?*) THE BOY WAS ALMOST DEAD.

Card Number 13MF. (Pause.) Well, the guy is crying because (pause) um, because his wife is dead and (long pause) she died in her sleep. (Long pause.) (*How does he feel about the wife?*) Sad, if she was still alive they would have really, really, really fun. (*How did the wife feel about him?*) Happy. (Long pause.) (*What happens to the man now?*) He dies too. (Long pause.) (*How does he die?*) He got shot. That's all. (*Title?*) THE WOMAN WHO DIDN'T GET TO LIVE LONG.

Card Number 17BM. Well, there's a rope and a guy is climbing it and he is naked and he's smiling at something. (Pause.) (*What else is there?*) Well, he's

QUADRANT ANALYSIS

NAME _Albert Doe_ DATE _10/21/88_

INTERPERSONAL ACTIVITY

1. Low level of aspiration
2. Demanding
3. Indiscriminately aggressive
4. Tends to expect the worst
5. Very challenging
6. Creative
7. Alternately impulsive & restrained
8. Jumpy

EARLY IDENTIFICATIONS
(FATHER)
1. Oral-Aggressive
2. Not particularly intellectual
3. Sometimes "mothers"
4. Not involved in details of child-rearing
5. Tempermental
6. Sometimes stable, sometimes not
7. A "doer"
8. Relates pretty well with children

(MOTHER)
1. Unable to see the inner needs of the child
2. Oral-Aggressive
3. Source of security
4. Not terribly nourishing
5. The motivator
6. Strong affection needs
7. More stable than the father
8. Trouble accomplishing things
9. Phobic

ANXIETY STRUCTURE

1. Poor school performance
2. Loss of attachments
3. Replacement of step-brother
4. Fear of future as dark
5. Believing what adults tell him
6. Knowing his own limits
7. Inadequacy of his physical size
8. Growing sexual interests
9. His own impulsive, angry thoughts & rage
10. Having family members angry at him
11. Embarrassed by creative needs
12. Father being killed

OUTLETS AND DEFENSES

1. Assertive
2. Angry openly
3. Oral dependent
4. Test limits
5. Shocks others
6. Early latency
7. Phobic
8. Expects failure
9. Pessimistic
10. Morbid preoccupation
11. Rich fantasy
12. Early depression
13. Displacement of fears to power objects (cars & motorcycles)

RECOMMENDATIONS

1. Test for diabetes
2. Cub scouts
3. Vocabulary flashcards
4. Own bank account & own bank at home
5. 4-6 weeks at camp this summer
6. Unrestricted positive regard from all adult family members
7. Behavior management to decelerate negative behaviors
8. Parent training techniques
9. Special reading material for parents
10. Emphasize the importance of being straightforward with him
11. Competitive swimming
12. A very regular, predictible schedule in all matters at both homes
13. Every effort by parents & teachers to be reassuring
14. Opportunity for creative activity
15. Sex education from the father
16. Male war games
17. Go-Kart
18. Set standards of discipline
19. Regular & consistent home-work times
20. A regular allowance
21. Special time with all parental figures - with listening
22. Prime adult make responsibility with stepfather confirmed & supported by the natural father
23. Efforts at social skill training by all parents with Albert
24. Re-evaluation at the end of sixth grade

FIGURE 13.7   Albert Doe's Quadrant Analysis Worksheet

strong, and he's got feet that are naked. (*What led up to all of this?*) Well, he heard a racket down on the first floor and he started to go down the first floor where his neighbor's on. (*What happened?*) There was this guy who had a gun and shot him. The end. (*Who is he smiling at?*) His wife. (*Why was he climbing with the rope?*) I told you! Because he heard something at the first floor. (*What did he hear?*) A guy with a gun. (Long pause.) (*Title?*) THE GUY WHO DIED.

These stories, which are rich with expressions of fear, wish, rage, and other responses that represent much of Albert's personality, confirm previously developed hypotheses. We can see in Albert a fairly demanding youngster with a low level of aspiration. His aggressiveness is almost indiscriminate. He is pessimistic and expects the worst, yet he is a creative youngster for his age.

The father figures are seen as persons who are in danger. Mixed feelings toward female figures are reflected in some of the stories. A growing awareness of sexuality, with concomitant embarrassment and unsureness, emerges. Albert repeatedly expressed fearfulness of loss of attachments, particularly in respect to the father possibly being killed. The seeming fear of the father being killed may represent some wish fulfillment, but it primarily appears to be fear of the loss of a positive figure. Pessimism and discouragement abound, and the conglomeration of fear and rage emerges in almost every story. Although Albert did very well and was quite creative, he seemed embarrassed when questioned.

Albert seemed to feel pleasure in shocking others as he presented his stories. There are indications that he may be approaching the preadolescent period somewhat earlier than expected. There are some signs that he struggles to contain his angry feelings, possibly predicting some early depression. The Thematic Apperception Test appears to be a rich source of material for describing Albert's personality.

Albert's Quadrant Analysis

Figure 13.7 presents Albert's quadrant analysis. As can be seen, the factors that were noted throughout the personality assessment are written in the appropriate quadrants. In some cases one could conceptualize some of the items under outlets and defenses as being either more appropriate or equally important for interpersonal activity. This is a matter of individual choice and judgment. The important thing is for the final report to represent Albert's personality in an understandable and meaningful way. In the next chapter, this quadrant analysis is used in the writing of the psychological report.

Developing and Presenting the Results and Recommendations

CHAPTER FOURTEEN

Constructing the Psychological Report

The result of the Basic Psychological Examination (BPE) should be a psychological report that is useful in advancing the best interests of the child. The psychological report can achieve a number of goals; the main goal is to present a realistic picture of the child. The report should describe the child in three general respects. First, the report should indicate *where the child has been.* It should indicate anything significant in the child's background or development that will help the reader understand what has brought the youngster to his or her present state of development. Significant elements of the family history, specific incidents in the child's life, medical history, indications of unusual psychological development, or any other special background factor should be included.

Second, the report should demonstrate *where the child is at the present time.* The formal test data and the personality analysis are the essential elements of this part of the report, although these may be expressed in terms of specific issues in the child's life. The presentation of the child in a realistic manner should give to the reader a picture of the child as he or she is likely to be known by anyone currently working with the youngster.

Third, the report provides *recommendations* that can be useful to those who are going to be in contact with the child or who are in a position to influence future growth, development, or rehabilitation. One might view the BPE and the resultant report as a navigational exercise: where the child has been, where the child is now, and what options exist for the child in the future.

Although not always possible, the report should attempt to answer most of the questions that were asked about the child and to address the issues that distress the child's parents. The report must communicate, to those who are in a position to help the child, all the information necessary, first, to understand the child and, second, to offer realistic opportunities to intervene in a positive manner.

STYLE AND FORMAT

Above all, the psychological report must communicate. Although most psychologists are very well educated, the quality of their writing skills varies. Fundamentals of clear communication should always be observed:

- Sentences should be short.
- Technical jargon should be avoided.
- No more should be written than is necessary to express the thought being presented.
- Material should not be repeated.
- Paragraphs should be relatively short, with only one concept presented per sentence.
- There should be a logical sequence in the presentation of material. The report should tell a story, beginning at the beginning and ending at the end.

Relatively few experienced professionals wonder about the quality of their usual reports. Almost anyone's technical reports can be improved, however. It is vital to keep in mind who will be receiving the report and whether they might be confused by complexities. Some of those who receive the report may have modest reading skills, and some will have little training in psychology. All of this should be considered in ensuring that the report communicates.

In almost every report, the same format can be used. By having a standardized format, the clinical child psychologist will begin to think in terms of the final report, from the very beginning of the BPE.

As previously noted, the report should tell a logical, direct story. The beginning should describe the reasons why the child is being seen, whereas the body of the report should present a thorough picture of what was done and what was found. The end of the report should answer questions and present recommendations. The good professional report is written throughout the assessment. From the time the psychologist first receives the intake information until the final report is done, the concept of the final report should be in the clinician's mind. In this way, meaningfulness, clarity, and completeness are more likely to characterize the report.

Conciseness is vital. Few reports have been written that could not have been shorter. It is neither practical nor meaningful for the psychologist to put everything that was found into the report. Key ideas and significant concepts should be emphasized, especially in the history and the personality description. Both of these areas seem to beg loquaciousness and redundancy. A report should awaken and keep the interest of the reader. The elements of a professional report that are recommended for the BPE are discussed in the following sections.

Heading

The heading of the psychological report should provide all of the basic information necessary to identify the youngster who is being examined. It should name the youngster's parents, state the youngster's address, and list the examination dates. This heading may be important for tracking the youngster through several examinations, for retrieving important information concerning the child and/or the family, or, in some instances, for legal purposes.

Introduction

The first paragraph or two of the report should clearly state how the child came to be examined. The significant persons involved and the route of referral should usually begin this paragraph. The introductory paragraph should also indicate something of the environmental press. The concerns of parents, the school staff, or other significant adults in the child's life should appear at this point. This is also a good place to list the questions that are to be answered by the BPE.

Background Factors

The background section should contain the traditional historical information that forms a part of most professional reports. The warning noted above should be heeded: This section should not be overwhelming. Only those elements that are important in understanding the child should be included. This section describes where the child has been; any previous examinations or evaluations should be summarized.

Examination Procedures

The examination procedures used in the BPE should be listed next. Abbreviations should not be used, since they may be unfamiliar to some readers.

Response to Evaluation

The next section should contain the clinical observations of the child. Here the clinician can describe how the child appears during the various phases of the examination. The experienced clinician may make observations of subtle behavior that can have considerable significance in understanding the child. This section should be relatively brief.

Intellectual Factors

The section describing intellectual factors is the first component of the report that describes actual testing procedures and findings. The objective results of intellectual evaluations should be presented, as well as subelements of the tests, where appropriate. This section may be short, medium, or long, depending on the significance of the results in respect to the child's situation.

The clinical child psychologist should do everything possible to reeducate teachers and parents concerning the description of intelligence. The IQ is not the desirable way to report intelligence. In this section, the clinician can help teachers and parents to understand that percentile, with reference to a specific normative group, is a much better way of understanding the youngster's intellect. The clinician may begin to make some statements as to how the youngster's functional intelligence relates to some of the difficulties that have appeared in the child's life.

Neuropsychological Status

A brief description of the neuropsychological tests given and their results belong in this section. The only reason for more than a sentence or two in this part of the report would be if the findings suggest any neuropsychological deficit; more extensive descriptions and implications may then be presented.

Achievement

Next, the child's functional potential in the academic setting can be demonstrated. Objective results should be presented in tabular form. Interpretation of the results and implications for the child's school life belong in this section.

Personality Factors

The quadrant analysis is presented last, with material listed under the appropriate subsections: interpersonal activity, early identifications, sources of anxiety, and outlets and defenses.

SUMMARY AND RECOMMENDATIONS

The report must contain a culmination of all of the work that has been done in the BPE. The busy professional, the puzzled parent, the pediatrician, or any other individual who reads the report should be able to find, on one or two pages, a summary of what has been done and the specifics as to what is recommended in the child's best interests. The experience and skill of the clinical child psychologist will be demonstrated in these two sections, first, in terms of summarizing very complex data and, second, in presenting practical recommendations to those involved in the child's life. (To the end of the chapter, "the clinical child psychologist" and "the psychologist" are used interchangeably.)

Summary

In most instances, the summary should consist of one or two paragraphs. This brevity proves to be difficult for some clinicians. Many reports contain extended repetitions of the report itself, which generally are not useful. The clinician should understand that everyone who receives the report will not read it thoroughly; some professionals have insufficient time or insufficient interest to peruse a 5- to 10-page report. The clinician must understand that the report should be flexible enough to communicate to as many of the adults in the child's life as possible, including those who seek a summary that briefly tells the whole story.

Some professionals prefer to read a summary and then go back and study the body of the report. A succinct summary helps such readers.

A good rule to follow in constructing a summary is to write about only those areas of the report that inform specifically about very significant elements of the child's psychological nature. Each major section of the BPE that reveals something of significance about the child should be represented by one sentence. Where the personality structure is complex or the results are convoluted, several sentences may be necessary.

The summary should be compiled so that the information leads to the section on recommendations. The reader should get a very concise picture of the child and the child's circumstances, and mentally pose questions such as, "So what?" or "Then what should we do?"

Recommendations

The recommendations made as a result of the BPE represent the usable product of the process. The recommendations should offer to all significant adults in the child's environment opportunities to enhance the youngster's development and to provide remedies for difficulties experienced by the child. The recommendations represent the keys to the youngster's future success, as well as to more integrated and satisfying family relationships. This issue, introduced in Chapter 13, is reemphasized here as a preparation for developing recommendations.

Recommendations should be keyed to the environmental presses presented during the intake process and aimed at resolving issues that are seen as problems by the parents, the school, the community, and the child. The clinical child psychologist has not only an opportunity but a duty to help all those who are involved in attacking these problems. The comprehensive psychological evaluation recommended in this book will generally produce information that can be used to enhance many elements of the child's function and development. It lies within the province of the skillful, experienced clinician to use this information to provide ideas as to how the significant adults who are involved with the child can be helpful.

There is no substitute for experience and skill in developing recommendations. The clinician must understand the child's growth and development, family structure, and the kinds of facilities available in the community. Before making recommendations for any case, the psychologist should consider a variety of factors. The following sections detail some of these factors.

Family Resources.   The clinician must understand what financial and time resources are available within the family. To ask a family of moderate income to support an expensive private school program may be unrealistic. Thus, during the intake process, the psychologist should learn about the family's resources.

The Child's Potential.   The clinician must always consider the youngster's capability. It is wise, particularly at the beginning of a remedial program, to make no recommendations that will tax the child to his or her limit. Early success is vital. The psychologist can help ensure this success by making recommendations that are well within the child's capabilities as they were measured during the assessment.

Community Opportunities.   The psychologist should consider remedial opportunities beyond those that he or she is able to control or deliver. To render appropriate professional service, the clinician ought to be familiar with the agencies and resources of the community, including treatment settings, remedial educational settings, medical facilities, and recreational opportunities. Knowing the availability of clubs and community centers, a zoo, a science center, and other learning opportunities within the community can help the clinician make recommendations.

Specifics for Significant Adult Figures.   It is of limited value to recommend generalities, such as suggesting that the adult figures in the child's life be more "accepting" or "tolerant." The clinician must strive to make specific recommendations as to what these adults should do, and how they can accomplish those tasks. Where necessary, specific training and/or reading materials can be suggested to increase the probability that the recommendations will be implemented.

Realistic Limits.   In many instances, the clinician will find that the family patterns and daily living routines are not in the best interests of the child being examined. Recommendations for a more stabilized pattern of life within the home may be very important, but the psychologist must take into consideration the realities of the family routine and structure.

Recommending consistency in eating and homework time may be very helpful for the child, but if both parents are on shift work, this may be impossible. The clinical child psychologist must be aware that recommendations that cannot be reasonably implemented can be iatrogenic or hurtful; they may provide additional frustration for the child or those who are implementing the recommendations.

Priorities.   The clinician should assign first priority to those issues that are most troublesome to the child and second priority to those that are most troublesome to the parents. The third priority is the child's current developmental stage. The psychologist should make recommendations that will be most easily implemented in respect to the child's capacities, needs, and opportunities, concurrent with that developmental stage.

Assets and Reinforcement.   The probabilities for early positive reinforcement of new behaviors, built on assets that the child already possesses, should be considered. Thus, the aggressive, competitive child who is in desperate need of vocabulary building should be challenged with word-card games, complete with rewards. A quiet child who is fearful of competition and who requires vocabulary building might be introduced to programmed instruction or computer-assisted instruction. Progress can be gauged by the child, in a quiet and sheltered setting. Again, the clinician's experience and creativity govern the range and variety of recommendations.

FOCUS OF RECOMMENDATIONS

Although each BPE is somewhat different, the focus of the recommendations tends to be the same. Almost all meaningful recommendations fall into three broad areas: recommendations *for the family, for the school,* and *for professional assistance.* The clinical child psychologist will have to let the situations of each child, each family, and each community guide the format of the recommendations. For the purpose of this volume, however, the trilogy noted above is followed.

Family Recommendations

Based on the material derived from the BPE, the clinician should choose recommendations that will help relieve uncomfortable symptoms and enhance the child's developmental course. Where the parents have been distanced from the child, recommendations to bring the family unit into closer communication and interaction are appropriate. Where discipline has been too harsh, recommendations to ease this pressure and to substitute better ways of eliminating unacceptable responses should be recommended.

Where the youngster has not had sufficient opportunity to develop self-esteem and mastery through independent activities, such activities should be recommended to the parents.

Some specific areas that are rich with potential to integrate the family and to help the child are described next.

Family Routine.   Most children who are having difficulty in school, or with behavior, function within a family where routine tends to be sporadic, unpredictable, and/or distressing to the child. Recommendations to establish a routine that becomes familiar to the child, within which the parents can provide security and support, include the life-style elements described in the following sections.

Bedtime.   Establishing a specific bedtime for the child, or one bedtime on school nights and another on weekend nights, can be helpful in cycling the child into a security-producing routine. The parent should also conduct activities before bedtime that are supportive and positive; these could include reading to the child, having a family conclave, or simply having some interactional playtime with the youngster.

Mealtimes.   Few families eat three meals a day together. The family meal can be an important time to give the child feelings of esteem and security. The psychologist should be aware of the family's mealtime schedules so that recommendations can be made to bring the family together for at least two meals a day. Recommendations should be made to help the parents ensure that this is a positive and reinforcing time for the child.

Television.   Evidence is accumulating to suggest that television watching may have negative impact on some children (Liebert & Sprafkin, 1988; Williams, 1986). For children with poor attention span, and for those having academic difficulty, it may be wise to recommend no television from 7 P.M. Sunday until 7 P.M. Friday. Many parents become almost terror stricken when such a recommendation is made; however, clinical experience suggests that within 3 or 4 days, parents often call and say, "It's unbelievable—he doesn't seem to miss it any more and enjoys playing outside."

The value of television as a teaching tool has probably been overrated. Until data can more clearly support such a claim, the negative aspects of television watching should be kept in mind by clinicians making recommendations to parents of children having problems, particularly academic difficulty.

Family Chores.   It is part of the American ethic that children participate in household chores. By doing things that the mother and the father do, a child can feel an important part of the family. Unfortunately, most children are handed the tasks that the parent would prefer not to do:

carrying out the garbage, cleaning up after the dog or the cat, and washing the bathroom floor. The clinical child psychologist should identify tasks assigned to the child, and suggest to the parents that odious or difficult tasks be shared with a parent to give a sense of cohesiveness and esteem to the child. The parents should be encouraged to provide chores that are somewhat prestigious so that the child may see these as rewarding rather than as an undesirable punishment-like responsibility. Preparing food, shopping, making repairs about the house, planning vacations, working with tools, and helping with cooking and baking are all tasks a child may approach positively if the parents are trained to present such activities in a positive manner.

For example, the psychologist might recommend that the parents teach the child to bake bread. Although many breads can be made from prepackaged ingredients, it can be a positive shared experience if the parent teaches the child to bake bread from ingredients available in almost every home.

Figure 14.1 presents a recipe for "Stephanie's Quick Bread." This is a simple, traditional white bread that can be easily baked by a child as young as 5, with the supervision of a parent. The result is several loaves of very good bread. This baking task will tend to enhance the child's sense of mastery and accomplishment, particularly if the task is undertaken with the cooperation of one or both parents.

Allowance.   The provision of an allowance should be routine. The child eventually has to face a world in which purchasing power is routine. The parents can help by teaching the child about money, earning, saving, and spending in accordance with the child's capacity to understand during the growing years.

Allowance may start as early as 5 years of age. Although allowance may be associated with chores and responsibilities, it is wise for the parent to provide a basic allowance simply because the child is living in an economic world and money is necessary to participate in this world. The older the child grows, the more the allowance should be associated with family participation and responsibility. There are no rigid rules, but good sense should prevail. The clinical child psychologist should examine the parents' attitudes about allowance and responsibility, and then make recommendations that would be helpful in the child's growth and development.

In relation to allowance, the child, even a young child, should have a secure place to keep his or her money. A bank with a combination lock or some other secure box will help the child have a sense of mastery and a sense of worth. In later years, the parents should help the child establish a bank account and to understand the value of saving and planning.

Guided Activities.   Consciously or not, parents guide their children's activities, particularly in the earlier years. The clinical child psychologist

STEPHANIE'S QUICK BREAD

1. Dissolve 3 packages yeast in 3 cups warm water.

2. Add 1/4 cup sugar or honey.

3. Add 5 cups flour and 5 teaspoons salt.

4. Beat hard with a spoon until batter is smooth.

5. Add another 4 or 5 cups flour and blend well.

6. Pour 5 tablespoons oil over the dough and knead in the bowl for 2 or 3 minutes. The dough will absorb most or all of the oil.

7. Cover the bowl and let the dough rise until doubled, about 45 minutes.

8. Punch down and turn out onto lightly floured board and knead slightly.

9. Shape into 2 large or 3 medium size loaves and place in buttered loaf pans.

10. Cover and let rise again until doubled, about 30 minutes.

11. Bake in 400° oven for 30 minutes, or until done.

FIGURE 14.1   A Formula for Baking Bread at Home

can help parents create situations that will be positive for the child. Some suggestions are described in the following sections.

Social Activities.   Participation in games, eating in restaurants, visiting other families, attending social functions, going to a circus or a fair, and other family activities provide opportunities for the child to understand behavior in relation to others. As the parent sets the model, the child is likely to follow. Family outings and other guided social activities can be an opportunity for the parents to provide the child with training in dealing with other people. This is particularly important for the child who has been phobic or shy. Gradually introducing social opportunities can be a way of resolving the child's fears.

Sports.   Western culture emphasizes the importance of sports. Children are encouraged to participate, and the child who knows nothing about a sport tends to be excluded. The parents should be guided by the clinical child psychologist in providing opportunities for the child to learn game rules and the positive aspects of physical activity and competition. In some instances, however, parents have provided an overstimulation of sporting activity for the youngster, which may be a source of distress. (The clinical child psychologist should explore this very carefully, being sure not to attempt to impart his or her values in this area.) Reasonable participation concordant with the child's developmental stage, physical skills, and emotional status should be recommended.

Peer Interaction.   Beginning at 2 years of age, the child is able to play with youngsters of a similar age, and seeks out such interactions. Where peer interaction has been a problem in the child's life, it is doubly important that the psychologist pay attention to what is happening and determine what might be done to create a more positive climate for the child to interact with others of a similar age. In the earlier years, visits with children, supervised by the parents, can be recommended. As the child moves up the developmental scale, having a special friendship, inviting school friends to a party, attending birthday parties of other children, and having the child invite one or two friends to family outings are all things that can be recommended to the parents to increase the child's socialization experience.

Independence Experiences.   For the younger child, visiting other children and going to parties are independence experiences. As the child grows, visits to relatives, going some places alone, and staying overnight with friends tends to increase independence striving. Beginning at about age 8, the child is ready for significant separation experiences. A well-established camp of good reputation is a way to introduce the child to his or her capability of "going it alone" and profiting from the experience. The camp should be carefully chosen. No matter who recommends the camp, the parents should personally talk to the parents of children who have attended the camp at an age similar to their child's. A series of positive reports generally supports the choice. No matter how favored the camp may be, if the parents receive a number of negative reports, this camp should be avoided. Being away from home can be either enhancing or traumatic. The clinician should help the parents decide the right time and the right place for such an independence experience.

Older children can profit from such experiences. As the child passes 11 and moves into the preadolescent/adolescent stage, the parent should be aware of specialty camps that provide unusual opportunities for children to make new friends and have new experiences.

Pets.   A pet can be a part of a routine the family establishes that can be helpful to the child. The child who has his or her "own" pet generally profits from such an experience. When it is possible for the family to have a pet, the parents should be guided in the choice of animal and the kind of responsibilities that the child, at his or her present age, can reasonably be expected to undertake. Again, the parents may be counseled that model setting is the best way for a child to learn responsibilities and routines.

Parental Attitudes and Interactions.   In many evaluations, the clinical child psychologist finds opportunity to make suggestions to the parents about changing their attitudes and their interaction with the child. Some parents keep at a distance from their children without realizing they are causing the child to believe that something is wrong or that the parent does not like the child. It may be the parents' own backgrounds and childhood experiences that dictate distance. Distance is not good for children, and the psychologist should encourage parents, wherever possible, to develop early attachments with the child (Bretherton & Waters, 1985). The following sections advise on some ways in which the psychologist can help parents to become closer to their children.

Positive Regard.   In some instances, it will be clear to the clinician that the parents limit the positive attitudes they demonstrate toward the child. It is very easy to raise children with 99% "don'ts" and only 1% "do's," but this is not good for children. Many parents are unaware that this is their general style. They should be encouraged to find opportunities to give the child regular positive regard.

Daily Interaction.   The parents should be encouraged to spend a small amount of time with the child every day in relatively meaningless interaction. Asking questions, playing games, and simply maintaining contact with the child can be very important in helping the child to establish a positive self-image and to feel a part of the family. Again, many families, busy as they are, tend to forget this, particularly when both parents work, and when there is a housekeeper, a relative, or a nanny in the home.

Discipline.   Most parents are concerned about discipline. The clinician will easily note during the intake process whether the parents are too harsh or too unstructured in respect to setting limits. Appropriate advice should be given during the interpretation to help the parents to create a climate with reasonable limits but without harshness that might damage the child's self-esteem or feelings of security.

Parental Interaction.   There is little that children do not know about their parents. Parents are often surprised when the clinical child psychologist presents an interpretation that describes the parental interaction, complete with details of the parents' behavior about which the parents thought the child was unaware. Children know when their parents fight, even though it is behind closed doors. The parents should be structured by the clinician to understand that children know almost everything that is going on. The importance of the parental interaction and its effect upon the child should be made an integral part of the interpretation and the recommendations to the parents.

Parental Training.   In making recommendations, the psychologist should help the parents to realize that there may be things that the parents should learn. Learning to deal with behavior problems, to decelerate negative responses in the child, to accelerate positive responses, and to interact more productively may require specific teaching materials. At the end of the interpretation, the clinician should provide the parents with literature that can show the parents things that they might do to help the child. Such literature often reassures the parents that some of the things they are doing are perfectly correct and helpful. Booklets, fact sheets, training guides, and other materials are available from private and governmental agencies. Appendix B provides a list of sources for such literature and materials.

The psychologist should have a supply of parent training literature available so that appropriate pamphlets can be provided to the parents at the time of the interpretation. Parents respond extremely well to being given materials that they can read between the interpretation of the results and any follow-up appointments. Not all parents are willing to do the reading or abide by the recommendations, but the psychologist has the responsibility to provide this training material to establish a basis for further discussion.

School Recommendations

Since very few maladjusted or disturbed children do well in school, this is an area that often requires recommendations. The scope of the recommendations is limited by the child's potential, the quality of the school opportunity, the parents' capacity to understand the recommendations and to cooperate, and the clinician's experience and knowledge. The following list includes a number of general areas under which recommendations can usually be made for improving school adaptation.

Remedial Work.   Where the tests indicate that a child is behind grade placement, remedial help should be recommended. To bring a child up to a level of function that is comfortable and competitive, the following procedures may be considered.

Professional Remedial Instruction.   In many communities, reading clinics or remedial clinics are available to provide children with individual and group instruction in the basics. Most of these clinics emphasize reading, since this subject is usually deficient when a child falls behind in school. The degree of sophistication of such clinics varies considerably, and the psychologist should visit these organizations to determine the quality and the style of services provided. Private services are relatively expensive, but if the family can afford such services, more immediate and more individual instruction is usually available than in nonprofit clinics.

Developmental Academic Services.   Some communities have schools that provide remedial services for children. The extent and quality of these services vary considerably from community to community. Where public school services are not available, junior colleges and universities may have remedial clinics where children can receive this kind of professional help. Again, to make such recommendations, the psychologist must know the community and the resources available.

Tutoring.   Traditionally, the child who falls behind is helped through tutoring. Sometimes tutoring is very effective, but at times it can be not only ineffective but iatrogenic. Much depends on the personality of the tutor and the interaction between the tutor and the child. Tutors who are unknown to the psychologist should not be recommended. Some effort should be made to assess the quality of the personal interaction likely to take place with a particular tutor. Tutoring may be the best way to bring the child up to speed academically, but the choice must be made carefully and monitored continually. The way the child feels about the tutor is often a good indicator as to whether the remedial procedure is working.

Peer Tutoring.   A movement in education during the past 40 years or so has been to provide as tutors to youngsters who are behind in their studies bright children who are slightly older than the student needing help. There are clear advantages to peer interaction, assuming that the older peer is sufficiently sensitive and supportive to provide a rewarding setting for the youngster who needs help. The psychologist can be very useful in assessing the peer tutor and deciding whether a good match is possible.

Parent Tutoring.   Parent tutoring can be helpful, but it can also lead to difficulties. The parent who is interested, sensitive, patient, and skillful can be an asset to the youngster having difficulty in school. This is particularly true with younger children who need such things as vocabulary building and basic arithmetic training. Using word cards, number cards, word and number games, and simple behavior management techniques, parents can do a great deal to build the child's basic skills. In complex instructional areas, this tutoring may not be as easy. If this method is to be recommended, the psychologist may wish to monitor the interaction to determine whether it is helpful.

Programmed Instruction and Computer-Assisted Instruction. Based on Skinnerian theories of reinforcement, programmed instruction and computer-assisted instruction are relatively modern techniques for allowing an individual to learn at his or her own pace. Material is presented, and a response is then required from the youngster, either in a workbook or on a computer screen. Once the youngster has made a response, the workbook or the screen provides the correct answer. If the child's response is correct, some kind of approval signal is given. If the child's response is incorrect, the correct response is provided or the child is encouraged to try again. Some programs "branch" and allow the child to move rapidly or slowly through remedial sections of the program. Research suggests that such programs are highly effective in remedial work. The psychologist who wishes to recommend such programs can write to a variety of publishers, such as those listed in Appendix A. Computer programs currently available are listed in a publication that can be ordered by writing to Educational Products Information Exchange (EPIE) Institute, P.O. Box 839, Watermill, NY 11976, or by calling (516) 283-4922.

Motivation and Responsibility. The further the child progresses academically and developmentally, the more the child should be involved in choosing what he or she will do and the amount of energy that will be expended in doing it. Although a third- or fourth-grade child can be "made" to do homework, forced study schedules are unlikely to be useful as youngsters approach adolescence. The wise parent will begin to create a positive attitude toward good work habits and good study habits early in the child's academic career. The psychologist will find that many parents have neglected to do this. Creating motivation and responsibility in youngsters is a difficult task. Some possible areas for recommendations include the following.

The Parental Model. Where the parents set the model for behavior, the child is more likely to follow. Certainly, expecting the child to behave in ways that are significantly different from the parents' style places an undue burden on the child. The psychologist must be aware of the parental values and life-style, and attempt wherever possible to fit recommendations for the child into that life-style. Where the child needs regularity, consistency, and application in a family where little exists, workable recommendations are hard to find. The parents may have to do some changing before success can be expected with the youngster. This change may have to be explained in some detail to the parents, or it may require a number of counseling sessions to convince the parents that setting a model is a first step in getting the child to be responsible and motivated.

The psychologist must be very careful to observe and assess the parents' true attitudes about recommendations. If the mother and father figures are not behind the program recommended, it is unlikely that the program will succeed.

School Attitudes.   Some schools require homework of very bright children who do not need to do regular homework, whereas other schools require no homework. Some children require the regularity and consistency of a homework schedule. It is the psychologist's job to assess the school's attitude and make recommendations that fit, as much as is practical, with this attitude. Where this is impossible, a great deal of work may be necessary to bring about compromise or consensus so that the recommendations for the child can go forward with some chance of success. Opposition from the school is never helpful. The clinician must bring to bear all skills possible to encourage the consensus or compromise.

In the event that a child has a relatively serious academic problem, a study habits program is probably going to be necessary. Figure 14.2 presents the Guaranteed Success Study Program, which was developed for youngsters just entering junior high school. It can be modified for younger children by changing the time sequences. This type of program should be acceptable to the parents, to the school, and to the child. One parent should supervise the program, using behavior management techniques, and providing or withholding rewards based on performance.

Behavior Management.   Behavior management, behavior modification, or token economy are systems for providing a scheduled series of reinforcements or rewards in response to accelerating acceptable activity on the part of the child. In some cases, the absence or deceleration of certain behaviors is rewarded. This technique has proven to be a very successful way of helping parents to help their children. The psychologist should be well aware of behavior management techniques and should have a variety of materials available to help the parents to conduct projects that increase positive behavior and decrease negative behavior. Appendix B provides a list of resources from which to obtain such materials.

School Contacts.   Although the psychologist may have contacted the school during the intake process to determine what needs existed on the part of the school for changes in the child's performance or behavior,

No two people study alike. Scientific research has suggested the ways in which different people can be successful in their academic work. Based on the previous psychological examinations which include evaluation of your intelligence, your personality, your special skills and your abilities, the following homework schedule will give you measurable success within a four to six-week period if it is applied exactly as recommended. The schedule is as follows:

    a.   Place. Homework must take place in the same setting each and every time it's done. A clear desk, facing unstimulating space (no pictures of naked girls directly in your line of vision). The chair should be fairly straight-backed, with a comfortable seat.

    b.   Time. All study should take place at the same time for each session. If you decide that you are going to study in the evening, begin at 7:00 o'clock each time. Do not split your studying time, part in the afternoon and part in the evening. This only works for children under the 7th grade.

        Each time you study, you should spend four sequences of 30 minutes each. Twenty-five minutes should be spent in studying, and then you should have a five-minute break. There should be four of these sequences, five times a week.

        The most efficient study schedule for you at this time in your life would be in the evening. Sunday through Thursday, a two-hour period, either 7:00 to 9:00, or 8:00 to 10:00, or something similar.

    c.   Conditions. The best study occurs in a quiet place, where no one is going to interrupt you with talking, questions, or phone calls. The door should be closed.

        Music is acceptable during studying. Rock and roll, and what have you seem to have no interfering effect with homework.

        Television, however, is absolutely destructive for any kind of studying. To get any kind of real results, television must be turned off from Sunday when studying starts, until Friday when you return from school. This means absolutely no television during that time.

        In order to make the studying most effective, you should acquire a kitchen timer, so that you can set your twenty-five minutes exactly, and when the bell rings, you should leave your room, drink a glass of milk, walk around or whatever for the five-minute break.

    d.   The sequence of studying. You will notice that teachers do not coordinate with each other, and they often load you on one day, and leave you empty on another. That should be their problem and not yours.

FIGURE 14.2 Guaranteed Success Study Program

The sequence of studying should be unequivocally and absolutely as follows:

1. The first studying task should be the hardest subject where an assignment is due tomorrow.

2. The second studying task should be the easier subjects where assignments are due tomorrow.

3. The third task should be difficult subjects where there is a long-range project or report due.

4. The next sequence should be easier subjects where there are long-range projects or reports.

5. When there is absolutely no homework, no projects, or no reports, you should then read ahead one chapter in your most difficult subjects.

6. When all of the above are taken care of, and there is absolutely no question in your mind that you are ahead at least one chapter in every subject, you should use the homework time to read for pleasure. Under no circumstances should you cancel your homework period because "everything is done".

    Once you have established these homework patterns, your work will improve measurably. At that time you should ask me for "Tricks of Testing". We can teach you some simple straightforward ways of taking tests that will improve your performance on any test that you take at least one letter grade. It is useless to teach this to you until your homework habits are established. As soon as you begin to see progress in school, let me know, and I will introduce you to the next step.

FIGURE 14.2 *(continued)*

follow-up is necessary. The parents should also be encouraged during the recommendation stage to maintain contact with the school and to demonstrate their concern and interest. Specific ways of interacting with the school include the following.

Contact with the Teacher and the Principal. Sometimes it is in the child's best interest for the psychologist to establish an ongoing interaction with the teacher and/or the principal of the child's school. This may be done through the modus operandi of delivering the report to the school. The complete report should not be sent to the school because academic institutions tend to make psychological reports part of the child's permanent record. When information is in the report that should not be in the school record, a "subreport" can be made in the form of a letter to the school.

The psychologist might wish to arrange a joint conference with the teacher and/or the principal and the parents. At this time all parties can discuss the recommendations and the parents' involvement. Teachers rarely see parents so thoroughly involved in helping their child; this conference may motivate school personnel to pay particular attention to the youngster and give more individual help.

School Visits.   The parents should be encouraged to take advantage of school visits, even though these tend to be *pro forma*. Because the psychologist has been involved, the teacher is likely to pay special attention to the visits from the child's parents. This is also a good way to maintain liaison, and to discuss whether difficulties are arising that were previously not apparent. The psychologist should, of course, direct the parents to report anything unusual that occurs during school visits.

Follow-Up.   In certain cases, the psychologist may want the parents' permission to telephone the teacher after a period of time to follow up on what has been happening in school. A careful clinical note should be made of this interaction, and a letter sent to the parents reporting what occurred. This is also a good way of monitoring the degree to which progress is being made by the child in the school.

Choice of a New School.   In some situations, it may be necessary for the child to enter a new school setting. The family may move, may choose an independent school, or may attempt to move the child to a public school other than the one attended at the time of the assessment.

Choosing a school for the youngster can be an interesting activity for the family. The United States Department of Education has researched this area and provides an interesting booklet to help parents choose a new school for their child (Weston, 1989). Figure 14.3 presents a checklist that can help parents in making this decision. The psychologist should be available for consultation when a new school is to be chosen.

Professional Recommendations

Many BPEs result in recommendations carried out entirely by the parents, the school, and the child. Little or no further professional activity is necessary. When dealing with children who are emotionally disturbed or with families in conflict, a wide range of professional interventions may be recommended. Some of the more common areas of professional assistance that can be rendered to the family are described next.

Family Therapy and Counseling.   The recommendations made by the clinical child psychologist may be sufficient to help the parents modify

Checklist

(Remove from
book and make
a photocopy for
each school you
consider.)
In looking at available schools, you may want to use the checklist below as a guide. During your school visit, you can confirm what you heard or read earlier. Once you select a school, you will want to doublecheck the admissions information you collected to make sure you meet all the requirements.

Curriculum

1. Thorough coverage of basic subjects?   ☐ Yes ☐ No

If no, which subjects are not covered completely?

2. A special focus or theme to the curriculum? ☐ Yes ☐ No

What is it?

3. Elective offerings (if appropriate)?

4. Extracurricular programs to enhance learning and character development?

Philosophy

5. Emphasis on a particular approach to teaching and learning?

6. Belief that every child can learn?   ☐ Yes ☐ No

7. Encouragement of attributes of good character?

☐ Yes ☐ No

*Important
Policies*

8. Discipline _____

9. Drugs _____

10. Homework, how much per subject?_____

11. Homework hotlines? ☐ Yes ☐ No

12. Tutoring? ☐ Yes ☐ No

If yes, by whom? _____

FIGURE 14.3   Checklist for Choosing a New School

13. Grades, feedback, and recognition: How often? _____

What type?_____

_____

14. Teacher opportunities and incentives?

_____

Proof of Results

15. Standardized test scores: Current _____ Past _____

16. Attendance rate: Students _____

Teachers_____

17. Graduation rate _____

18. How many leave school in a year? _____

Why?_____

19. Special achievements or honors for the school?

_____

School Resources

20. Staff backgrounds and qualifications _____

_____

_____

21. Library? ☐ Yes ☐ No

22. Classroom books for independent reading? ☐ Yes ☐ No

23. Auditorium or other meeting room? ☐ Yes ☐ No

24. Physical education facilities? ☐ Yes ☐ No

If yes, what type? If no, what alternatives?

_____

Parent and Community Involvement

25. Parent volunteers in school? ☐ Yes ☐ No

Doing what?_____

_____

26. Teachers enlist parent cooperation on home learning?

☐ Yes ☐ No

If yes, how?_____

_____

FIGURE 14.3 (continued)

27. Other community members involved in school?

☐ Yes   ☐ No

28. Partnerships with local businesses or other institutions?

_____

_____

Reputation

29. Views of parents with children in the school

_____

_____

_____

30. Views of friends and neighbors

_____

_____

_____

31. Views of community leaders

_____

_____

_____

Special Questions for Private and Church-Affiliated Schools

Financial obligations, including

32. Tuition? $_____

33. Other fees? $_____

34. Uniforms?   ☐ Yes   ☐ No

35. Book purchases?   ☐ Yes   ☐ No

36. Required participation in fundraising?   ☐ Yes   ☐ No

Financial assistance, including

37. Scholarships up to what percent of tuition? _____

38. Loans?_____

39. Reduced fees if more than one child enrolls?_____

40. State aid available to families?_____

41. Apply how and when?_____

FIGURE 14.3 (*continued*)

Other

42. School's age and financial status?

43. Religious instruction and activities?

Admissions Requirements and Procedures

For a public, church-affiliated, or other private school of choice

44. List of materials to submit (application form, transcript, test scores, references, etc.)

45. Interview required?   ☐ Yes   ☐ No
Date _____   Time _____
46. Date school will decide? _____
47. How will school select students?

For other public schools

48. Borders of the attendance area the school usually serves?

49. Does State law give you a right to transfer your child to another public school?   ☐ Yes   ☐ No
50. Tuition or other charges for transferring students? $ _____

51. Facts considered important in deciding whether to grant a request for a transfer?

52. When will a decision be made on transfer requests? _____

53. Names of district officials who can permit a child to transfer to a school outside that child's attendance area

FIGURE 14.3 (*continued*)

their interaction with the child. In some cases, although a comprehensive psychological assessment may provide new and important information about the child and the child's condition, parents may have powerful and painful resistance to the information. The greater the impact upon individuals, the more strenuously it is likely to be resisted (Newcomb, 1965).

Particularly in families in which the children exhibit conduct disorders, when the parents agree to be counseled concerning marital discord or interaction with the child, considerable improvement occurs in the youngster's response (Dadds, Schwartz, & Sanders, 1987). The frequency of parental counseling or family therapy, as well as the number of family members participating in the procedure, depends on the circumstances and the psychologist's judgment in this matter.

Psychotherapy. Some clinicians feel that psychotherapy for young children is relatively ineffective, because the primary goal of psychotherapy is independence. Very few children can become independent within the context of psychotherapy and carry this trait into their home and school lives. Others believe that when the child shows significant emotional disturbance, play therapy or activity group therapy with other children is helpful. With children between 8 and 17, in particular, intervention is important for the child who shows depression or hopelessness (Kashani, Reid, & Rosenberg, 1989).

When recommending psychotherapy for a youngster, it is extremely important to try to enlist the youngster's participation in the process, even though this may take some specific counseling by the psychologist before the psychotherapy starts. The need for this kind of intervention should be presented less as a "treatment" and more as a learning opportunity to make more friends and be more comfortable both at home and in school. The more the clinician focuses on psychopathology, the less immediate results can be expected (Wedell, Parducci, & Lane, 1990). The more volitional the child's involvement, the more likely it is that success will occur in the psychotherapy with the child (Noll & Segull, 1982).

Parent Training. During the past three decades there has been a strong movement to develop training for parents. This training focuses on ages and stages of development in the child, the needs of children at various ages, appropriate forms of discipline and control, and ways of building a child's self-esteem. The growth of the parent effectiveness training movement testifies not only to its popularity but also to its probable effectiveness. Many clinical child psychologists provide parent training groups in which parents of children who exhibit various disorders may meet together, learn how to work with their youngsters, and share common concerns. Whether the parent is seen in this kind of quasi-therapeutic setting depends on the philosophy and the clinical intuition of the psychologist.

Behavior Management Training. Sometimes referred to as behavior modification, the application of principles of learning to the modification of a child's behavior is accepted as an effective form of treatment. There is a double satisfaction in that the youngster's behavior changes and the parents feel that they have been instrumental in creating a positive situation (Chadez & Nurius, 1987).

There are many forms of behavior modification. Sometimes this form of management is taught in parent effectiveness training classes. The psychologist uses his or her clinical judgment to decide whether to help the parents develop and execute a variety of behavior management plans to deal with negative behavior that the child exhibits, or to create a more positive response from the child.

Social Modeling Training. The research suggests that youngsters who withdraw from social interaction have increasingly more problems as they develop (Rao, Moely, & Lockman, 1987; Serna, Shumaker, Hazel, & Sheldon, 1986; Wierzibicki & McCabe, 1988). Children aged 7, and in some cases younger, can be given social problem-solving training. Follow-up study suggests that withdrawal is reversed and later pathology is decreased when youngsters have such training. This training may be offered by the clinical child psychologist, or a referral may be made to a community mental health center or a university where social modeling training is available. Most of the methods use a classroom-type situation in which the children participate in lessons and exercises concerned with understanding feelings, recognizing the growth of problems, generating solutions, and evaluating consequences (Yu, Harris, Solovitz, & Franklin, 1986).

Medical Treatment. Many children who are seen by the clinical child psychologist are also under the care of a physician, either a pediatrician or, because the youngster is learning disabled, a specialist (Rourke, 1988). Many medications are available for children who suffer behavioral problems, central nervous system deficits, depression, agitation, and other symptoms that are distressing to adults in the child's environment (Campbell, Green, & Deutsch, 1985). The effectiveness of medications, particularly for youngsters who are "hyperactive," is a matter of some controversy. Some clinicians believe such medication to be effective, whereas others cite research that suggests that the medication not only is ineffective but also may interfere with the child's learning and development (Hinshaw, Buhrmester, & Heller, 1989; Hinshaw, Henker, Wahlen, Erhardt, & Dunnington, 1989).

The clinical child psychologist must always keep as positive a relationship as possible with the youngster's physicians. Consultation, reports, and sharing of research reprints can create an atmosphere of cooperation. When medication is to be used, the psychologist should offer objective procedures for tracking the effects of the medication. If there is no significant effect after

3 or 4 weeks, this issue should be discussed with the physician and the parents. The psychologist may wish to use standard behavioral rating scales to evaluate the changes or may wish to rely on clinical evaluation of the reports of parents and teachers. When medication is used over a long-range period, tracking with standard measures of intellectual capacity and neuropsychological response should be recommended in order to determine any objective changes that may occur as a result of the use of the medication.

Residential Treatment Care.   When a child is so disturbed that the parents are helpless or feel hopeless about being able to cope with the youngster, a residential treatment placement may be indicated. Many more such facilities are available for adolescents than for younger children. When such a situation occurs with a child or an adolescent, the clinical child psychologist can be extremely helpful by utilizing the BPE to guide the choice of placement and the kinds of treatment that are most likely to facilitate the youngster's return to a stable status and to the family.

Reevaluation and Tracking.   If the youngster shows significant behavioral, emotional, or academic difficulties, the clinical child psychologist may recommend a reevaluation at some future time. Reevaluations are best conducted after the child reaches a "next stage" in development. Thus, a child evaluated at age 5 should probably be reevaluated at the end of the first year of school. A 6- or 7-year-old who is evaluated during the first or second grade should probably be reevaluated at the end of either the fourth or the sixth grade, depending on whether significant academic problems were a part of the difficulty that brought about the first BPE. The more school problems are involved, the more likely it is that the child should be reevaluated before the fourth grade and before the seventh grade. Where the problems are primarily behavioral, consultation with the parents and brief contacts with the child may be sufficient to track progress and to modify the original recommendations.

Second Opinions.   Parents may have some difficulty accepting the results of the BPE. The clinical child psychologist should always strongly encourage the parents to seek a second opinion. Some parents may wish to choose a professional who would be willing to receive a report of the BPE before rendering the second opinion; others may prefer to take the child to a professional who has no access to the original BPE so that this second opinion will be free from any influence that might be exerted by the first clinician. These situations are relatively rare; however, the psychologist should be prepared to encourage such a procedure in the best interests of the child.

ALBERT'S PSYCHOLOGICAL REPORT

As a demonstration of how the report is actually constructed, the material that has been previously presented from the BPE of Albert is brought together to form the basis of a psychological report. To follow the sequence used to construct this report, the reader is referred to the information about Albert that was presented in chapter 8. In particular, the reader can see the sources of the report by reviewing the previous figures that present the test responses and test results of Albert's BPE. Albert's BPE report is presented on pages 224–231.

The psychological report does not complete the BPE. The information must be conveyed to the parents. The clinical child psychologist must make every effort to help the parents understand the results of the examination, and to implement those recommendations that seem appropriate to the parents. It should be noted that a considerable number of recommendations were made. There is no way for the psychologist to know in advance which recommendations are likely to be most easily implemented by the parents. The philosophy of the psychologist should be that a sufficient number of recommendations ought to be made so that the parents have some choice in this matter. The manner in which the interpretation is given to the parents is the subject of the next chapter.

PSYCHOLOGICAL REPORT

OCTOBER 20, 1988

NAME: Doe, Albert

DATES OF
EXAMINATIONS: 9/20, 10/17,
10/18, 10/19,
11/09, 11/23,
1988

ADDRESS: 1651 Biltmore Road
Winston, Florida 33601
(Mother)

TELEPHONE: (M) 661-3121
(F) 407/219-3664

BIRTHDATE: 7/22/81

AGE: 7-2

EDUCATION: 2.2

SCHOOL: WILLOW ELEM.

REFERRAL

Albert is referred originally by his father, a detective with the Grogan County
sheriff's office. The father initially states that Albert is not doing well in
school. Albert has both behavioral problems and problems completing his
work. The father has been told that the child may be "hyperactive" or may
have a "learning disability."

The parents are divorced, but both the natural mother and the natural
father agree that psychological evaluation is necessary. Both parents have
remarried. A fairly positive relationship seems to exist among the parents and
the stepparents. Albert's mother has recently given birth to a half brother.

On interview, attended by both natural parents and both stepparents, they
agreed that they would like help in answering the following questions:

1. Is Albert hyperactive?
2. Is he learning disabled or abnormal in any other way?
3. What can the parents do to help him in his adjustment?
4. How can Albert's attention span be improved?

BACKGROUND FACTORS

The mother, Jane Smith, is a 32-year-old executive secretary with a high
school education. She reports herself to be in good health. In describing her
personality, she says that she likes it best when Albert is on his good behavior. She tries to be fair and to correct him constructively. She married Bill, a
29-year-old insurance executive with 14 years of education. He is in good
health and describes himself as "easygoing." The stepfather and the natural
father know each other and seem to get along pretty well. The father, Jack, is

a 38-year-old detective. He has an associate's degree in criminal justice. He describes himself as somewhat stern. He believes he has a good time when he sees Albert. They play and laugh a lot. The stepfather is somewhat quieter with Albert, enjoying T.V. with the boy, and helping him with his homework.

The stepmother is relatively new on the scene. Mary Doe is a 31-year-old correctional officer with a high school education. She admits to being short-tempered, but believes herself to be "honest."

The natural mother appeared to be a person who very much wanted to help. The natural father seemed traditional, fairly dominant but flexible. The stepmother was uncomfortable in the situation, but this may well be because she is the newest parent. The stepfather seemed relatively quiet and pleasant. All of them seemed anxious to participate in helping the youngster.

The half brother is almost 1 year old. They described Albert as having no problems with the half brother, and they believe he loves him very much. Albert sees his stepgrandparents and his paternal grandparents on a fairly regular basis. He seems to get on well with them. He has regular contact with a maternal aunt and her children, his cousins. They all get on fairly well according to the reports presented during the history.

The mother has formal custody of Albert, but the families are very comfortable and relaxed about visitation. The parents divorced when Albert was just under 2 1/2. The mother remarried when Albert was about 4, and the father remarried when he was 6.

The parents and stepparents presented an almost ideal cooperative situation, considering the difficulties experienced by many children of divorce. The father said that he sees Albert almost every week, and they take fishing trips together throughout the year.

GROWTH AND DEVELOPMENTAL FACTORS

Albert weighed 8 pounds, 4 ounces at birth. He seemed to have developed over the first year in a normal way. Toilet training took place between 1 and 1 1/2. The parents were satisfied with his first year's development and with the developmental milestones between ages 2 and 5.

His pediatrician is Dr. William Jason of Winston. Albert broke his clavicle at age 2. He has sinus problems and nosebleeds. He had a bad case of chicken pox. He used to complain of aches and pains, but this stopped last year.

Neuropsychological deficits are denied. He does have occasional headaches. In the father's hereditary chain there is redheadedness, and on the mother's side there are twins. Mixed cerebral dominance and left-handedness are denied.

He attended preschool and did well. First grade was at the Willow Elementary School, and he was said to be hyperactive. He did well academically. Pretty much the same performance has been described, to date, in the second grade.

He makes friends easily and he tends to be a follower. He has his own room at home and puts up posters. He has had friends sleep over with him, but he has not slept over with his friends. Albert enjoys movies, television, soccer, and riding his skateboard. He likes to collect stickers. He is somewhat of a picky eater. The mother describes him as loving his half brother. When father disciplines him, he uses deprivation. The mother uses deprivations and occasionally spanks him. Albert has been to day camp and he enjoys it. Albert had an allowance, but this has been stopped. During the school year his bed time is 8:30 and he gets up about 6:30. He has chores that include keeping his room, making his bed, dusting, and sweeping.

Albert has always sucked his thumb. He has wet the bed on and off since the age of about 3. He has occasional tantrums. He is generally uncooperative and has a high energy level. The parents feel he lacks self-confidence and is overly sensitive.

His performance is said to be below his potential, he is frequently socially embarrassing, his emotional behavior is quite variable, and he seems to experience irritability without apparent cause. He creates war in the family and doesn't seem to learn from experience. He is impulsive and stubborn, cannot complete projects, has trouble following directions, but is extremely kind to small animals and those less fortunate than himself.

EXAMINATION PROCEDURES

Peabody Picture Vocabulary Test–Form L, Wechsler Intelligence Scale for Children–Revised, Graham–Kendall Memory for Designs Test, Torque Test of Cerebral Laterality (repeated), Hand Dynamometer, Metropolitan Achievement Test–Primer, Metropolitan Achievement Test–Primary I, Thematic Apperception Test, House–Tree Test, Draw-a-Person Test, Child Sentence Completion Test, Family Drawing, History, Interview, and Clinical Observations.

RESPONSE TO EVALUATION

Albert is a tall youngster for his age. He has blonde hair and blue eyes. Several front teeth are missing. He sucked his thumb periodically throughout the examination. He speaks in a high, crackly voice. Hearing is within normal limits. During the course of the assessment, he drank a lot of liquids.

He is a friendly youngster but seems immature for his age. His ability to cooperate varied considerably. When his agitation and jumpiness was tolerated, he did better. When limits were set, he would tend to regress and come close to tears. Clearly, his confidence is poor and he gets upset easily. He seems to be a needful child who requires concrete evidence of approval and acceptance.

RESULTS OF EVALUATION

Intellectual Factors

Objective results of the Wechsler Intelligence Scale for Children–Revised (WISC-R) were as follows:

Factor	Percentile
Verbal Scale	84th
Performance Scale	96th
Full Scale	94th

The above results indicate that Albert falls in the superior range of intellectual capacity. His poorest performance, which is well within the average range, was on Vocabulary and Digit Span Subtests. This suggests that he is having some difficulty with immediate memory and expressive language skills.

On the Peabody Picture Vocabulary Test, Albert's performance was average, falling in the 50th percentile. This is rather strange in view of his excellent results on the WISC-R. This suggests that there is a good bit of "on and off" or distractibility which influences the quality of his intellectual performance.

Neuropsychological Factors

This youngster is able to pull between 11 and 12 kilograms with the right hand, and between 11 and 13 with the left hand. He seems to be right-handed, but this information suggests that there is a lack of development in the sensory–motor strips concurrent with his lateral dominance. On the Torque Test, he was found to be Type O on both trials.

On the Memory for Designs, he achieved a raw score of 3 and a difference score of 1. This would suggest that there are some visual–motor anomalies, but they are not inconsistent with his age and development.

Achievement Factors

Here again we found on-and-off behavior. He was given two forms of the Metropolitan: the Primer and the Primary I. Since he is in the second grade, the Primary I will apply, and the results are as follows:

Factor	Grade Equivalent	Percentile (Fall of Grade 2)
Reading	1.9	38th
Mathematics	2.3	52nd
Language	2.1	46th

The above results show that he is within acceptable limits for his present grade placement. He was not able to do the vocabulary requirements in reading. He had great trouble in literal–specific and inferential–specific reading, as well as in inferential–global reading. This may well reflect his difficulty in vocabulary.

Personality Factors

Interpersonal Activity. Young Albert appears to be a demanding, active, jumpy youngster. He is very challenging as he becomes comfortable. His aggressiveness seems indiscriminate. As one gets to know Albert, one finds that beneath the facade of aggressiveness is a great fear of setting goals for himself and a very low level of aspiration. In facing new things, he expects the worst.

Early Identifications. Albert's primary identification is with a father figure. The unconscious picture of the father, as expressed in projective techniques, is that of an oral–aggressive, temperamental person. The father is seen as a person who is somewhat anti-intellectual, and exceedingly practical and aggressive. In spite of this, the father is seen as sometimes stepping in and mothering the child in place of the mother. The father is seen as a person who has never been strongly invested in the details of child rearing.

The mother figure is the love object. The unconscious picture from the projective techniques is that of a person unable to see the inner needs of the child. She can be oral–aggressive. She is a person who is very security minded. Apparently, she has had great difficulty in being spontaneously nourishing, perhaps because she herself had difficulty in establishing a warm and nourishing relationship with her own mother. The mother is clearly the motivator and the setter of goals in the family. She is seen as an individual who has very strong affection needs.

Anxiety Structure. The deepest sources of anxiety for Albert relate to the fractured marriage, as they do in all children of divorce. He is very fearful of the loss of attachments. He feels that everyone in the family is angry at him and that most difficulties are his fault. He is very discouraged. He feels he will be replaced by his half brother.

He is made very anxious by his poor school performance. He finds that he believes what adults tell him, and then finds that they do not tell him the truth. He is very unsure of the limits in his environment and what is expected of him. He is quite embarrassed by his creative interests and needs.

His sexual interest is quite high for his age, probably based on his good intellect. He is very embarrassed and frightened of these thoughts and feelings. He is very fearful of his own anger.

Outlets and Defenses. Albert rids himself of intolerable tension through his assertive manner. He tests limits to try to understand new environments. He tries to elicit the degree of anger held toward him by others by shocking them. He is very pessimistic about his life and about the future. He has relatively few intellectual outlets and defenses.

His more labile defenses include outbursts of anger, strong oral depend-ency, and strong phobic reactions when he feels guilty. He is desperately trying to hold his anger inward and is beginning to show the signs of early depression. He tries to displace some of his angry feelings to power objects, such as his fantasies of powerful vehicles. He is moving into early latency and seeks the company of those his own age to express his feelings and seek approval.

SUMMARY AND RECOMMENDATIONS

Psychological evaluation of Albert Doe indicates that he is a youngster of Superior intellectual capacity and potentially Very Superior function. At the present time, his intellect varies considerably. It is suspected that part of this variability results from a neuropsychological basis because of the developmental changes now occurring, and part of it is because of the considerable stress under which he operates. He is sometimes able to pro-duce superior functional productivity. At other times he spoils his own responses.

The personality structure is that of an extremely tense, pressured young-ster who is suffering the aftermath of being a member of a fractured family. His parental models have not been sufficient and his environment has not been enriched enough for his strong intellectual and creative needs. He blames himself for his failures and expects little in the future. The following recommendations would seem appropriate for this youngster.

The Father's Role

The father has a limited amount of time with Albert. The focus of his attention during this time should be in the following areas:

1. Provide sex education. Appropriate material will be given.
2. Interact competitively at Albert's level. Games of cards, checkers, and dominoes.
3. Take Albert on regular visits to the go-kart track.
4. Arrange to have special time with Albert, and to listen to him. Give advice rarely.
5. Provide Albert with unrestricted positive regard.
6. Give behavior management techniques, when necessary to shape Albert's behavior. Emphasize the positive and ignore the negative.
7. Make specific expectations for Albert's academic work, behavior, and productivity.
8. Always tell the truth to Albert.
9. When Albert is visiting, aim for a specific schedule and predictable events to make Albert feel more comfortable.

10. Try to give Albert a great deal of assurance in all of his creative efforts.
11. Create a sense of territoriality by use of a calendar, room furniture, or other things so that there is some reasonable equivalence or similarity in Albert's rooms in the two households.

The Stepfather's Role

The stepfather can be a very important adult in Albert's life. He is not a replacement for the father, but he can provide some of the security and confidence that Albert so badly needs. He can be particularly helpful in the following ways:

1. Reinforce the sex education given by the father, and appropriate materials will be provided.
2. Like the father, provide games of competition.
3. Set the limits within the home, and the disciplinary measures that are necessary.
4. Set the homework schedule and ensure that this schedule is followed.
5. Provide a regular allowance on Monday mornings for Albert.
6. Provide special time for Albert to listen and be interested in Albert's everyday activities.
7. Like the father, provide a lot of reassurance and positive regard.
8. Use behavior management to shape Albert's behavior.

The Mother's Role

The mother should be the provider of security, warmth, and philosophy of life. Specifically, the mother should do the following to help Albert:

1. Provide unrestricted positive regard.
2. Offer reassurance at every opportunity.
3. Avoid discipline whenever possible except as father's "lieutenant."
4. Always tell the truth to Albert.
5. Provide a very regular schedule for him in all significant matters.
6. Provide Albert with an opportunity for creative activity.
7. Try not to take the father role, allowing the father and stepfather to be the masculine images and setters of limits.

The Stepmother's Role

The stepmother is the most serious "interloper" in Albert's life. Every child has a fantasy of the parents reuniting. When one parent remarries, this myth and hope is pretty well dashed, and when the second parent remarries, the last stepparent holds the role of the "clincher." The stepmother could be most helpful if she is willing to do the following:

1. Provide Albert with as much positive regard as possible.
2. Avoid all discipline and criticism.
3. Understand the nature of behavioral management and use it whenever possible.
4. Help the father to arrange a fairly rigid schedule that Albert can count on whenever he visits.
5. Give Albert as much reassurance as possible.

GENERAL RECOMMENDATIONS

The following recommendations should be acceptable to all parties. When this is not so, some negotiation should take place to make sure that all parties understand the implications of either fulfilling the recommendations or rejecting them.

1. Albert should have an evaluation for the possibility of early diabetes. His excessive drinking of water should be checked out by a physician.
2. Albert should be entered into the Cub Scouts as soon as possible. This kind of activity is likely to be helpful for him.
3. Albert should be entered into competitive swimming as soon as a facility is found. Some programs operate year-round and some start in the spring.
4. Albert should have 4–6 weeks of camp next summer.
5. He should have a bank in his home of residence where he can keep his money privately.
6. Any of the parents who feel they have run into a difficulty should be willing to accept developmental counseling for parents by a professional.
7. The parents should read the reading materials provided.
8. It would be helpful for Albert to be reevaluated at the end of the sixth grade.

Prognosis is guarded. This is a complex and difficult situation for Albert. There are four parental figures and a new baby. The success of the program will depend on the capabilities and the willingness of all parental parties to cooperate.

Theodore H. Blau, Ph.D.

CHAPTER FIFTEEN

Interpretation of Results

The results of the Basic Psychological Examination (BPE) should be interpreted directly to the child's parents and/or to other significant adults who shepherd the child's development. The direct oral presentation of the results to the parents can achieve a number of goals, as discussed in the following sections.

GOALS AND OBJECTIVES

Clear Transfer of Information

Meeting directly with the parents and giving them the results of the BPE is very important to ensure that they understand what was done, what was found, and what is recommended. No matter how clear a written report may be, there is no way to be sure that the parents read the report and comprehend it. By scheduling an interpretation session, the clinical child psychologist has an opportunity to present in a holistic manner the entire process and its outcome. During the presentation, the parents can be encouraged to ask questions, explore unclear areas in depth, and add commentary. Also, the clinician can observe the parents and determine whether they have any difficulties in accepting the results. Their understanding and acceptance can be helpful when it comes time to encourage the parents to participate in the implementation of recommendations.

Bonding Significant Adults to Implementation

Critical to the BPE is the bonding of the significant adults in the child's life to the process. By having the parents begin the process during the intake procedures and then hear the results at the end, the psychologist creates a total information loop. By the time the interpretation session is scheduled, the clinician should have done everything possible to include the parents, and to indicate that everybody is working together in the child's best interests.

The manner in which the psychologist makes the interpretation can enhance this bonding. Using the concept of "we" in describing how the BPE was conducted and, in particular, how the information can be used by following the recommendations, can help in this process. The psychologist must, of course, be committed to the concept that an alliance has been formed. Should the clinician develop antagonisms or distance from the parents during the course of the BPE, this bonding that is so necessary to carry out recommendations may not occur.

Provide Resources to Support Implementation

Simply presenting results and recommendations to the parents may be overwhelming to them. In giving a direct oral interpretation, the psychologist can indicate that he or she not only has conducted the BPE, but is available to provide continuing guidance and support. During the interpretation, the clinician can also be constantly aware of any distress that the parents may show concerning the results or the recommendations. Encouragement, support, and availability can be indicated during the process, encouraging the parents to take a positive attitude toward the entire process.

Reinforcement of What Has Been Done

It is vital that the clinical child psychologist understand that literally no parent has done everything wrong and that no school has been totally inadequate for a child. Certain things have been done well and in the child's best interests. Although a statement to this effect may not appear in the formal written report, the interpretation session is a time for the clinician to point out, particularly to the parents, that many things have been "done right." Almost every parent who brings a child for examination has doubts and fears as to the quality of his or her parenting. Whether these doubts are very obvious and expressed or simply implied, the psychologist should be aware that the interpretation session is the time to assuage the parents' unrealistic fears. It is a time to give positive reinforcement for those things that have helped the child in his or her development. It is also a time to make positive statements about things that are being done correctly in school. An interpretation presentation that includes as much positive reinforcement as possible can lay the groundwork for parents and teachers to continue doing those things that are helpful in implementing additional recommendations in the child's best interests.

THE FIRST INTERPRETATION SESSION

The clinician should allow sufficient time before the first interpretation session to analyze the test data carefully and to construct the written report properly. The interpretation to the parents should never be given before the report is completed. Once the report is written, the psychologist can review the report from the perspective of all the available material and make any final changes to ensure correctness.

Two hours should be allowed on the clinician's schedule for the first interpretation. Although the presentation may take only 1 hr, 15 min, the parents may have questions or concerns that will require the additional time.

The psychologist can expect that the parents and/or others who attend the interpretation are likely to be nervous. Every effort should be made to start the appointment on time to avoid increasing the participants' nervousness through delay.

The first interpretation session should be put on audiotape. The clinician should explain to the participants that so much information is to be presented that the tape will allow them to review what has been said as they consider the report and the recommendations later. This tape should be used by the parents and other significant adults in a family setting to discuss what has been found and to make plans for implementation and integration of the results.

Another reason for taping the session is that when the parents play the tape, probably several times, they are likely to develop questions that require some clarification. This is also the reason why the interpretation is given in at least two sessions. The parents should be told that the tape is theirs, and that they may wish to listen to it in the future as other questions or difficulties arise. Parents report that this procedure is extremely useful in helping them to focus their attention on the critical aspects of their youngster's development and how best to participate in future growth.

The first interpretation session should begin with a review by the clinician of the reasons why the youngster was brought in, and the goals or purposes of the BPE. The parents should be encouraged to relax and to listen to the entire presentation. The parents should be reassured that there will be time to discuss the results, not only during the first session, but in great depth during the second session after they have been given all of the results as well as time to review these results on the tape.

The clinician should follow the written report quite closely, beginning with the history and background, highlighting the questions that were asked at the beginning, and focusing on the outcomes that were expected. The child's history and the parents' involvement should then be reviewed briefly. The greatest amount of time should be spent in presenting the results of the BPE. The clinician should describe the tests that were given and focus on the results in terms that the parents are likely to understand.

After describing the youngster's intelligence, neuropsychological status, academic factors, and personality, the clinician should carefully and thoroughly summarize and make the recommendations. Each psychologist develops his or her own style for giving the recommendations. It is probably unwise to simply read the report to the parents; they can do this at their leisure. Each significant element of the BPE should be explained with appropriate metaphors or analogies. When possible, the findings should be associated with behavior that has been described during the intake process.

The clinician should end the presentation by reassuring the parents that there will be plenty of time for questions and that the most pressing ones will be addressed right then and there. Once the parents seem to accept that the first session is finished and that they will be reviewing this information between the first and second sessions, the clinician should end the session by giving the parents appropriate materials that will help them to understand their child's situation, as well as some simple advice on instituting a few of the recommendations that were made, particularly those that are likely to yield early results. The pamphlets, appropriate to the child's stage of development and the child's needs, amount to a kind of "homework" for the parents. Selecting the appropriate materials will help the parents view the child in any new ways that the clinician deems necessary. Also, the parents will read things in many of the materials that will reassure them that much that has been done with the child was correct and helpful.

The recommendations that the clinical child psychologist asks the parents to try between interpretation sessions should be chosen very carefully. They should be simple, be easy to initiate, and fit appropriately with the family's schedules and capabilities. Early success with several recommendations will provide some positive reinforcement during the time the parents are reviewing the report and recommendations, and preparing for the second session.

At this first interpretation session, the clinician should not get signed permission to send reports. The school ultimately will receive some information concerning the comprehensive evaluation; however, the parents should be told to digest the information, think about it, and then at the second interpretation session decide who should receive what information about the child.

Whether the psychologist gives the parents the written report at the end of the first interpretation session is a matter of choice. Some parents straightforwardly ask for a written report. The clinician should be prepared to provide a report if the parents so request.

Every effort should be made to end the first session on a positive note. The clinician should underscore his or her availability for telephone consultation should any urgent questions rise between sessions. Whenever it is possible and realistic, the clinician should end the session by positively emphasizing the things that the parents have done in the past that have been helpful to the child.

THE SECOND INTERPRETATION SESSION

The second interpretation session with the parents should be scheduled about 2 weeks after the first interpretation session. The parents must have some time to digest the findings and, in some cases, to share the results with other significant adults in the child's life. In most instances, the second interpretation session can be scheduled for 1 hour of conference time. The psychologist will have done literally all of the talking in the first interpretation session. The second session is for the parents to ask questions, express their views, and obtain clarification about any elements of the report that seem obscure.

The second interpretation session should begin with the clinical child psychologist's asking the parents and other adults who may be in attendance to verbalize their thoughts regarding the results and recommendations. Thus the clinician can get a picture of whether the significant adults have accepted the interpretation and recommendations, and how well invested they are in proceeding. During this discussion, the clinician can ask the parents to describe what has happened as a result of their following the recommendations that were made in the previous session. By having the parents talk about what they have tried and what they have observed, the clinician can determine whether to modify the recommendations that were made in the first interpretation session.

When the parents have no further questions, the clinician should suggest who should receive the results. In most instances, the complete report should go to the child's pediatrician and any other physicians who work with the child, as well as any psychologist who will be working with the child if such a referral is made.

The entire report probably should not be sent to the school, or to remedial reading clinics. These organizations rarely have the facilities to maintain the kind of confidentiality that is promised by the clinical child psychologist to the parents. For schools and other places that require some information about the child in order to provide remedial work, a summary of test results and a letter are recommended.

Figure 15.1 presents a form that can be used to request the parents' permission to release the report to specific individuals. The form shown in Figure 15.2 can be used to forward basic intelligence and achievement data to remedial clinics or tutors. A cover letter should, of course, always accompany either the report or the basic data. This letter should encourage the person working with the child to communicate with the clinical child psychologist regarding any results of the work done or any questions that should arise.

During the second, and in many cases final, interpretation session, the clinician should indicate to the parents his or her availability to continue to consult should questions arise in the future. In the event that the child will continue to work with the clinical child psychologist, or if the parents plan to receive counseling or other clinical services, this is the time that scheduling can take place.

Sometimes the parents appreciate the entire process, but require some time to think about implementation. The psychologist should encourage the

---

PERMISSION TO RELEASE CONFIDENTIAL RECORDS

Permission is hereby given to Doctor Theodore H. Blau, to release clinical information and/or test results to:

_____

about _____

Date _____

Signed _____

Relationship _____

FIGURE 15.1   Permission Form to Release Records

parents to take their time and to think carefully about following recommendations or implementing treatment plans. The clinician should be very aware that he or she is a resource person, and that it is unwise to press the parents to take action before they are ready.

FOLLOW-UP

Some parents will want to retain a relationship with the clinical child psychologist. Follow-up contact should certainly be encouraged. If no specific treatment recommendations have been made, the clinician should offer the parents the opportunity to schedule counseling sessions whenever they feel they would like to review what has occurred. Figure 15.3 presents a form that can be used to keep a record of what occurs during a follow-up conference with the family.

Telephone Conferences

The clinical child psychologist will find that parents often make telephone calls to ask questions about particular recommendations, or about specific incidents that have occurred with the child. Most psychologists find that this is an efficient way to deal with residuals from the evaluation process. Few parents abuse the privilege, and the calls maintain the alliance between the clinician and the parents. This is also true of any telephone calls that may be made by the youngster's teachers, guidance counselors, tutors,

CONFIDENTIAL

BASIC REFERRAL DATA

NAME _____ AGE _____

EDUCATION _____ BIRTH DATE _____

REPORT TO _____ DATE OF THIS REPORT _____

INTELLIGENCE: ACHIEVEMENT:
  Instrument _____   Instrument _____

  Form _____   Form _____

  Date of Adm _____   Date of Adm _____

Factor   Percentile   Factor   Grade Equivalent or Percentile

ADDITIONAL:

SPECIAL PROBLEMS OR SUGGESTIONS:

By: _____

_____

FIGURE 15.2   Basic Referral Data Sheet

_____ Phone

_____ In Person

FAMILY CONFERENCE

Name _____ Date _____

Age _____ GR _____

PARTICIPANTS

_____ Mother   _____ Other

_____ Father

_____ Sibs

PURPOSE

DISCUSSION

INTERPRETATION/RECOMMENDATIONS

FIGURE 15.3 Family Conference Record Sheet

or remedial specialists. Clinical child psychologists are advised to be generous in allowing such consultations.

Reevaluation

Reevaluations can occur at any time when there is an apparent need for current information. For youngsters who have had very severe problems, such as lag in neuropsychological growth and development, severe behavior problems, divorce situations, or severe trauma, the reevaluations may occur as frequently as every 6 months. If youngsters seem to be doing well, reevaluation may occur rarely or not at all. The decision about recommending a reevaluation should be based on the psychologist's judgment as to whether such a reevaluation will serve the child and the parents. The likeliest time for a reevaluation in youngsters without severe problems would be just after they pass into a significant developmental stage. In terms of academic placement, such evaluations are best done at the end of the first grade, at the end of the third grade, at the end of the sixth grade, and at the end of the eighth grade. At these particular times in the developmental sequence, considerable changes can be expected in the youngster's social, academic, and family life; the latter two stages also include very significant physiological changes that occur just before adolescence.

Many clinical child psychologists report that when parents are pleased with the BPE, they return, with the child, during the last years of secondary school. The parents may bring in the 11th grader who was seen originally when in the 2nd grade. They will report that everything has gone well, and that the child has done well. The purpose of the visit is to seek help from the clinical child psychologist in planning for the major separation of going off to college. If the psychologist feels that he or she has the skills and training to participate in this educational–vocational–developmental guidance process, a reevaluation is certainly indicated. The clinician who does not have the skills or who is uninterested in this kind of work should refer the family to a competent psychologist who can meet their needs for this particular service.

In considering reevaluation, the clinician must always balance between a natural curiosity to see how the child is doing and conducting a reevaluation only when it is clearly indicated. As the psychologist gains experience, recommendations to try specific things for a period of time may precede reevaluation. Where clinical judgment suggests that the youngster is simply passing through a "phase," questions from the parents can probably be resolved successfully with only a conference.

Closing Notes

When the case is finished, and it is clear that all services have been rendered, the clinical child psychologist should formulate a closing note which

END OF CONTACT

NAME _____   DATE OF CLOSING _____

SERVICE _____

_____

_____

ADDITIONAL COMMENTS: _____ SESSIONS INDIV.

_____ SESSIONS GROUP

_____ FAMILY

FIGURE 15.4   End of Contact Form

is the final page in the case folder. Its purpose is to describe briefly what has happened and when it happened. This note is extremely valuable in the event that the parents call at a later date. A telephone call 4 years after the child was seen requires that the clinician have some brief review of what happened. The closing note also provides an opportunity to jot down notes about telephone calls, conferences, or reports that were sent. Figure 15.4 presents an end of contract form.

THE FIRST INTERPRETATION SESSION
WITH ALBERT'S PARENTS

A verbatim account of the first interpretation session with the significant adults in Albert's life is presented here to illustrate the process. The first interpretation session was scheduled approximately 2 weeks after Albert's testing was finished. The clinical child psychologist used Albert's psychological report as the basis for the interpretation. The reader will notice that the oral interpretation to the parents very closely follows the report that was presented in the last chapter, beginning on page 224.

Both of Albert's natural parents and his stepparents had planned on being at this first session. Because of a change in shift schedules, the stepmother could not be present. This illustrates another good purpose for taping the sessions, since the tape enabled her to hear exactly what was said about Albert at a later time.

At several times during the session, a parent interrupted to ask a question or to make a comment. These interruptions are not included in the verbatim dialogue so that the presentation can have uninterrupted continuity. The clinical child psychologist should, however, encourage these interruptions and answer questions as they arise. Experience dictates that interruptions seldom occur during the first interpretation session.

After the two natural parents and the stepfather were comfortably seated in the consultation office, and were served beverages, the psychologist proceeded as follows:

> I am glad to see all of you here today. Sorry that we all couldn't be here, but we're going to tape this session so that you'll have a chance to go over the results, and everyone can think about what I have to say at their leisure.
>
> We're making a tape because what I'm going to tell you is very complicated. We've done a very thorough examination of Albert and found many interesting things about him. At the beginning, you asked a number of questions about Albert, and I think we have answered most of them. Let me start by telling you what we've done, what we found, what it means, and what we recommend.
>
> We originally saw Albert because Dad was somewhat concerned. He had been told that Albert was not doing too well in school, and that he might be "hyperactive" or perhaps having a "learning disability." It was agreed among both parents and stepparents that a complete psychological evaluation would be helpful. We all met, and I took an extensive history.
>
> We found that both parents have divorced, but have remarried. I must tell you that the children of divorce in almost all cases suffer consequences affecting their schoolwork, their self-concept, and their behavior for many years after the divorce. I am going to give you some special literature to read to help you understand the kinds of things that Albert is facing as a child of divorce. This will help you to lessen the effect.
>
> A number of questions were raised, including "Is Albert hyperactive?" "Is he learning disabled or abnormal in any other way?" and "What can parents and stepparents do to help Albert in his adjustment?" Mother in particular wanted to know, "How can Albert's attention span be improved?"
>
> We took an extensive history and learned that Mother is a 32-year-old executive secretary with a high school education. She describes herself as a person who is happiest when Albert is on his best behavior. She tries to be fair and to correct Albert constructively. Recently, she has remarried to Bill, a 29-year-old insurance executive. He describes himself as an "easy going" person. He thinks he gets along pretty well with Albert.
>
> The natural father, Jack, is a 38-year-old detective. He describes himself as kind of a stern guy. He does say that he and Albert have a good time and that they spend quite a bit of time together. They play and laugh a lot. Stepfather enjoys a more quiet relationship with Albert, watching TV and helping him with his homework.

Stepmother is relatively new to the scene. Mary is a 31-year-old correctional officer who has a short temper but believes herself to be honest.

There is a newcomer on the scene—Bill, a half brother who is almost 1 year old. All of you say that Albert seems to love his brother and there are no obvious signs of sibling rivalry.

Albert gets to see his grandparents, both on the natural side and on the stepparents' side on a pretty regular basis. He seems to get a lot out of these relationships. He also has a chance to see the mother's sister (his aunt) and her children (his cousins). They all get along pretty well.

Mother has the formal custody of Albert, but the families are very comfortable with shared responsibility, and natural father and stepmother see Albert frequently. There has been no stress about this.

The parents were divorced when Albert was about 2 1/2, and Mother remarried when Albert was about 4. Dad remarried when Albert was about 6.

I have to tell you that you present almost an ideal cooperative situation for a divorced child. You are not angry at each other, you have very little or no unfinished business, you're very cooperative, and you all seem to be anxious to help Albert.

Our history showed that Albert was a big boy at birth, over 8 lbs, and that his early growth and development seemed to take place within normal limits. His pediatrician, Dr. Jason, finds him in good health. Albert broke his clavicle at age 2. He's had some sinus problems and nosebleeds. He had a lot of aches and pains, but they stopped last year.

There may be some mixed cerebral dominance or left-handedness within the family, and we will check that out with Albert.

Albert had preschool and he did well. During the first grade when he was at the Willow School they said he was hyperactive. He seemed to do pretty well academically. Now that he is in the second grade they say that he still seems fairly hyperactive.

You report that Albert makes friends easily and he tends to be a follower. At Mother's home he has his own room and he's put up a lot of posters. He's had some friends sleep over with him, but he has not slept over with his friends. You've told me that Albert likes the movies, TV, soccer, and riding his skateboard. He collects stickers. He's been a picky eater, and discipline has been very mild. Dad uses deprivation, and Mother does the same. Mother also will occasionally spank Albert.

Albert has been to day camp and he enjoyed it. He had an allowance for a while but this has been stopped. It's unclear to me why this was so, but I have some recommendations later to deal with this.

His bedtime is about 8:30 during school nights and he gets up at about 6:30. He does have chores at both houses.

You report that Albert has always sucked his thumb, and he wet the bed on and off since the age of about 3. He has occasional tantrums. He has been generally uncooperative and has a high energy level. You believe that he lacks self-confidence and is overly sensitive.

His performance at school is considered by everyone to be below his potential. You find that he's socially embarrassing. His emotional behavior is variable, sometimes seeming to be mature and sometimes childlike. He has occasional periods of irritability where there is no apparent cause. He does cause conflict in the family. He is impulsive, stubborn, cannot complete projects, has trouble following directions, but you notice that he is a kind youngster and doesn't have any bad responses to animals or small children.

I have to tell you that most of the things that you've mentioned are perfectly normal for first-born male youngsters between the ages of 5 and 9. I know that these behaviors are troublesome, but they do come and go, and every indication is that they will pass from Albert's life.

Well, with this history we would say that the information is "equivocal." This means that it may mean something and it may not. To really get at the answers, we gave Albert a very comprehensive psychological examination that we call the Basic Psychological Examination. We gave him a large number of tests of his intellect, his neuropsychological brain–behavior interactions, his achievement, and his personality.

As you all know from many years of living, the human being is an extremely complicated creature. There is the outside individual that you see and respond to. I'm working at that level now. I wear clothes in a certain way, talk in a certain way, and present myself. All of you sitting here and listening are functioning at a middle level. You're listening, weighing, judging, and evaluating what you hear. There is a third level, sometimes called the unconscious or the subconscious. It causes us to do things without our thinking. For example, some mornings you wake up irritable and if you are asked, "Why are you irritable?" you will probably answer, "I got up on the wrong side of the bed!" Well, you got up on the same side you always get up on. We don't really know why certain reactions occur, but they do. In my interpretation I'm going to try to tell you all the levels of Albert's psychological life. The more you understand about him, the easier it's going to be to help him.

I'd like to start with the way Albert looks to us. This is called the "clinical picture." We don't think it means very much, but people are very concerned about the way they look on the outside. People spend billions of dollars a year on clothing, hairdos, contact lenses, and so forth. So let's start with that.

We noticed that Albert seems tall for his age. He has blond hair and blue eyes, and has several front teeth missing. This is perfectly normal for his age. During the examinations he would suck his thumb occasionally. He speaks in a high, kind of crackly voice, which is characteristic of 7-year-old boys. His hearing is within normal limits. We did notice, during all of the examination sessions, that Albert had a tendency to drink an unusually large amount of water. I've talked to all of you about this, and you agree that he is always drinking water. We want to suggest that Dr. Jason be informed about this, but I'll talk to you about this when we talk about sending copies of the report to appropriate people.

We found that Albert was a friendly youngster, but in some ways he seemed immature for his age. Sometimes he would cooperate extremely well, and sometimes he would be so agitated and jumpy that it was hard for him to pay attention to what we were doing. When we accepted this and allowed him to move around the room, he calmed down quickly and did better. If we set limits too strictly, he would tend to regress, and several times he came close to tears. We quickly found that criticism was not the way to work with Albert. We gave him a lot of positive regard and he did much better. It seems that his confidence is pretty limited and he gets upset easily. We have the feeling that

Albert is a needful child who has to have some pretty clear evidence, on a regular basis, that he is loved and accepted.

He really doesn't look too much different from a lot of second-grade youngsters we've seen. I can understand how some of his teachers might think of him as hyperactive. He does have a lot of exuberance and energy. In my opinion, he is no different from a lot of intelligent youngsters who have more energy than they can use, and who may be somewhat worried about things.

That's what he looked like. Now I would like to get into the actual examination and what we found about Albert psychologically. The first thing we'd like to look at is intelligence. We like to think of this as "horsepower." How much energy does the youngster have that requires stimulation and opportunity to learn? The first thing I'd like to do is ask you to try to get rid of the concept of "IQ." One single number can never really describe a child. Even a youngster of 7 is quite a complicated individual, and, to understand him well, I'd like you to think of another concept that we have for describing children. It is called "percentile." A percentile is not a percentage. It is a way of characterizing any human trait in a very exact way. Let me give you an example: If an adult male is 5 ft 7 1/2 in. tall, we could say that he is "average." That would be okay, but "average" in height for adult males might range between 5 ft 4 in. and 5 ft 10 in. To be more exact, we could say that our man who is 5 ft 7 1/2 in. tall falls at the 50th percentile. This would mean that if we randomly selected 100 adult males, off the street, and lined them up military fashion from the shortest to the tallest, our man would be taller than 50 of the 100 and shorter than 50. He would fall at the *50th percentile.* I would like to use this concept throughout, comparing Albert with youngsters his age and his grade.

Looking at 11 different tests of his ability to learn and do things, we found that Albert fell at the 94th percentile. This means he is in the superior range of intellectual capacity. Only 5 out of 100 youngsters could do these tests as well as Albert did them.

We found that in some things he was able to perform at a much more competent level than in others. In none of his tests did he fall below the average range. Let me go through the 11 subtests of the Wechsler Intelligence Scale for Children—the Revised version—and tell you how he stood in comparison with other 7-year-old youngsters.

In his ability to collect general information, he was at the 63rd percentile. This is within the average range. In his ability to do analogous reasoning and make comparisons, he was at the 84th percentile. Arithmetic reasoning fell at the 99th percentile. His vocabulary skills were found to be at the 50th percentile. This was the lowest level to which Albert's intellect fell. Now, the 50th percentile is average, but for a boy of superior ability, this is somewhat low. Verbal comprehension, the ability to understand concepts through the use of words, fell at the 75th percentile. Albert's attention span, his ability to focus and use short-term memory, fell at the 50th percentile.

He was able to pick out key ideas equal to or better than 91% of youngsters his age. His social intelligence and his ability to predict his own behavior in comparison with others according to his age fell at the 75th percentile. Eye–hand coordination and design ability were at the 75th percentile. Albert's ability to manipulate large objects into a meaningful array fell at the 91st percentile. His ability to do small motor movement and new learning fell at the 98th percentile.

You can see that using IQ to describe a youngster leaves an awful lot out. In this description I just gave you, we see that Albert is an absolute whiz in arithmetic reasoning, assembling of objects, picking key ideas, new learning, and small motor movement. He is average, which is far below his basic ability, in vocabulary and his ability to concentrate. These results suggest that Albert may have some difficulty with immediate memory and expressive language skills.

To do a kind of cross-check on Albert's intellectual function, we gave him the Peabody Picture Vocabulary Test. In this, he didn't have to use any words. He simply had to point to one of four pictures that best described a word that was given by the examiner. On this he fell at the 50th percentile. This is very far below his excellent results on the Wechsler scales. This suggests that Albert's intellectual efficiency fluctuates and sometimes he is "on" and sometimes he is "off." He may also be the victim of distractibility, which influences the quality of his intellectual performance. This kind of response is not unusual for youngsters at this age. Albert is in a stage of considerable physiological growth. You can expect on-and-off response throughout his growing years. Sometimes it's better and sometimes it's worse.

We gave Albert a number of neuropsychological tests. We found he could pull between 11 and 12 kg with his right hand and between 11 and 13 kg with the left hand. Even though he is right-handed, the lack of difference in strength with the dominant hand and with the nondominant hand suggests that indeed he is in a stage of growth. We thought he might have mixed cerebral dominance. We gave him several tests of this and found that he is left-brain–dominant, which essentially means right-handed. On a test of visual memory, he showed some slight difficulty. We found this pretty consistent for his age, which, as I said, is an age of growth. In short, we found no reason to believe that Albert has any kind of neuropsychological deficit.

To determine whether Albert has a specific learning disability, we gave him a standardized achievement test to measure the three basic elements of his academic world: reading, arithmetic, and language. On the test that we gave him, compared with youngsters beginning the second grade, his reading fell at the 38th percentile. This is within the average range, but quite low for a youngster as bright as Albert. It is consistent, however, with the lowered intellectual factors on vocabulary and attention span that we found on his Wechsler scales. In arithmetic, where Albert showed himself to be extraordinarily skillful on the intelligence tests, he fell at the 2.3 grade level, which placed him at the 52nd percentile. Albert's language skills were at the 46th percentile.

His test results are within acceptable limits for his grade placement, but they are considerably below his potential. We evaluated each of the tests and found that in the reading tests, he lacks the vocabulary skills that are required to read at the level of his own potential. He also had trouble with literal–specific reading and inferential–specific reading. These may reflect his difficulty in vocabulary, and that's something that we want to address later on when we make recommendations.

The final area that we examined very thoroughly was Albert's personality. Personality is a very complex thing, as we all know. It involves "Who am I?"

"What influences brought me to where I am?" "What things frighten me?" and a host of other questions. Personality is one of the psychological areas that really makes individuals different from each other.

We gave Albert a number of tests including projective techniques. A projective technique is an opportunity for the youngster to express things in personality that are at the lower levels of awareness.

I'd like to go through all the levels that we found. I've taken all of the tests and divided them into four elements. The first is interpersonal activity. Here, we'll talk about Albert and how he appears to people. At the second level we'll look at early identifications. Here, we'll try to determine the effects and the impact of his exposure to the important people in his life—you. In the third portion of the personality analysis, we'll look at his anxiety structure. These are the energies that Albert has delivered to him daily, and with which he must do something. We'll finally look at outlets and defenses, where we have measured what Albert does with the energies that he has. We will show you what he does that works in his best interests, and what he does with his energies that work against his best interests.

First let's look at his interpersonal activity. At this first level, we found that Albert appears at first to be a demanding, active, jumpy youngster. He tends to be pretty challenging as he becomes comfortable. It's as though he's testing his environment. His aggressiveness seems pretty indiscriminate—it can be toward adults or toward children, males or females. As one gets to know Albert, one finds that beneath his outside aggressiveness, Albert has a great fear of setting goals for himself and not reaching them. He has what we call a low level of aspiration. When he faces new things, Albert expects the worst. So we might say that Albert approaches life with a certain pessimism.

Next let's examine Albert's early identifications. In looking at our projective techniques, we attempt to find what we call identification and love objects. The identification object is the person whom the youngster seeks to imitate, and to whom the child looks as a model of what he's likely to be when he matures. The love object is the person he is drawn toward, feels safest with, and will eventually tend to mate with.

We found that primary identification for Albert was with a father figure. I'll tell you what we found, and then you can decide which of his father figures has had the greatest influence. The unconscious picture of the father figure as expressed in the projective techniques is that of a rather oral-aggressive person. That means an individual who says what he thinks when he thinks it and doesn't much mind who's listening. He sees the father as being somewhat of a temperamental person. He is seen as somewhat anti-intellectual, seeing people with a lot of education as not particularly practical. He himself is very practical and very aggressive. In spite of this picture of outer aggressiveness and roughness, the father is also seen as able to step in and do some mothering when the youngster is with him—feeling his head to see how much fever he has, cautioning him to be careful, taking care of him when he's hurt, and feeding him. The father is seen as loving his child, but the father has never been seriously invested with tiny details of child rearing. [At this point the mother and the stepfather looks smilingly at the natural father, who was grinning sheepishly and nodding his head.]

The mother figure is seen as a love object. The unconscious picture from the projective techniques is that of a person who has some trouble seeing the inner needs of the child. What she sees on the surface is what she responds to. Like the father, she can be verbally aggressive. He sees the mother as a security-minded person who is always worried about details of being safe. He sees her as having trouble being spontaneous in her nourishment or giving of warmth and affection. There are some indications that it may be because she herself had some difficulty establishing a warm and nourishing relationship with her own mother. We see this frequently—one learns to mother from one's own mother [at this point the mother began dabbing at her eyes with a tissue as she became teary]. Mother is clearly the motivator in the family, asking "Wouldn't you like to do this?" or "Why don't you give it a try?" She seems to be the one who has set the goals in the family. She is seen as a person who has very strong affection needs and is seriously uncomfortable if these are not met.

This information does not indicate specifically who has given him this impression of mothers or fathers. Albert himself would be surprised that we got this much information. We did not ask him, "What is you mom like?" or "What is your dad like?" These images came from the test results. [At this point there was a discussion of how accurately these descriptions fit the natural mother and the natural father.]

What I have described about the personality so far is essentially "yesterday." The last two portions of the personality relate to "today" and "tomorrow." Let me take up Albert's anxiety structure. Anxiety means the energies that are developed as a person sees something wrong in his or her environment. Anxiety is a warning signal that something ought to be done to change things. When the anxiety is realistic, it helps us. You certainly want Albert to be anxious about crossing the street without looking. On the other hand, anxiety about things that are not very realistic can be very painful. It does not help Albert a great deal to be afraid that monsters will break into his room at night and kidnap him. I would like to look at Albert's anxieties and tell you what I believe they represent, and then we will see what he does about them. I want to clearly emphasize the point that anxiety by itself is not a bad thing. A certain amount of anxiety is very normal, and very necessary for healthy growth and development.

Albert's deepest sources of anxiety relate to the fractured family situation, and in this he is like all children of divorce. I will give you some things to read about this when we finish. He is fearful of the loss of attachments. He is afraid that everyone in the family is angry at him and that most of the difficulties that Mom and Dad have experienced are his fault. I want you to understand that this is the most common thing we find in children of divorce. It is unrealistic, and it does not make sense to a lot of parents, but the child believes that whatever happened was his or her fault. He tends to feel very discouraged. He is frightened that he will be replaced in the affection of his mother by the new half brother. This again is very normal, but is painful to Albert. Many children this age overdo the "loving" behavior toward a new sibling to disguise or deny this anxiety.

We also found that Albert is very tense about poor school performance. He is afraid that he won't do well. He is frightened now that he has discovered that many things that adults tell him are not the truth. Until recently, he has believed every single thing his mother, father, stepmother, stepfather, and teachers have told him. It is at about at age 7 that children realize that parents do not always tell the truth. This comes as a shock to some parents. You must remember that when the telephone rings and you say "If it's Mr. Jones, tell him I've left already," this may seem to you a perfectly acceptable fib. To the child it is a behavior that he has been told is absolutely unacceptable—lying. It is very difficult for young children to discriminate shades of gray. The brighter the child, the more confusing this can be. Albert is a very bright child and he is confused about this behavior.

Albert is unsure of the limits of his environment, so he is always testing them. He doesn't know really what is expected of him.

Albert often feels creative. He wants to build things, draw things, and make new things. In some ways, he is very embarrassed about this and tries to hide it. This makes him quite tense.

He has strong, natural, healthy sexual interests for his age. You must remember that he has a mental age that is about 2 years greater than his chronological age. He is thinking of some things like 9- and 10-year-old boys. He is quite frightened by these thoughts and feelings. He clearly has not had sufficient sex education. We will give you some material to ease this situation for Albert.

Albert has a great deal of difficulty with the concept of anger. He does not understand that anger is a natural part of everyone's life, and it occurs when a person is fearful and is unable to do anything about the fear. That in effect represents all of Albert's angers. Most of them are perfectly normal for his age. That does not mean they aren't painful.

Now let's look at what he does with the emotional energies that are delivered to him. We'll look at his outlets and defenses.

Albert tries to rid himself of intolerable tension through his assertive manner. He follows the policy of "when unsure, attack." In this he is very much like his dad. He tests limits to try to understand new environments and new situations. Sometimes Albert is frightened of what people think of him, and he tries to get them angry at him by shocking them. This way he can be relieved of the fear that someone is thinking badly about him and not saying it.

Albert is pretty pessimistic about his life and very cautious about the future. As we can see, he has relatively few of what we call intellectual outlets and defenses. These are ones that he can organize and control.

Most of the outlets for anxiety that Albert has are what we call "labile." They come out suddenly, and they relieve tension quickly. They generally distress the people around Albert. These labile outlets include outbursts of anger, and strong oral-dependency, which includes his demands for candy, ice cream, food, and drinks. When he feels very guilty he will become quite phobic. I noticed that he is afraid of lightning, thunder, and "boogeymen."

Albert is desperately trying to hold his anger inward and is beginning to show the signs of early depression. This happens quite early in bright children. He is trying to display some of his angry feelings to power objects, such as fantasies of driving powerful vehicles, and he is beginning to attach himself to science fiction presentations on the TV. In this he is certainly more like a 9- or 10-year-old. He is moving into the next stage of development, and very much seeks the company of youngsters his own age, particularly boys, to express his feelings and to seek approval. He hasn't had a lot of chances to do this yet, but when he does, he is going to feel much better.

Well, that's the story of Albert. What does it all mean? Let me put it all together briefly and then tell you about some of the things we recommend.

Essentially, we find that Albert is a youngster who has potentially superior intellectual capacity. His intellect varies considerably, and this is probably based on developmental changes that are occurring. There are some indications that Albert is going to be a very big boy. Some of his stress and tension are based on the pressure under which he operates. So he has up-and-down performance, as well as up-and-down emotional responsiveness. Sometimes he does very well, and sometimes he spoils his own responses.

The personality structure is that of a very tense, pressured youngster who is suffering the aftermath of being a member of a fractured family. The parental models have had troubles of their own, and there has been no real chance to enrich Albert's strong intellectual and creative needs. He blames himself for the failures of the family.

To help Albert, I have a number of recommendations, and I would like to split them into individual things that each of you can do and things that you can agree on and do together. I'd like to start with Dad. Dad has a limited amount of time with Albert. I would like to suggest certain things that can be done that can be really helpful for the youngster. First of all, Albert needs sex education. I have here a booklet called "All About You." I would like you to read this book to Albert and then set up some times that you can talk about this, using the book to illustrate your discussions. You should mostly listen. Once you read the book to Albert, he will know what's in it.

Second, I'd like you to start some competitive games with Albert, but be sure that they are games at his level. If you would play cards, eventually teach him to play poker, but start with simple games such as "Go Fish." Dominos, checkers, and other such games will be helpful.

Third, I'd like you to take Albert to the go-kart track. You can tell Albert you're teaching him to steer and compensate in preparation for the age when he can get a license. This will have an enormously positive effect on Albert.

When you have to change Albert's behavior, I would like you to use behavior management techniques. This essentially means accentuating the positive and eliminating the negative. When he does something you like, give him a lot of praise and support. When he does something you don't like, turn away. I'm going to give you some literature to read which will help you to understand how it works.

I think it's important that the father should have specific expectations for academic work, for Albert's behavior, and for chores. I think you should make it clear what you expect of him, but do it in a supportive, kindly manner.

Father is the identification object, and I think you must always be careful, as much as possible, to tell Albert the truth about things. Even in little things, deception is painful to Albert.

When Albert is with you, having a regular, consistent schedule is very important. The more predictable breakfast, lunch, dinner, and recreational activities are, the more comfortable Albert is going to be.

I know it's not easy for you to give spontaneous assurance. I think you must try to work with yourself to develop the ability to give Albert as much support and approval as possible.

Finally, I would like you to get a couple of calendars with some theme such as Star Trek so that he can have one in his room at your house and one in his room at home. If there can be some piece of furniture, a bulletin board, or other things that give him a sense of territoriality, this also will be helpful. You will notice that I gave Albert two pictures of himself with Harry the Bear when he first came. This is a way of establishing territoriality that gives children security. [At this point the parents very enthusiastically said that Albert asked to have both pictures framed and put up in his two rooms.]

I would now like to talk to Stepdad. Your role can be extremely important as a model for Albert. You are not a replacement for Dad, but you're an additional important male figure that can provide the security and confidence that Albert really needs. There are some specific things I'd like to recommend. First, I'd like you to reinforce the sex education given by Dad. I'm going to give you a copy of the same book. Second, I'd like you to follow through with games of competition. At your house I'd like you to be the one that sets the limits on when Albert goes to bed, and what he must do and must not do. He is getting too old for any kind of physical discipline. It would be much better if you set the limits clearly and then follow them with behavior management techniques. I'd like you to set a regular homework schedule for Albert and make sure that this schedule is followed. I think it should be 5 nights a week, Sunday through Thursday. I think it should be from 7:00 P.M. to 8:00 P.M.. I think it should be in 10-min segments, with 5 min between each segment. You might want to have a kitchen timer set so that when the bell goes off he takes his breaks and when the bell goes off again he goes back to his homework. Often he won't have homework, but I'd like you to have him read for pleasure, at his desk, to get used to the idea that this is the place and time that he will do his schoolwork.

I think it's important that you provide him a regular allowance on Monday morning. At this age, 50¢ a week is enough. If you want to associate it with chores at home, that would be okay.

I'd like you to give him 10 or 15 min every evening when you and he can be alone. Try to get Albert to talk about what he has done. In all instances provide him with as much reassurance and positive regard as you can.

I'm going to give you some booklets on behavior modification so that you can learn how to shape Albert's behavior to increase positive responses and decrease the things you don't like.

Mother is going to be very important. You are the traditional provider of security, warmth, and philosophy of life. I think it's very important that you take the position that Albert needs a lot of unrestricted positive regard. Compliment him as often as you can. Accentuate the positive. When he is stressed, give him reassurance. I would like you to try to avoid discipline whenever possible except when carrying through what father has set down as the limits. As I mentioned with Dad, you must always tell Albert the truth. That's harder to do than you think, and you may have to practice this. We as adults don't realize how literally children take our words.

A regularity of schedule is going to be vital. Every effort should be made to have the family eat at least two meals together. These should not be rushed or pressured times. Try to make mealtime a positive, friendly, supportive experience. Bedtime and other responsibilities should be scheduled pretty strictly so that Albert knows just what's going to happen.

I'd like you particularly to provide some creative opportunities for Albert. Whether it be finger painting, modeling with clay, or going to a children's creative workshop at one of the local community centers, I believe that Albert has really got to have a chance to see how creative he is.

I think it would be easier for Albert if you could help your husband to be the setter of limits and the masculine image. You've worked very hard with Albert, and it may be time for you to lean back a little and let your husband do some of the work as stepdad.

Stepmother is the most recent adult figure in Albert's life. I'm sorry she isn't here, but I will talk to you directly on the tape, Mrs. Doe. I hope you can realize that every child of every divorce situation has a fantasy of the parents reuniting. This should not be held against Albert. Now that Dad has married you and you are the stepmother, his myth and hope are pretty well shattered. You happen to be the last one to clinch the end of the marriage. That puts you in sort of a difficult spot for a short period of time. This can be overcome, and you can be really helpful. I think, first of all, by ignoring Albert's efforts to get you angry you will do a lot of good. Give him a lot of positive regard and avoid all discipline and criticism. I am going to give you some of these materials on behavior management and behavior modification. If you will read these booklets you will see how to change Albert's behavior without resorting to discipline or criticism. I hope that you can take part in arranging a fairly predictable schedule for Albert so that he knows what is going to happen.

There are some general recommendations I want to give that apply to Albert. Some of them may be practical, and some may require some consensus or negotiation. I am going to give these and then let you think about them. If they raise any conflicts, we will try to work these out and do those things that are most comfortable for all parties. First, I'd like you to take Albert to his pediatrician so that he can check to see if there is any basis for this excessive water drinking that we have noticed.

Second, I would hope that you could enter Albert into the Cub Scouts. That program gives a lot of opportunity for creative work, and Albert certainly needs this.

Third, I think Albert would profit from competitive physical activity. Your community offers a number of competitive swimming clubs for youngsters of Albert's age. Some of them operate all year long and others start in the spring. I would recommend that you start Albert in this activity. He's at the right age and he has a long, thin body, so he might do quite well in this sport. That would certainly build his confidence and use up a lot of his energy.

I think that next summer Albert is going to be ready for a camping experience away from home. As much as 4–6 weeks would be helpful. If you decide on this, I'd be happy to help you look at the camps in your area and select those that are likeliest to be helpful for Albert.

Albert doesn't have a place to keep his money, and I think he should have a little lockbox or bank in both of his homes.

Many of these recommendations may put some pressure on you. If any of you believe that you're running into a difficulty that can't be settled with a phone call, I would urge you to be willing to come in for a session to look over the situation, see where the difficulty is, and work out some solutions.

I've got a lot of material for you. These little pamphlets will give you the latest that we know about how to bring about the best kind of circumstances for your youngster. I've got a booklet called "Your Child from Six to Twelve." This will tell you a lot of things that are happening now to Albert and will show you that in some ways he is behaving in a manner more like a 9- or a 10-year-old. Here are some booklets on sex education that I mentioned. Here are several things on behavior modification that will help you to plan behavior management projects that will increase the behavior that you want Albert to show and decrease the behavior that is annoying to you. I also have some literature here on the kinds of things that children of divorce seem to feel as a group, and some things that can be done about this.

There is probably a total of about 3 hr of reading in these pamphlets. If you read all of them, you're going to be better informed about children and what you can do with children than 99% of parents. You have a very bright and capable youngster. It should be a pleasure and a rewarding experience to raise him. These materials will help you.

Finally, I believe that Albert ought to be reevaluated at the end of the sixth grade. If all is well at that time, you might want to consider selecting a special junior high school experience for him. If he has finished his development through the 12th year as we expect, he might be ready for some extra stimulating experiences. At that time we can tell you what he is ready for and make such recommendations.

I really don't know what's going to happen in the future. I've given you more recommendations than are necessary to straighten things out. I think the answers to your questions are clear. Albert is a normal, healthy boy of superior intelligence, and is not hyperactive. He is not abnormal, but he is like almost all of the 60% of youngsters who live in the residuals of a fractured family. The answer to your third question is clear: Each of you can help Albert in his development. Your concern about his attention span should be resolved as you institute these recommendations, and as Albert becomes more comfortable. A certain amount of patience will be required because some of Albert's so-called "problems" have to do with development. These will take care of themselves with time.

I hope that you will have a chance to play this tape two or three times between now and our next appointment. Make a note of any questions that you might have, and we will try to answer them at that time. Please feel free to call me between now and then if anything specific comes up. Perhaps at this point you would like to ask some questions that have arisen during my presentation.

The family interrupted in only a few instances during this presentation. After the presentation, they all made remarks suggesting that the picture of Albert that was presented indeed was an accurate one, and they were amazed at how much emerged from the psychological tests. They seemed enthusiastic, and it was suggested that they try some of the recommendations in the

2-week interim period before the second interpretation session. Plans were made to ensure that a second copy of the tape was made so that each family could have one. The families left on a very positive note.

During the 2 weeks between the first and the second interpretation sessions, one call was received from the stepmother, who asked a technical question about a behavior management project. She was distressed about Albert's jumping up from the table. She was counseled by telephone and seemed enthusiastic about carrying forth the behavior management project.

THE SECOND INTERPRETATION SESSION
WITH ALBERT'S PARENTS

All four parental figures attended the second session. They chatted pleasantly before the conference began, and seemed to be pretty excited about the program.

They reported that they had tried a number of the recommendations, and they were delighted. The mother was particularly excited about how easily Albert was willing to give up TV in the evening and start his study program under the guidance of the stepfather. They found a swimming club, and Albert was enrolled. He was already enthusiastically participating. Plans to start Cub Scouts in about 2 weeks had been made.

The family had no specific questions concerning the evaluation. An extremely positive tone emerged from each of the parents and stepparents. They requested that a full report go to the pediatrician. They agreed that a letter to Albert's second grade teacher, summarizing the intellectual findings and the achievement test findings and giving a brief statement about his stage of development, would be sufficient. Interestingly, they asked that a similar letter go to his first-grade teacher who continued to show interest in Albert.

The appropriate letters were sent, and copies of these were provided to the parents. The parents were also given a copy of the report of the BPE.

About 6 months later, the father called to tell the clinical child psychologist that Albert was doing exceedingly well and appeared to be at the head of his class. He had won a number of ribbons as a member of the swimming team, and had made some new friends. He was now going overnight to his friends' homes.

A letter was received from the natural mother reflecting much of what the father had said by telephone. She was particularly pleased with Albert's academic progress and his rising position as a leader in the class. Interestingly, she gave much of the credit to her new husband for creating a stable environment that gave Albert a great deal of security.

About 7 months after the assessment, a call was received from Albert's teacher. She mentioned how pleased she was with Albert's progress, but she specifically wanted to say that she had never received a letter from a professional person who had been consulted by one of her students. She appreciated this gesture and referred a family of one of her other students.

The case of Albert represents the kind of situation that is quite common in the practice of the clinical child psychologist who conducts Basic Psychological Examinations in the community.

CHAPTER SIXTEEN

Epilogue

The Basic Psychological Examination that has been presented in this book is applicable to the entire range of children likely to be seen in clinical practice. The same format can be applied in examining normal youngsters whose parents seek guidance in providing the best possible developmental course for their children, as well as deeply disturbed youngsters, brain damaged children, and those children who suffer various handicaps. Different testing instruments may be chosen, to focus on the specific difficulty presented by the child. The format, however, can remain the same.

No specific setting is required to utilize the BPE. It can be applied in community mental health centers, child guidance clinics, academic settings, and private settings and practice. It does however, require that a trained and experienced clinical child psychologist be in charge of the process. To conduct a comprehensive psychological examination of the child, and then to have the interpretation given to the parents by an individual who has not seen the child or conducted the examinations, is likely to result in a rather bland process in which the alliance between the parents and the professional is weak or missing. The clinical child psychologist should join the parents at the beginning, during the examination, and at the conclusion of the process, working together in the child's best interests.

Even though more people today know what psychologists do than ever before, there is still a hesitancy about seeking psychological services. Apparently, adults are more willing to bring their children to the psychologist than they are willing to seek services for themselves. The use of the BPE in practice leads to some interesting results. Often, when a need for adult services arises, those who have been involved as parents seek the help of the clinical child psychologist for themselves or to make referrals to other psychologists who may provide adult services. Psychologists who have used the BPE in clinical child psychology consistently report that they have become the "family psychologists" in the years following the examination of the child and the family.

In the 18 months following Albert's examination, some interesting things developed. Within 3 months of the interpretation session, the parents referred the child of a relative for a similar examination. Then, within 6 months, they referred a neighbor whose teenager was a source of difficulty. Within 1 year, one of the parent figures sought personal psychotherapeutic services from the clinical child psychologist, as a result of the experience of participating in Albert's BPE. Recently, a couple requested marriage and family counseling, referred by one of the stepparents who participated in Albert's assessment.

This phenomenon has been reported by numerous clinicians who have used the BPE in their practice. The satisfaction that comes from participating in an event that has major positive influence on the growth and development of one's child has a very strong effect. The esteem that parents develop for the clinical child psychologist tends to be considerable, and the alliance formed during the BPE continues for years.

The first form of the BPE was developed during 1953 and 1954. Since that time, we have examined the children and grandchildren of hundreds of adults who were originally seen as children in the 1950s. This procedure has proven to be seminal, and apparently it meets the approval of consumers.

Perhaps the greatest advantage of this procedure is the considerable professional satisfaction that comes from seeing troubled youngsters and concerned parents achieve higher levels of personal integration and satisfaction within a relatively short time following the application of the BPE.

Test Publishers and Distributors of Materials for the Assessment of Children and for Remedial Education

Advanced Ideas
2902 San Pablo Avenue
Berkeley, CA 94702
(415) 526-9100

American Guidance Service
Publisher's Building
P.O. Box 99
Circle Pines, MN 55014-1796
(800) 328-2560

Blue Lion Software
90 Sherman Street
Cambridge, MA 02140
(617) 876-2500

Britannica Software
345 Fourth Street
San Francisco, CA 94107
(415) 546-1866

Broderbund Software
17 Paul Drive
San Rafael, CA 94903
(800) 521-6263

College Board Publishers
45 Columbus Avenue
New York, NY 10023

Consulting Psychologists Press, Inc.
577 College Avenue
Palo Alto, CA 94306
(800) 624-1765

CTB/McGraw-Hill Publisher's
  Test Service
Del Monte Research Park
2500 Garden Road
Monterey, CA 93940

Degrees of Reading Power
The College Board
45 Columbus Avenue
New York, NY 10023-6917
(212) 713-8080

DLM Teaching Resources
P.O. Box 4000
One DLM Park
Allen, TX 75002
(214) 248-6300

Educational Testing Service
Rosedale Road
Princeton, NJ 08541

EPIE Institute
P.O. Box 839
Water Mill, NY 11976
(516) 283-4922

First Byte
Clauset Centre
3100 South Harbor Blvd., Suite 150
Santa Ana, CA 92704
(714) 432-1740

Halstead-Reitan Neuropsychological
  Batteries
Reitan Neuropsychology Laboratory
1338 East Edison Street
Tucson, AZ 85719
(602) 795-3717

Institute for Personality and Ability
  Testing, Inc.
P.O. Box 1602
Champaign, IL 61820-0188
(217) 352-4739

Integrated Professional Systems, Inc.
5211 Mahoning Avenue, Suite 135
Youngstown, OH 44515
(216) 799-3282

Jastak Associates, Inc.
P.O. Box 4460
Wilmington, DE 19807
(302) 652-4990

Lafayette Instrument Co., Inc.
P.O. Box 5729
Lafayette, IN 47903

MECC (Minnesota Educational
  Computing Corporation)
3490 Lexington Avenue North
Saint Paul, MN 55126
(800) 228-3504

Charles E. Merrill Publishing Co.
1300 Alum Creek Drive
Box 508
Columbus, OH 43216

Multi-Health System
908 Niagara Falls Boulevard
North Tonawanda, NY 14120-2060
(416) 424-1700

National Computer Systems
P.O. Box 1416
Minneapolis, MN 55440
Professional Assessment Services
(612) 933-2800

Neuropsychology Press
1338 East Edison Street
Tucson, AZ 85719

PRO-ED
8700 Shoal Creek Boulevard
Austin, TX 78758
(512) 451-3246

Psychological Assessment Resources, Inc.
P.O. Box 98
Odessa, FL 33556
(813) 968-3003

Psychological Test Specialties
P.O. Box 1441
Missoula, MT 59805

Reitan Neuropsychology Laboratory
1338 East Edison Street
Tucson, AZ 85712
(602) 795-3717

Scholastic, Inc.
730 Broadway
New York, NY 10003
(212) 505-3000

Science Research Associates
155 North Wacker Drive
Chicago, IL 60606

Slossen Educational Publications, Inc.
P.O. Box 280
East Aurora, NY 14052
(716) 652-0930

Stanford University Press
Stanford, CA 94305

Stoelting Co.
1350 South Kostner Avenue
Chicago, IL 60623

The Learning Co.
6493 Kaiser Drive
Fremont, CA 94555
(800) 852-2255

The Psychological Corporation
P.O. Box 839954
San Antonio, TX 78283-3954
(800) 233-5682

The Riverside Publishing Co.
8420 Bryn Mawr Avenue
Chicago, IL 60631
(312) 693-0040

Teachers College Press
P.O. Box 939
Wolfeboro, NH 03894-0939
(603) 569-4576

Test Corporation of America
4050 Pennsylvania, Suite 310
Kansas City, MO 64111-9897

Weekly Reader Software/Optimum
  Resource, Inc.
10 Station Place
Norwalk, CT 06058
(203) 542-5553

Western Psychological Service
12031 Wilshire Boulevard
Los Angeles, CA 90025
(213) 478-2061

Sources of Information for Parents

Association for Childhood Education International
3615 Wisconsin Avenue Northwest
Washington, DC 20016

Provides various publications having to do with child growth and development. Creative presentations on using ordinary activities such as cooking and eating to help children learn about themselves and their families. A publication entitled "Play—Children's Business" is very helpful for parents.

Channing L. Bete Co. Inc.
200 State Road
South Deerfield, MA 01373

Many different publications concerning families, stressful events, and ways of dealing with difficulties. Includes such publications as "What Kids Should Know About Divorce" and "What Every Family Should Know About Getting Along at Home." Much of the script is illustrated with very understandable cartoons.

Division of Communications & Education
"Plain Talk" Series
National Institute of Mental Health
5600 Fisher's Lane
Rockville, MD 20857

Regularly publishes a series of three- and four-page pamphlets such as "Raising Children," "Your New Child," and "Understanding Adolescence."

Johnson & Johnson Consumer Products Inc.
P.O. Box 836
Somerville, NJ 08876

Publications related to the earlier developmental years. A book entitled "Advances in Touch—New Implications in Human Development" is very good for the parents of young children.

Lindemann, J., & Lindemann, S. (1988)
Growing Up Proud: A Parent's Guide to the Psychological Care of Children With Disabilities. New York: Warner Books.

First, this book reviews normal growth and development. Second, it goes into what the parents can do to help the child adapt when there are disabilities ranging from mild to severe.

Mount, G., & Walters, S. R. (1988)
Effective Parenting (rev. ed.).
Practical Renovations Press
6750 Hillcrest Plaza Drive, Suite 304
Dallas, TX 75230

127-page booklet contains short chapters covering pitfalls in the child's world, principles for changing behavior, communicating effectively, early social training and development, emotional reactions of children, early development of the child, language, intelligence and creativity, treatment of adjustment problems, additional principles of child management, and ideas for behavior programs. Brief and instructive.

National Educational Association
1201 16th Street, N. W.
Washington, DC 20036

Publishes a wide range of booklets about children of school age. Includes four booklets that have received wide acclaim in the area of sex education.

Office of Educational Research & Improvement
c/o U.S. Department of Education
Washington, DC 20208

Short booklets to help parents, including "Help Your Child Improve in Test Taking," "Help Your Child Become a Good Reader," "Help Your Child Do Better in School," and "Help Your Child Learn Math," and "Help Your Child to Write Well."

Parenting Press
P.O. Box 15136
Seattle, WA 98115

Publishes such titles as "Without Spanking or Spoiling," "Kids Can Cooperate," "Pick Up Your Socks," "Bully on the Bus," and "I Can't Wait." Each book focuses on different issues. Several dozen titles.

Public Affairs Pamphlets
381 Park Avenue South
New York, NY 10016

Small, concise booklets on a wide range of topics including family life, social problems, health, and child growth and development. Very readable and interesting.

Includes such important topics as "You and Your Adopted Child," "Divorce," "Discipline," and "Helping the Slow Reader."

Research Press
2612 North Mattis Avenue
Champaign, IL 61820

Excellent publications about helping children through behavior management. A particularly good publication is "Living With Children—New Methods For Parents and Teachers."

U.S. Department of Health and Human Services
Office of Human Development Administration Series for Children,
    Youth & Families—Children's Bureau
Order from: Superintendent of Documents
U.S. Government Printing Office
Washington, DC 20402

Publishes two booklets, "Your Child From One to Six" and "Your Child From Six to 12." Reviews ages, stages, and issues of importance to parents.

U.S. Government Pamphlets
c/o The Consumer Information Center—N
P.O. Box 100
Pueblo, CO 81002

Consumer information catalogs are printed four or five times a year. These list a variety of government publications. Many of these relate to helping children: "Choosing a School for Your Child," "School Without Drugs," "Helping Your Child Do Better in School," "Helping Your Child Become a Good Reader," and others.

Winter Communications Inc.
1007 Samy Drive
Tampa, FL 33616

Approximately 35 titles having to do with children, drug abuse, alcoholism, child development, and parental guidance. Under $1 per booklet.

References

Achenbach, T. (1985). *Assessment and taxonomy of childhood and adolescence in psychopathology*. Newbury Park, CA: Sage.

Achenbach, T., & Edelbrock, C. (1983). *Manual for the Child Behavior Checklist and the Revised Child Behavior Profile*. Burlington, VT: University Associates in Psychiatry.

Aiken, I. R. (1987). *Assessment of intellectual functioning*. Boston: Allyn and Bacon.

Alberts, F., & Edwards, R. (1983). A longitudinal analysis of torque and its relationship to achievement and educational classification among normal, disturbed and learning disabled children. *Journal of Clinical Psychology, 39*, 998–1006.

Alberts, F., & Tacco, T. (1980). Torque, lateral dominance and handedness in normal, disturbed, and learning disabled children. *Clinical neuropsychology, 2*(4), 157–160.

American Psychiatric Association. (1980). *Diagnostic and statistical manual of mental disorders* (3rd ed.). Washington, DC: Author.

American Psychological Association, American Educational Research Association, and National Council in Measurement of Education. (1985). *Standards for educational psychological testing*. Washington, DC: American Psychological Association.

Anastasi, A. *Psychological testing.* (1982). New York: Macmillan.

Balow, I., Farr, R., Hogan, T., & Prescott, T. (1978). *Metropolitan Achievement Test* (5th ed.). San Antonio, TX: Psychological Corporation.

Bangs, T. E., & Dodson, S. (1979). *Birth to Three Developmental Scale manual*. Allen, TX: DLM Teaching Resources.

Bayley, N. (1969). *Bayley Scales of Infant Development:* Birth to two years. San Antonio, TX: Psychological Corporation.

Bellak, L. (1975). *The TAT, CAT and SAT in clinical use* (3rd ed.). New York: Grune & Stratton.

Binet, A., & Simon, T. (1905). Me'thodes nouvelles pour le diagnostic du niveau inte'llectuel des anormaux. *L'Année Psychologique, 11*, 191–244.

Binet, A., & Simon, T. (1909). L'intelligence des imbeciles. *L'Année Psychologique, 15*, 1–47.

Blau T. (1974). *The sinister child.* Presidential address, division of clinical psychology, presented at the 82nd annual meeting of the American Psychological Association.

Blau, T. (1977a). Torque and schizophrenic vulnerability. *American Psychologist, 32*, 997–1005.

Blau, T. (1977b). The Torque Test: A measure of cerebral dominance. *JSAS Catalog of Selected Documents in Psychology, 7*(16), MS#1431.

Blau, T. (1979). The diagnosis of disturbed children. *American Psychologist, 34.*

Blau, T. (1984). An evaluative study of the role of the grandparents in the best interests of the child. *American Journal of Family Therapy, 4*(2), 46–50.

Boake, C., Salmon, P., & Carbone, G. (1983). Lateral preference and cognitive ability in primary grade children. *Journal of Abnormal Child Psychology, 11,* 77–83.

Bretherton, I., & Waters, E. (Eds.). (1985). Growing points of attachment theory and research. *Monographs of the Society for Research in Child Development (Vol. 50,* 1 & 2, serial number 209).

Buck, J. (1948). The H-T-P technique, a qualitative and quantitative scoring method. *Journal of Clinical Psychology Monograph Supplement Number 5,* 1–20.

Buck, J. (1981). *The House-Tree-Person Technique: A revised manual.* Los Angeles: Western Psychological Services.

Burks, H. (1977). *Burks' Behavior Rating Scales.* Los Angeles: Western Psychological Services.

Buros, O. K. (Ed.). (1960–1985). *Third through ninth mental measurements yearbooks.* Lincoln: University of Nebraska Press.

Buros, O. K. (Ed.). (1970–1975). *Personality tests and reviews (Vols. I–II).* Highland Park, NJ: Gryphon Press.

Byar, H. (1983). *Mother's reports of behavior problems among treatment and non-treatment children: An outgrowth of the MacFarlane study.* Unpublished doctoral dissertation, School of Human Behavior, U.S. International University, San Diego.

Campbell, M., Green, W., & Deutsch, S. (1985). *Child and adolescent psychopharmacology.* Beverly Hills, CA: Sage.

Campus, N. (1976). A measure of needs to assess the stimulus characteristics of TAT cards. *Journal of Personality, 40,* 248–258.

Chadez, L., & Nurius, P. (1987). Stopping bedtime crying: Treating the child and the parents. *Journal of Clinical Psychology, 16,* 212–217.

Conrad, N., & Hammen, C. (1989). Role of maternal depression in perceptions of child maladjustment, *Journal of Consulting and Clinical Psychology, 57,* 663–667.

CTB/McGraw-Hill. (1977). *California Achievement Test: Test coordinator's handbook.* Monterey, CA: Author.

Cummings, N. (1988). Emergence of the mental health complex: Adaptive and maladaptive responses. *Professional Psychology: Research and Practice, 19,* 308–315.

Dadds, M., Schwartz, S., & Sanders, M. (1987). Marital discord and treatment outcome in behavioral treatment of child conduct disorders. *Journal of Consulting and Clinical Psychology, 55,* 396–403.

Dana, R. (1982). *A human science model for personality assessment with projective techniques.* Springfield, IL: Thomas.

Demarest, J., & Demarest, L. (1980). Does the "torque test" measure cerebral dominance in adults? *Perceptual and Motor Skills, 50,* 155–158.

Diamond, S. (1954). The house and tree verbal fantasy. *Journal of Projective Technique, 18,* 316–325.

Drotar, D., & Crawford, P. (1987). Using home observation in the clinical assessment of children. *Journal of Clinical Child Psychology, 16,* 342–349.

Dunn, L., & Dunn, L. (1981). *Peabody Picture Vocabulary Test-revised.* Circle Pines, MN: American Guidance Service.

Elbert, J., & Holden, E. (1987). Child diagnostic assessment: Current training practices in clinical psychology internships. *Professional Psychology: Research and Practice, 18,* 587–596.

Elkin, F. (1960). *The child and society.* New York: Random House.

Ellsworth, R. (1981). *The child and adolescent adjustment profile scale: The measurement of child and adolescent adjustments.* Palo Alto, CA: Consulting Psychologists Press.

Exner, J. (1974). *The Rorschach: A comprehensive system* (Vol. 1). New York: Wiley.

Exner, J. (1978). *The Rorschach: A comprehensive system, current research and advance interpretation* (Vol. 2). New York: Wiley.

Field, T. (1987). Interaction and attachment in normal and atypical infants. *Journal of Consulting and Clinical Psychology, 55,* 1–7.

Filskov, S. (1975). *Prediction of cerebral impairment and lateralization from figure copying.* Unpublished doctoral dissertation, University of Vermont, Burlington.

Fletcher, J., Smidt, R., & Satz, P. (1979). Discriminant function strategies for the kindergarten prediction of reading achievement. *Journal of Clinical Neuropsychology, 1,* 151–166.

Freud, S. (1933/1966). *The complete introductory lectures on psychoanalysis.* New York: Norton.

Gardner, E., Rudman, H., Karlsen, B., & Merwin, J. (1982). *Stanford Achievement Test* (7th ed.). San Antonio, TX: Psychological Corporation.

Goldberg, P. (1965). A review of sentence completion methods in personality assessment. In B. Murstein (Ed.), *Handbook of projective techniques.* New York: Basic Books.

Golden, C. (1987a). *Luria–Nebraska Neuropsychological Battery: Children's revision.* Los Angeles: Western Psychological Services.

Golden, C. (1987b). *Screening tests for the Luria–Nebraska Neuropsychological Battery.* Los Angeles: Western Psychological Services.

Golden, C. (1987c). *Screening tests for the Luria–Nebraska Neuropsychological Battery: Children's form.* Los Angeles: Western Psychological Services.

Goldfried, M., & Zax, M. (1965). The stimulus value of the TAT. *Journal of Projective Techniques, 29,* 46–48.

Goldman, J., Stein, C., & Guerry, S. (1983). *Psychological methods of child assessment.* New York: Brunner/Mazel.

Graham, F., & Kendall, B. (1960). Memory for Designs Test: Revised general manual. *Perceptual and Motor Skills, 11,* 147–188; [Monogram Supplement], 2–7.

Hammer, E. (1978). *The clinical application of projective drawings.* Springfield, IL: Thomas.

Hartlage, L. C., & Telzrow, K. F. (1986). *Neuropsychological assessment and intervention with childhood and adolescents.* Sarasota, FL: Professional Resource Exchange.

Hinshaw, S., Buhrmester, D., & Heller, T. (1989). Anger control in response to verbal provocation: Effects of stimulant medication for boys with ADHD. *Journal of Abnormal Child Psychology, 17,* 393–407.

Hinshaw, S., Henker, B., Wahlen, C., Erhardt, D., & Dunnington, R. (1989). Aggressive, prosocial and nonsocial behavior in hyperactive boys: Dose effects of methylphenidate in naturalistic settings. *Journal of Consulting and Clinical Psychology, 57,* 636–643.

Hoch, E., Ross, A., & Winder, L. (1966). *Professional preparation of clinical psychologists.* Washington, DC: American Psychological Association.

Hodges, K. (1985). *Manual for the child assessment schedule (CAS)*. Available from K. Hodges, Department of Psychology, Duke University Medical Center, Durham, NC 27710.

Horowitz, F., & O'Brian, M. (Eds.). (1985). *The gifted and talented: Developmental perspectives*. Washington, DC: American Psychological Association.

Incagnoli, T., Goldstein, G., & Golden, C. (1986). *Clinical application of neuropsychological test batteries*. New York: Plenum.

Ireton, H., & Thwing, E. (1980). *Minnesota infant development inventory*. Minneapolis, MN: Behavior Science Systems.

Jarman, F., & Nelson, J. (1981). Torque and cognitive development: Some further investigations of Blau's proposals. *Journal of Clinical Psychology, 37,* 542–555.

Jastak, J., & Jastak, S. (1984). *Wide Range Achievement Test–revised*. Wilmington, DE: Jastak Associates.

Johnson, G., & Boyd, H. (1981). *Non-verbal tests of cognitive skills*. Columbus, OH: Merrill.

Johnson, J. H., & Tuma, J. M. (1983). Training in clinical child psychology: A brief overview of selected issues. *Journal of Clinical Child Psychology, 12,* 365–368.

Jolles, I. (1983). *A catalog for the qualitative interpretation of H-T-P*. Los Angeles: Western Psychological Services.

Jones, E. (1953). *The life and work of Sigmund Freud* (Vol. 1). New York: Basic Books.

Kashani, J., Reid, J., & Rosenberg, T. (1989). Levels of hopelessness in childhood and adolescents: A developmental prospective. *Journal of Consulting and Clinical Psychology, 57,* 496–499.

Kaufman, A. (1979). *Kaufman Infant and Preschool Scale*. Chicago: Stoelting.

Kaufman, A., & Kaufman, N. (1985). *Kaufman Test of Educational Achievement*. Circle Pines, MN: American Guidance Service.

Kaufman, R., & English, F. (1979). *Needs assessment: Concept and application*. Englewood Cliffs, NJ: Educational Technology Publications.

Kessler, J. (1966). *Psychopathology of childhood*. Englewood Cliffs, NJ: Prentice-Hall.

Keyser, D. J., & Sweetland, R. C. (Eds.). (1987). *Test critiques* (Vols. 1–6). Kansas City, MO: Westport.

Knoff, H. (1986). *The assessment of child and adolescent personality*. New York: Guilford.

Kolb, B. (1989). Brain development, plasticity and behavior. *American Psychologist, 44,* 1203–1212.

Koppitz, E. (1968). *Psychological evaluation of children's human figure drawings*. New York: Grune & Stratton.

Lewis, R., Dlugokinski, E., Caputo, L., & Griffin, R. (1988). Children at risk for emotional disorders: Risk and resource dimensions. *Clinical Psychology Review, 8,* 417–440.

Lezak, M. (1983). *Neuropsychological assessment* (2d ed.). New York: Oxford University Press.

Liebert, R., & Sprafkin, J. (1988). *The early window: Effects of television in children and you* (3d ed.). Oxford, England: Pergamon.

Luria, A. R. (1973). *The working brain*. New York: Basic Books.

Luria, A. R. (1980). *Higher cortical functions in man*. New York: Basic Books.

Lyle, J. (1968). Performance of retarded readers on the Memory-for-Designs Test. *Perceptual and Motor Skills, 26,* 851–854.

MacFarlane, J., Allen, J., & Honzik, M. (1954). *A developmental study of behavior problems of normal children between twenty-one months and fourteen years*. Berkeley: University of California Press.

Machover, K. (1949). *Personality projection in drawings of a human figure.* Springfield, IL: Thomas.

Markwardt, F. (1989). *Peabody Individual Achievement Test–revised.* Circle Pines, MN: American Guidance Service.

Masoth, N., Kalmar, D., Westerveld, M., Lanzi, A., D'Amico-Novaky, D., & Riley, E. (1987). Torque as an indicator of reduced cerebral laterality. *International Journal of Clinical Neuropsychology, 9,* 62–67.

Matheny, A. P. (1979). Hereditary determinants of manual torque. *Perceptual and Motor Skills, 49,* 751–755.

Menninger, K. (1959, August). Verdict: guilty—Now what? *Harper's Magazine,* pp. 60–64.

Meyers, J. (1989). Human figure drawing unfairly underrated by psychologists. *California Psychologist, 23*(4), 12–13.

Mitchell, J. V., Jr. (Ed.). (1985). *The ninth mental measurements yearbook.* Lincoln: University of Nebraska Press.

Murphy, G. (1949). *Historical introduction to modern psychology.* New York: Harcourt, Brace.

Murray, H. (1938). *Explorations in personality.* New York: Oxford University Press.

Murray, H. (1943). *Thematic Apperception Test–manual.* Cambridge, MA: Harvard University Press.

Murstein, B. (1963). *Theory and research in projective techniques (emphasizing the TAT).* New York: Wiley.

Myers, D., Jr., Sweet, J., Deysach, R., & Myers, F. (1989). Utility of the Luria–Nebraska Neuropsychological Battery–children's revision in the evaluation of reading-disabled children. *Archives of Clinical Neuropsychology, 4,* 201–215.

Newcomb, T. (1965). *New directions in psychology.* New York: Holt, Rinehart.

Noll, R., & Seagull, A. (1982). Beyond informed consent: Ethical and philosophical considerations in using behavior modification or play therapy in the treatment of enuresis. *Journal of Clinical Child Psychology, 11,* 44–49.

Palmer, J. (1983). *The psychological assessment of children.* New York: Wiley.

Peterson, C., & Schilling, K. (1983). Card pull and projective testing. *Journal of Personality Assessment, 47,* 265–275.

Piaget, J. (1962). *Play, dreams and imitation in childhood.* New York: Norton.

Porter, R., & Cattell, R. (1975). *Manual for the Children's Personality Questionnaire "CPQ" Ages 8–12.* Champaign, IL: Institute for Personality and Ability Testing.

Prescott, G., Balow, I., Hogan, T., & Farr, R. (1978). *Metropolitan Achievement Tests.* New York: Psychological Corporation.

Rabin, A. (Ed.). (1981). *Assessment with projective techniques: A concise introduction.* New York: Springer.

Rao, N., Moely, B., & Lockman, J. (1987). Increasing social participation in preschool social isolates. *Journal of Clinical Child Psychology, 16,* 178–183.

Rapaport, D., Gill, M., & Schafer, R. (1968). *Diagnostic psychological testing.* New York: International Universities Press.

Reitan, R. (1981). *Halstead–Reitan neuropsychological test battery.* Tucson, AZ: Reitan Neuropsychology Laboratories.

Reitan, R. (1984). *Aphasia and sensory–perceptual deficits in children.* Tucson, AZ: Neuropsychology Press.

Rhue, J., & Lynn, S. (1987). Fantasy proneness and psychopathology. *Journal of Personality and Social Psychology, 53,* 327–336.

Rogolsky, M. (1968). Artistic creativity and adaptive regression in third grade children. *Journal of Projective Techniques and Personality Assessment, 32,* 53–62.

Rorschach, H. (1942). Psychodiagnostics, a diagnostic test based on perception. New York: Grune & Stratton.

Rourke, B. (1988). Socioemotional disturbances of learning disabled children. *Journal of Consulting and Clinical Psychology, 56,* 801–810.

Rourke, B. P., Bakker, D., Fisk, J., & Strang, J. (1983). *Child neuropsychology.* New York: Guilford.

Rourke, B. P., Fisk, J., & Strang, J. (1986). *Neuropsychological assessment of children.* New York: Guilford.

Routh, D. K. (1985). Training clinical child psychologists. In B. Lahey and A. Kazdin (Eds.), *Advances in clinical child psychology* (pp. 309–324). London: Plenum.

Sattler, J. M. (1974). *Assessment of children's intelligence.* Philadelphia: Saunders.

Sattler, J. M. (1982). *Assessment of children's intelligence and special abilities* (2d ed.). Boston: Allyn & Bacon.

Sattler, J. M. (1988). *Assessment of children* (3d ed.). San Diego: Author.

Satz, P. (1973). Left-handedness and early brain insult: An explanation. *Neuropsychologia, 11,* 115–117.

Satz, P., & Fletcher, J. (1979). Early screening tests: Some uses and abuses. *Journal of Learning Disabilities, 12,* 43–50.

Satz, P., & Fletcher, J. (1982). *The Florida Kindergarten Screening Battery.* Odessa, FL: Psychological Assessment Resources.

Satz, P., Taylor, H., Friel, J., & Fletcher, J. (1978). Some developmental and predictive precursors of reading disabilities: A six year follow-up. In A. L. Benton & D. Pearl (Eds.), *Dyslexia: An appraisal of current knowledge.* New York: Oxford University Press.

Satz, P., & Fletcher, J. (1980). *The Florida kindergarten screening Battery.* Odessa, FL: Psychological Resources.

Serna, L., Shumaker, J., Hazel, J., & Sheldon, J. (1986). Teaching reciprocal social skills to parents and their delinquent adolescents. *Journal of Clinical Child Psychology, 15,* 64–77.

Silver, A. (1978). Prevention. In A. L. Benton & D. Pearl (Eds.), *Dyslexia: An appraisal of current knowledge.* New York: Oxford University Press.

Simeonsson, R. J. (1986). *Psychological and developmental assessment of special children.* Boston: Allyn & Bacon.

Smith, S. (1978). *No easy answers—the learning disabled child* (Department of Health, Education, and Welfare publication number ADM 77-526). Washington, DC: U.S. Government Printing Office.

Sparrow, S. S., Balla, D. A., & Cicchetti, D. (1984). *Vineland Adaptive Behavior Scales: Expanded form manual, interview addition.* Circle Pines, MN: American Guidance Service.

Spreen, O., & Gaddes, W. (1969). Developmental norms for 15 neuropsychological tests for ages 6 to 15. *Cortex, 5,* 171–191.

Stein, M. (1981). *Thematic Apperception Test* (2d ed.). Springfield, IL: Thomas.

Terman, L. (1921). A symposium: Intelligence and its measurement. *Journal of Educational Psychology, 12,* 127–133.

Thorndike, R. L., Hagen, E., & Sattler, J. (1986). *Stanford–Binet Intelligence Scale* (4th ed.). Chicago: Riverside.

Tolan, P., Ryan, K., & Jaffe, C. (1988). Adolescents' mental health service use and provider, process and recipient characteristics. *Journal of Clinical Child Psychology, 17*, 228–235.

Tolpin, M., & Kohut, H. (1978). The disorders of the self: The psychopathology of the first years of life. In G. Pollock & S. Greenspan (Eds.), *Psychoanalysis of the life cycle* (NIMH) pp.?–?. Washington, DC: U.S. Government Printing Office.

Tomkins, S. (1947). *The Thematic Apperception Test.* New York: Grune & Stratton.

Turnbow, K., & Dana R. (1981). The effects of stem length and directions on sentence completion. *Journal of Personality Assessment, 45*, 27–32.

Wallach, M., & Kogan, N. (1965). *Modes of thinking in young children.* New York: Holt, Rinehart, Winston.

Walters, C. (1961). Reading ability and visual–motor function in second grade children. *Perceptual and Motor Skills, 13*, 370.

Watson, R. (1963). *The great psychologists.* Philadelphia: Lippincott.

Wechsler, D. (1974). *Manual for the Wechsler Intelligence Scale for Children*–Revised. San Antonio: Psychological Corporation.

Wechsler, D. (1981). *Wechsler Adult Intelligence Scale–Revised: WAIS-R manual.* San Antonio: Psychological Corporation.

Wechsler, D. (1989). *Wechsler Preschool and Primary Scale of Intelligence–Revised.* San Antonio: Psychological Corporation.

Wedell, D., Parducci, A., & Lane, N. (1990). Reducing the dependence of clinical judgement on the immediate context: Effects of number categories and type of anchors. *Journal of Personality and Social Psychology. 58*, 319–329.

Wenck, S. (1984). *H-T-P drawings: An illustrated diagnostic handbook.* Los Angeles: Western Psychological Services.

Weston, S. (1989). *Choosing a school for your child* (Report No. PIP89-833). Washington, DC: Office for the Improvement of Practice, U.S. Department of Education, Superintendent of Documents.

Wierzibicki, M., & McCabe, M. (1988). Social skills and subsequent depressive symptomatology in children. *Journal of Clinical Child Psychology, 17*, 203–228.

Williams, T. (Ed.). (1986). *The impact of television: A natural experiment in three communities.* Orlando, FL: Academic Press.

Wirt, R., Lachar, D., Klinedienst, J., Seat, P., & Broen, X. (1984). *Multidimensional description of child personality: A manual for the Personality Inventory of Children Revised–1984.* Los Angeles: Western Psychological Services.

Woods, D., & Oppenheimer, K. (1980). Torque, hemispheric dominance and psychosocial adjustment. *Journal of Abnormal Psychology, 89*, 567–572.

Wyatt, F. (1949). The case of Gregor: Interpretation of test data. *Journal of Projective Techniques, 13*, 155–205.

Yama, M. (1990). The usefulness of human figure drawings as an index of overall adjustment. *Journal of Personality Assessment, 54*, 78–86.

Yu, P., Harris, G., Solovitz, B., & Franklin, J. (1986). A social problem-solving intervention for children at high risk for later psychopathology. *Journal of Clinical Child Psychology, 15*, 30–40.

Zendel, I. H., & Pihl, R. (1980). Torque and learning and behavioral problems in children. *Journal of Consulting and Clinical Psychology, 48*, 602–604.

Zucker, L. (1948). A case of obesity: Projective techniques before and after treatments. *Journal of Projective Techniques, 12*, 205–215.

Name Index

Subject Index

(*continued from front*)

Agoraphobia: Multiple Perspectives on Theory and Treatment *edited by Dianne L. Chambless and Alan J. Goldstein*

The Rorschach: A Comprehensive System. Volume III: Assessment of Children and Adolescents *by John E. Exner, Jr. and Irving B. Weiner*

Handbook of Play Therapy *edited by Charles E. Schaefer and Kevin J. O'Connor*

Adolescent Sexuality in a Changing American Society: Social and Psychological Perspectives for the Human Service Professions (Second Edition) *by Catherine S. Chilman*

Failures in Behavior Therapy *edited by Edna B. Foa and Paul M.G. Emmelkamp*

The Psychological Assessment of Children (Second Edition) *by James O. Palmer*

Imagery: Current Theory, Research, and Application *edited by Aneés A. Sheikh*

Handbook of Clinical Child Psychology *edited by C. Eugene Walker and Michael C. Roberts*

The Measurement of Psychotherapy Outcome *edited by Michael J. Lambert, Edwin R. Christensen, and Steven S. DeJulio*

Clinical Methods in Psychology (Second Edition) *edited by Irving B. Weiner*

Excuses: Masquerades in Search of Grace *by C.R. Snyder, Raymond L. Higgins and Rita J. Stucky*

Diagnostic Understanding and Treatment Planning: The Elusive Connection *edited by Fred Shectman and William B. Smith*

Bender Gestalt Screening for Brain Dysfunction *by Patricia Lacks*

Adult Psychopathology and Diagnosis *edited by Samuel M. Turner and Michel Hersen*

Personality and the Behavioral Disorders (Second Edition) *edited by Norman S. Endler and J. McVicker Hunt*

Ecological Approaches to Clinical and Community Psychology *edited by William A. O'Connor and Bernard Lubin*

Rational-Emotive Therapy with Children and Adolescents: Theory, Treatment Strategies, Preventative Methods *by Michael E. Bernard and Marie R. Joyce*

The Unconscious Reconsidered *edited by Kenneth S. Bowers and Donald Meichenbaum*

Prevention of Problems in Childhood: Psychological Research and Application *edited by Michael C. Roberts and Lizette Peterson*

Resolving Resistances in Psychotherapy *by Herbert S. Strean*

Handbook of Social Skills Training and Research *edited by Luciano L'Abate and Michael A. Milan*

Institutional Settings in Children's Lives *by Leanne G. Rivlin and Maxine Wolfe*

Treating the Alcoholic: A Developmental Model of Recovery *by Stephanie Brown*

Resolving Marital Conflicts: A Psychodynamic Perspective *by Herbert S. Strean*

Paradoxical Strategies in Psychotherapy: A Comprehensive Overview and Guidebook *by Leon F. Seltzer*

Pharmacological and Behavioral Treatment: An Integrative Approach *edited by Michel Hersen*

The Rorschach: A Comprehensive System, Volume I: Basic Foundations (Second Edition) *by John E. Exner, Jr.*

The Induction of Hypnosis *by William E. Edmonston, Jr.*

Handbook of Clinical Neuropsychology, Volume 2 *edited by Susan B. Filskov and Thomas J. Boll*

Psychological Perspectives on Childhood Exceptionality: A Handbook *edited by Robert T. Brown and Cecil R. Reynolds*

Game Play: Therapeutic Use of Childhood Games *edited by Charles E. Schaefer and Steven E. Reid*

The Father's Role: Applied Perspectives *edited by Michael E. Lamb*

A Developmental Approach to Adult Psychopathology *by Edward Zigler and Marion Glick*

Handbook of Behavioral Assessment (Second Edition) *edited by Anthony R. Ciminero, Karen S. Calhoun, and Henry E. Adams*